SHAKESPEARE AT STRATFORD

ROMEO AND JULIET

RUSSELL JACKSON

The Arden website is at
http://www.ardenshakespeare.com

Shakespeare at Stratford: *Romeo and Juliet*
first published 2003 by The Arden Shakespeare
in association with The Shakespeare Birthplace Trust

© 2003 Russell Jackson

The Arden Shakespeare is an imprint of Thomson Learning

Thomson Learning
High Holborn House
50/51 Bedford Row
London WC1R 4LR

Typeset by LaserScript, Mitcham, Surrey

Printed by Zrinski in Croatia

British Library Cataloguing in Publication Data
A catalogue record for this book is available from the British Library

Library of Congress Cataloguing in Publication Data
A catalogue record has been applied for

ISBN 1-903436-14-1 (pbk)
NPN 9 8 7 6 5 4 3 2 1

THE AUTHOR

Russell Jackson is Director of the Shakespeare Institute and Professor of Shakespeare Studies at the University of Birmingham. His publications include critical editions of plays by Oscar Wilde, a translation and edition of Theodor Fontane's account of London Shakespeare productions in the 1850s and a volume of documents of the Victorian Theatre. He edited *The Cambridge Companion to Shakespeare on Film* (2000) and co-edited (with Jonathan Bate) the *Oxford Illustrated History of Shakespeare on Stage* (2001). With Robert Smallwood he edited two volumes in the series *Players of Shakespeare* (Cambridge University Press, 1988 and 1993), and since 1994 his reviews of Stratford-upon-Avon productions have appeared each year in *Shakespeare Quarterly*. As text adviser he has worked on many stage, film and radio productions of Shakespeare's plays, including the 1993 Radio3/Random House Audiobooks production of *Romeo and Juliet*, with Kenneth Branagh and Samantha Bond.

FOR

THE STRATFORD COMPANIES 1947–2000:

THE ACTORS, STAGE CREWS, DRESSERS,

CRAFT WORKERS, HOUSE STAFF,

DESIGNERS AND DIRECTORS

WHOSE SKILLS AND COMMITMENT

HAVE GIVEN THE PLAY LIFE

CONTENTS

LIST OF ILLUSTRATIONS

SOURCES

Joe Cocks Studio: The Joe Cocks Studio Collection, The Shakespeare Centre Library, Stratford-upon-Avon. Copyright Shakespeare Birthplace Trust

Malcolm Davies: The Shakespeare Centre Library, Stratford-upon-Avon. Copyright Shakespeare Birthplace Trust

Gordon Goode: The Shakespeare Centre Library, Stratford-upon-Avon. Copyright Royal Shakespeare Company

Thomas Holte: The Tom Holte Theatre Photographic Collection, The Shakespeare Centre Library, Stratford-upon-Avon. Copyright Shakespeare Birthplace Trust

Angus McBean: The Shakespeare Centre Library, Stratford-upon-Avon. Copyright Royal Shakespeare Company

Ernest Daniels: The Shakespeare Centre Library, Stratford-upon-Avon

John Bunting

Laurence Burns

Donald Cooper

Mark Douet

John Haynes

Richard Mildenhall

Solihull News

Every effort has been made to contact copyright holders and the publishers will be happy to include further acknowledgements.

GENERAL EDITOR'S PREFACE

The theatre archive housed in the Shakespeare Centre Library here in Stratford-upon-Avon is among the most important in the world; for the study of the performance history of Shakespeare's plays in the twentieth century it is unsurpassed. It covers the entire period from the opening of Stratford's first Shakespeare Memorial Theatre in 1879, through its replacement, following the fire of 1926, by the present 1932 building (renamed the Royal Shakespeare Theatre in 1961) and the addition of the studio theatre (The Other Place) in 1974 (closed, lamentably, in 2000), and of the Swan Theatre in 1986, and it becomes fuller as the years go by. The archive's collection of promptbooks, press reviews, photographs in their hundreds of thousands, and, over the last couple of decades, archival video recordings, as well as theatre programmes, costume designs, stage-managers' performance reports and a whole range of related material, provides the Shakespeare theatre historian with a remarkably rich and concentrated body of material. The wealth and accessibility of this collection have sometimes tended to give general performance histories of Shakespeare's plays an unintentional Stratford bias; the aim of this series is to exploit, and indeed revel in, the archive's riches.

Each volume in the series covers the Stratford performance history of a Shakespeare play since World War II. The record of performances at Stratford's various theatres through this period unquestionably offers a wider, fuller, and more various range of productions than is provided by any other single theatre company. It may fairly be said, therefore, that a study of the Stratford productions since 1945 of any Shakespeare play provides a representative cross-section of the main trends in its theatrical interpretation in the second half of the twentieth century. Each volume in the series will, however, begin with an introduction that sets this Stratford half-century in the wider context of the main trends of its play's performance history before this period and of significant productions elsewhere during it.

The organization of individual volumes is, of course, the responsibility of their authors, though within the general aim of the series to avoid mere chronicling. No volume in the series will therefore offer a chronological account of the Stratford productions of its play: some will group together for consideration and analysis productions of similar or comparable style or approach; others will examine individual aspects or sections of their plays across the whole range of the half-century of Stratford productions' treatment of them. Illustrations are chosen for what they demonstrate about a particular production choice, a decision that, on some occasions, may be more important than photographic quality. Given the frequency with which individual plays return, in entirely new productions, to the Stratford repertoire, most volumes in the series will have some ten or even a dozen productions' approaches and choices to consider and contrast, a range that will provide a vivid sense of the extraordinary theatrical diversity and adaptability of Shakespeare's plays.

The conception and planning of this series would not have been possible without the support and enthusiasm of Sylvia Morris and Marian Pringle of the Shakespeare Centre Library, Kathy Elgin, Head of Publications at the Royal Shakespeare Company, Jessica Hodge and her colleagues at the Arden Shakespeare, and above all, my two Associate Editors, Susan Brock of the Shakespeare Centre Library and Russell Jackson of the Shakespeare Institute. To all of them I am deeply grateful.

ROBERT SMALLWOOD
The Shakespeare Centre, Stratford-upon-Avon

ACKNOWLEDGEMENTS

I am grateful to the staff of the Shakespeare Centre Library, the Shakespeare Institute Library and Birmingham Shakespeare Library, whose expert and generous support has made this work possible. I have also benefited from the advice of my colleagues and friends Peter Holland, Patricia Tatspaugh and Stanley Wells, and from the meticulous attention of Robert Smallwood, the General Editor of the series, and Jessica Hodge and her colleagues in the Arden team. I am particularly grateful to Hannah Hyam for her patient and meticulous copy-editing.

My account of the Shakespeare Memorial Theatre and (since 1960) the Royal Shakespeare Company is generally indebted to the works by David Addenbrooke, Sally Beauman, Cicely Berry, Colin Chambers and Marian J. Pringle listed in the bibliography. Peter Holland's *English Shakespeares* (Cambridge, 1997), a lively and acute survey of English Shakespeare productions in the 1990s, provides a valuable context for some of the later productions I have discussed here. The studies of the play in performance by Peter Holding and Jill L. Levenson, and the editions by Levenson, Brian Gibbons and T.J.B. Spencer are particularly informative and stimulating. In addition to critical works on the play referred to in what follows, readers are commended to the account of the play's gestural language given by Peter Donaldson in his *Shakespearean Films / Shakespearean Directors* (Boston, 1990). I am grateful to students in a seminar on the play in performance at the Shakespeare Institute, and to my students and colleagues there and elsewhere, for keen and informed responses to productions we have seen and discussed together: any ideas they have contributed unwittingly have been incorporated unconsciously – but also unrepentantly – in this book.

RUSSELL JACKSON

Stratford-upon-Avon, May 2002

INTRODUCTION

On 5 April 1947 the curtains of the Shakespeare Memorial Theatre parted to reveal a dark, empty stage, on which a solitary figure began a slow walk towards the front, speaking the lines of the prologue to *Romeo and Juliet* to the accompaniment of melancholy horn music. On 5 July 2000, at the press night of Michael Boyd's production of the same play, the audience sat looking at a bare white stage with two curving walls and a runway into the left-hand aisle of the auditorium: a chair was thrown on from the right-hand wing, followed by a dangerous-looking man who bawled 'A dog of the house of Montague moves me' and made a violent and explicit gesture in the direction the chair had come from.

This book examines productions of *Romeo and Juliet* at Stratford-upon-Avon between 1947 and 2000, attempting to measure the ground travelled not only in terms of response to the script in question, but as evidence of changes in theatrical and social sensibilities. The productions are not dealt with one by one in chronological order. Rather, the chapters address the play in terms of a series of topics, the central ones being accounts of the play's leading characters. This is done not in the spirit of 'character criticism', but because at one level the play works through a series of situations, dilemmas and moments of behaviour and (critically) choice. These derive their potency from the vividness and poetic force of the figures portrayed. 'Passion lends them power', and the

1

play's account of the passions – specifically love and hate – depends on the way its central characters are represented and understood. It also reflects the different priorities with which actors and directors and reviewers have approached the script. The first chapter discusses different ways in which designers and directors have represented 'Fair Verona', which afford an overview of the general tendency of the productions.

The times change, and Shakespearean performance at Stratford has changed with them – even if not sufficiently for some commentators. The fifteen productions of *Romeo and Juliet* staged there between 1947 and 2000 constitute an intriguing commentary on the range of the text's possibilities, and at the same time reflect the changing aims and circumstances of the organizations that produced them. The period embraces the aftermath of World War II, with its varied hardships and optimism, the social and political upheavals of the 1950s and 1960s, the changes in political and social definition of the 1970s and 1980s, and a new, 'post-modern' sense of irony and disenchantment at the turn of the second Christian millennium. 'A case could easily be made', writes Peter Hennessy, 'for mid century Britain as the most settled, deferential, smug, un-dynamic society in the advanced world' (Hennessy, 434). In the course of the next five decades, assumptions about class, public speech and behaviour, sexual morality and government would be challenged and overhauled, although not according to any systematic plan and without the total destruction or rebuilding of society as the discernible result. Among the issues on which 'smugness' was exercised were gender politics, the ethnic composition of the country, and the centrality of Shakespeare to the cultural life of the nation. In the late 1940s, professional careers for women were still widely regarded as incompatible with marriage, the influx of immigrants from Empire (subsequently, Commonwealth) countries had barely begun, and the primacy of English culture in the sense of national identity went largely unquestioned. Shakespeare was central to that culture, and it was expected that the Stratford theatre would fulfil its duty by providing accomplished and authoritatively faithful interpretations of his works.

CHANGES AT STRATFORD

In the 1940s and 1950s Stratford seemed almost immune to the new ideas. 'Eccentric' or tendentious productions, devised according to some literary or theatrical theory, were regarded as the province of outsiders and, especially, foreigners. 'Intellectual' was not a word associated with the kind of high-definition classical theatre against which Stratford measured itself. Men, and occasionally women, of sound judgement could assess the degree of faithfulness to the playwright's intentions, which might be deduced with confidence from the texts. Fifty years later, notions of excellence and vitality in theatre have been overhauled, and few academics or theatre workers believe that 'right' interpretations should even be sought, still less that they might be arrived at.

In 1947 the twenty-one-year-old Peter Brook, whose *Love's Labour's Lost* had been the success of the 1946 season, 'produced' (that is, directed) *Romeo and Juliet* at the Shakespeare Memorial Theatre at the invitation of its artistic director, Sir Barry Jackson. The years immediately following World War II were the period of 'Austerity' in a Britain still crippled by the cost of the war and not yet divested of its imperial possessions and responsibilities. The winter months of 1947 were a remarkable combination of severe weather and economic misery: snowstorms in February, gales and flooding in March, a fuel and transport crisis, reductions in food rations and social unrest. In late April the government banned the use of coal and gas fires until September, food rations were cut back further during the summer and in August the convertibility of sterling was suspended and the basic petrol ration was abolished to discourage 'pleasure motoring'. The first night of *Romeo and Juliet* was on 5 April. A local paper, under the headline 'Pre-War Crowds for Opening of Festival', noted that two major

hotels, the Falcon and the Welcombe Manor, had reopened for the
season (although the Red Horse and the Shakespeare were still
requisitioned by the government), and that there was already
'evidence of American visitors coming . . . in pre-war numbers'
(*Coventry E. Tel.*). The correspondent of the *Irish Times* described
the festival enthusiasts, undiscouraged by poor weather, queuing
damply for seats in the gallery, and the more glamorous scenes in
the main foyers, 'all the signs of peace – sleek limousines outside
the door, stiff shirts and long dresses, cigars passed freely in the
foyer from film producer to ambassador and back again'. Inside
the theatre, Brook's production offered a world of heat, light and
passion. His iconoclasm and lack of concern for the more
hallowed romantic style associated with the play displeased some
conservatives. 'No boy of 21', fumed Beverley Baxter in the
Evening Standard, 'should even try to direct the balcony scene . . .
Only a man in his fifties can understand the tenderness of young
love.' Brook's production, with a Romeo aged twenty-four and a
Juliet aged eighteen, was scandalously successful.

By 1954, when the theatre offered its next production of the
play, Barry Jackson had left: he had brought in interesting
directorial talent, but maintained a degree of remoteness from
the theatre's work that made him uncongenial to the governors,
and he seemed to lack the sense of 'leadership' that the chairman,
Sir Fordham Flower, admired. Now the festival was under the
direction of Anthony Quayle, who was experimenting with a
'young' company with a sprinkling of established actors. After one
season this experiment was abandoned, and Quayle committed
the festival, for the sake of its survival, to a policy of handsome
productions 'led' (as the phrase went) by established stars. Glen
Byam Shaw directed the 1954 *Romeo and Juliet*. According to the
Observer's drama critic, Ivor Brown, he could be relied on 'for an
honest production faithful to the text, just to the story and helpful
to the actors'. Byam Shaw (born 1904) was hardly an *enfant terrible*,
but he was not unadventurous. Quayle, for his part, was anxious to
find new ways for the festival to develop (Beauman, 211–15). The

1954 season was announced as a 'youth' season, with few established stars and some fresh new faces in leading roles. A very young actress, Zena Walker, was cast opposite a film star with relatively little Shakespearean experience, Laurence Harvey.

Unfortunately, it was soon clear that Stratford did need stars to survive. The 1954 season fared poorly at the hands of the press, and box-office percentages fell to a level (the lower nineties) then regarded as deeply troubling (Beauman, 219). It was indicative of the need for security, and of the social and theatrical position aimed for by the annual Stratford festival, that Laurence Olivier and Vivien Leigh were already being announced as having agreed to 'lead' the next season's company. These plans, with the Oliviers at Stratford and John Gielgud on tour with Peggy Ashcroft, united, in Ivor Brown's words, 'the sovereign players of our time'.[1] Shaw's 1954 *Romeo and Juliet*, like his second Stratford production four years later, was designed by Motley, the design team responsible for the famous Gielgud–Olivier–Ashcroft production in London in 1935. Continuity and West End professionalism were the key to success. Quayle, a pragmatic and accomplished actor and manager, was not given to proclaiming artistic credos. In 1952 he outlined succinctly the problems facing the Memorial Theatre, and argued that in order to compete with London it needed proper financing, and would have to expand its operations to include the regular London transfer of productions.[2] In 1950, in less pragmatic vein, he had acknowledged a vision of Stratford's role in the 'Cold War':

> Two great wars have been fought, and painfully won, in the space of a single generation. A third, and even greater war, looms ahead. As he looks into the future, and prepares himself to face what it may bring, the Englishman needs to be in touch with his country's past; he needs to remind himself of the things he holds dear, of the kind of men from whom he is sprung. So he turns to the magic of Shakespeare's words and the fellowship of Shakespeare's characters as to old and well-worn friends. There they are in his theatre by the Avon, filling the air with echoes of that astonishing age of Elizabeth.[3]

Such convictions were usually implicit rather than expressed directly in public statements by Quayle and Byam Shaw, who had become Quayle's co-director in 1953 and succeeded him as artistic director in 1956. They certainly had little to do with the ferment of ideas and experiment in contemporary theatre and politics, except as a reaction against it.

In 1961 when he directed the fourth post-war *Romeo and Juliet* at Stratford, Peter Hall, a new 'Young Turk' of the theatre world, was in his second season as artistic director of what had recently become the Royal Shakespeare Company. When the production opened, it was known that proposals had been discussed for incorporating the RSC with the as yet unformed National Theatre. Stratford was anxious, and assurances were sought that its identity as a centre for Shakespearean theatre would not be jeopardized. 'Memorial' had been replaced by 'Royal' in the name of the main house in March 1961: it neatly conveyed a sense of national centrality while discarding the deadly connotations of the old name. A settled policy of government subsidy was soon to follow, though not without continual struggle on a season-by-season basis. Rehearsal time was lengthened from three to five weeks, and new talent was brought into every department of the company's activities: the sets for the new *Romeo and Juliet* were by Sean Kenny, an aggressively radical designer with ambitions to redefine rather than decorate theatrical spaces (Addenbrooke, 243). Opposite Dorothy Tutin, Hall cast Zia Mohyeddin, a Pakistani actor who had recently made a hit in a stage adaptation of E.M. Forster's novel *A Passage to India*. Unfortunately, Mohyeddin had to withdraw, and the RSC's first 'colour blind' casting in a major role did not reach the public. Nevertheless, Hall was setting down a marker for a forward-looking company that would be run on ensemble lines, with long contracts to retain and nurture talent with performances in Stratford and London rather than rounding up fresh casts to support established 'names' every spring. Famous actors would still be engaged (in *Romeo and Juliet* Dame Edith Evans played the Nurse, Max Adrian the Friar) but the seasons would no longer be built round them. Artistic vision and a sense of company identity, rather than stars, would lead in Stratford. Unlike Quayle's understanding of Shakespeare as a support for the morale of a threatened nation, Hall's credo was determinedly aesthetic and social in quite a different sense from that of his predecessors, and looked outwards and forwards. 'A highly-trained group of actors, constantly playing Shakespeare, but with antennae stretched towards our world of contradictions can, perhaps, be expert enough in the past and alive enough to the present to perform the plays' (*Royal Shakespeare Company, 1960–63*, 43). In 1966 the special 'Swinging London' issue of *Time* magazine quoted Hall's social vision:

> We've got to get rid of that stuffy middle-aged lot that go to the theater as a sop for their prejudices. We're getting a young audience who are looking for experiences and will take them from the latest pop record or *Hamlet*.   (15 Apr)

The 'In' Hamlet of the season, the magazine reported, was 'David Warner, 24, who plays the Dane with a Beatle haircut and a Carnaby Street slouch' (Hewison, 1986, 78; see also Addenbrooke, 112). This was unfair to the thousands of young people who had trekked to Stratford for many seasons past and lined up, often in foul weather, to buy the cheapest tickets. However, it was appropriate for Hall to align his company with the renewed anti-Establishment mood, an aspect of the political and social change that was elevating the energy and self-expression of youth above 'mature' visions of stability and authority. Warner's aggressively ungracious Hamlet in a production (directed by Hall and designed by John Bury) that emphasized the national and familial politics of the play, was regarded as a touchstone of this, a successful extension into the supposedly more sublime area of tragedy of the quasi-Brechtian techniques that had already been applied to the history plays (Wells, 1977, 23–42)

The RSC soon began to develop a diversity of activities similar to those that might be expected of a National Theatre. Hall initiated a 'Studio' under the direction of Michel St Denis, the company acquired a regular London base at the Aldwych Theatre, and in 1962 staged an experimental season at the Arts Theatre. The 1964 'Theatre of Cruelty' season (from which Brook's production of Peter Weiss's *Marat/Sade* emerged) fuelled what became known in 1965 as the 'Dirty Plays' controversy, in which the RSC came under attack for staging allegedly subversive and indecent work. From 1965 a small-scale touring enterprise, 'Theatregoround', was launched, and in 1971–75 seasons were put on in London at The Place, a small venue near Euston. The RSC also sponsored the annual 'World Theatre Seasons' organized by Peter Daubeny at the Aldwych. It was after his own company had appeared under these auspices that Karolos Koun, director of the National Theatre of Greece, was invited to direct *Romeo and Juliet* at Stratford in 1967.

Romeo was to be played by Ian Holm, a distinguished product of the first wave of RSC-nurtured actors, and Juliet by Estelle Kohler, a young actress from South Africa. Six years later she appeared in a production of the play by Terry Hands, one of a group of directors attracted to the company by Hall's successor, Trevor Nunn. Nunn, together with Hall himself and John Barton, was a Cambridge graduate, and a company style seemed to have emerged. Behind them Hall, Barton and Nunn had the Cambridge approach to English studies, combined with a longstanding tradition of amateur theatricals whose presiding spirit was George Rylands. Among Nunn's innovations was the addition to the company's support staff of a full-time voice teacher, Cicely Berry. The poetic coherence of the plays and their formal qualities were elicited in a theatrical equivalent of the methods of current trends in literary criticism: staging, design, direction and programme notes – now more voluminous than ever before – were considered as 'readings' of the plays, rather than being simply appropriate and picturesque frames for good acting. The project was to identify and embody the thematic strands that, wound together, constituted the unity of the theatrical and poetic effect. At the same time an element of Brechtian rigour in staging and design was softened by the values of Stanislavskian character-creation in the acting. Throughout the 1960s the company faced a series of threats to its economic and artistic independence: government subsidy, when it came, was never as generous or predictable as it was for the continental European companies with which the RSC hoped to challenge comparison.

Until the early 1970s the company's Shakespearean work was done on the proscenium-arch stages of the Royal Shakespeare Theatre in Stratford and the Aldwych Theatre in London, which were poorly adapted to the plays' stagecraft. From 1971 small-scale productions, some of them of plays by Shakespeare and his contemporaries, were performed in a metal shed in Stratford, converted into a studio theatre with rudimentary facilities and dubbed 'The Other Place'. This was a double reference to the company's fringe venue in London and Hamlet's suggestion to Claudius that if his messenger could not find Polonius in heaven, he might seek him 'i'th'other place' himself. The Other Place was very much the brainchild of a brilliant young assistant director, Buzz Goodbody. After her production of *Hamlet* in 1975, with Ben Kingsley in the title role, the metal shed became one of the most prized venues available to the company, to the point where actors were insisting that roles there should be included in their contracts. Productions in theatres other than the main house also became a centre of radical thinking, both in terms of production values and repertoire, and as a corrective to what many perceived as an increasingly corporate ethic in the RSC's administration (Chambers, 17–19). The influence of this studio theatre was felt in work at the main house, combining with a growing dissatisfaction with the larger theatre's limitations. The 1976 season, with a 'permanent' setting that amounted to a partial reconstruction of an Elizabethan stage, was in some measure a response to this pressure – but the economies it allowed also reflected a financial crisis more severe than those of the previous decade.

In 1975 the company had declared a centenary for itself as a fund-raising venture. This was a time of economic crisis and industrial unrest in Britain and across the world, and the subsidized theatres were once again feeling the pinch. Des Wilson, formerly director of the housing charity Shelter, was employed to mastermind an operation that included at one end of the scale the dedication of a 'centenary garden' by the Queen, and at the other a sign over the foyer fountain suggesting that theatre-goers might throw in a donation of 50p. (Most of us didn't.) That year's production of *Henry V*, directed by Terry Hands, was made into a figurehead for this campaign, with its image of a country (or company) united behind a king (or director) battling against the odds to win a famous victory (or stage a season). In 1976, a permanent 'Elizabethan' stage setting in wood was claimed as a response to the economic situation of the company and the country. 'Financially, we're down to the bone', Trevor Nunn told a reporter. 'I enjoy simplicity. I'm grateful in a grudging way to Mr Healey [the Chancellor of the Exchequer] for forcing me to get my priorities straight.'[4] The free cast list for the *Romeo and Juliet* that opened the season carried a summary of the annual accounts for 1975–76, designed to demonstrate what good value for money the public was getting. Crises of this kind, often the result of uncertainties in the level of Arts Council funding, continued to harass the company. Not only was subsidy subject to the vagaries of the economic and political climate, but a high percentage at the box office remained (as it had in Quayle's time) an absolute necessity.

In 1980, as Ron Daniels's *Romeo and Juliet* opened in the main house, the company's General Manager, David Brierley, described the uncertainties and inadequacies of funding, and pointed out that sponsorship was proving to be the only means by which such activities as touring could be maintained.[5] (Before long, as it turned out, even the 'core' of main house Shakespeare productions would need this support.) In 1989, shortly after the opening in the new Swan Theatre's fourth season of his second *Romeo and Juliet*, Terry Hands, who had succeeded Nunn as artistic director in 1986, announced that he would be leaving in 1992: 'RSC boss exits as cash battles rage on', as the *Daily Mail* headline declared (6 Apr). In fact Hands's tenure was due to expire in two years, but this was a way of dramatizing the company's plight. Defending himself against his critics, he reminded them that 'Sponsorship theatre is safe theatre.'[6] Under the headline 'RSC "First Lamb to the Slaughter"' in the *Stage*, a 'leading theatre finance expert' was quoted to the effect that only 'the collapse of a major national company such as the RSC' would convince the government and the Arts Council that the policy of reduced state funding and increased private sponsorship would result in a Britain 'awash with bankruptcies and liquidations' (27 Apr 1989). In the mid- to late 1980s the company was performing a repertoire for ten months in three theatres in Stratford, occupying two spaces at the Barbican in London, touring to Newcastle-on-Tyne (where the whole Stratford repertoire was given) and other venues at home and abroad, and seeking commercial transfers of some of its shows. This expansionism was reflected in the buoyancy of the reports in the series of illustrated *Yearbooks* published between 1978 and 1986, where the company presented itself as experimental, far ranging and socially responsible and responsive. The season schedule for 1986, when Michael Bogdanov staged his *Romeo and Juliet*, announced five Shakespeare plays in the main house, four from the period between the 1580s and the 1670s in the first season of the Swan, and four new plays in The Other Place. The season lasted from March to the middle of the following January.

By the turn of the century, the picture was less encouraging. Since the 1980s, the RSC had suffered from the vagaries of changes in Arts Council policy and unpredictability in private funding. Securing business sponsorship was now a complex and demanding activity, with intense competition between arts organizations. Terry Hands's attack on 'sponsorship theatre' had its point. In return for their money, companies expect not only credit for altruism but also confidence that they are being associated with a prestige product. *Hamlet* at the Royal Shakespeare

Theatre with a 'name' in the lead is one thing, but would Jaguar or Allied Domecq wish to be known as sponsors of another Theatre of Cruelty season? In response to an Arts Council policy of regional development, reduction in the commitment to the London base at the Barbican was accompanied by 'residencies' in Plymouth as well as Newcastle – from which in 2000 the RSC announced its intention to retreat. The pattern of the seasons in Stratford had already altered in the mid-1990s, causing some confusion and culminating in a return by 1998 to a 'Summer Festival Season' redolent of the 1940s and 1950s. Touring productions mounted outside Stratford now dominated plans that were announced for the new century. Shorter contracts for principal actors would attract 'names' away from their London base by not endangering other more lucrative commitments. This seemed inconsistent with the ambition to create a semi-permanent ensemble, led by company work rather than stars.

In the autumn of 2001 plans were announced for demolishing and replacing the main house, and turning The Other Place into part of a new, larger theatre with a flexible audience/stage configuration and more seating. Over the years the Memorial Theatre had undergone several structural alterations, all designed to bring the audience into a more intimate relationship with the stage (Pringle; Beauman). By 2001 the recurrent financial and artistic problems of the company had become a matter of bricks, mortar and contracts to a degree not anticipated in previous decades. The departure of Adrian Noble from the post of artistic director, announced in Spring 2002, has left the future uncertain, as it is not clear at the time of writing (May 2002) which elements of the proposed changes to the theatres themselves, the manage-ment structure and the organization of seasons might be implemented by his successor, whose identity is not yet known. It does seem likely that some radical changes (possibly short of demolition) will be made to the 1500-seat Royal Shakespeare Theatre, and that perhaps The Other Place (about 120 seats) might be reprieved: the 450-seat Swan would in any case be untouched.

ROMEO AND JULIET:
CHANGING EXPECTATIONS

Romeo and Juliet carries with it a formidable reputation as a transcendent story of romantic and tragic love, largely derived from the enthusiasms and impassioned readings of nineteenth-century composers, painters and critics. Hector Berlioz, whose 'dramatic symphony' *Roméo et Juliette* (1839) includes one of the most extravagant and ecstatic musical readings of the balcony scene, is an extreme but not unrepresentative example. In 1827 the performances of an English company in Paris, and in particular of their leading actress, Harriet Smithson, had galvanized the young composer. The performance of *Hamlet* had so shaken him that he resolved not to expose himself again to 'the flame of Shakespeare's genius', but he gave in to temptation and bought a ticket for *Romeo and Juliet*. This time he was able

> to steep [him]self in the fiery sun and balmy nights of Italy, to witness the drama of that immense love, swift as a thought, burning as lava, radiantly pure as an angel's glance, imperious, irresistible, the raging hatreds, the wild, ecstatic kisses, the desperate strife of love and death contending for mastery.   (Berlioz, 111)

It was, he admitted, 'too much'. His exposure to Shakespeare in English resulted in some astonishing musical works – the *Symphonie Fantastique* as well as *Roméo et Juliette* – but also led to a disastrous marriage with Harriet Smithson.

The qualities admired by Berlioz, particularly the 'fiery sun and balmy nights' of Italy, remained priorities for more decorous theatrical interpretations throughout the century, with the text trimmed to favour the two lovers, hasten the onrush of romantic catastrophe and allow for the shifting of elaborate realistic scenery. It was common practice (deriving from Garrick's version) to stage Juliet's funeral and end the play with the death of the lovers (Levenson, 1987, 17–30). In the early twentieth century other dimensions of the play began to be valued, as the theatre discarded the pictorial priorities of the picture frame and explored the unlocalized staging and swifter and less cluttered action of the playwright's original theatres. In 1935, John Gielgud directed himself, Laurence Olivier, Peggy Ashcroft and Edith Evans in what became a benchmark production, able to explore the variety of expressive modes of a full text. The graceful and eminently practical setting designed by Motley was a structure which placed elements of a quasi-Elizabethan stage in a West End proscenium-arch house (Levenson, 1987, 57–60; Mullin, 47–52). It set a standard for negotiations between Shakespeare's stage and those available to most British and American companies. Gielgud's production was an uncluttered, impassioned and elegant perfor-mance, romantic but accommodating the variety of the play's challenges. One performance in particular, that of Evans as the Nurse, proved particularly influential: it was unsentimental, richly comic and persuasive in realistic detail. The Stratford productions of the 1930s (that of 1936 was restaged in 1945) suffered from the customary lack of glamour in comparison with those in London, and were less radical in their adaptation of Shakespeare's stage-craft to the Memorial Theatre's somewhat intractable proscenium arch. A sense predominated of the pictorial values associated with the Renaissance, and of idealized social and sexual behaviour.

Since the 1940s the expectations that audiences bring to productions of *Romeo and Juliet* have changed in ways that this book will document. Both critical writing and the theatre have recently acknowledged the play's vitality in ways that complement the Romantic model. Michael Goldman, in *Shakespeare and the Energies of Drama* (1972), writes eloquently of the play's power on stage:

> Against the play's general background, its rapidly assembling crowds, its fevered busyness, its continual note of impatience and the quick violence of its encounters, the image that remains most strongly in our minds is not of the lovers as a couple, but of each as a separate individual grappling with internal energies that both threaten and express the self, energies for which language is

inadequate but that lie at the root of language, that both overturn
and enrich society. (Goldman, 43)

This reads like a late twentieth-century revisiting of the storm and
stress of Berlioz's experience, with a blending of the societal and
personal psychology that is very much of its own time. Coppélia
Kahn provided a notable analysis of the social processes at work in
a seminal essay on 'Coming of age in Verona' (Kahn, 1983). Other
critics, notably Susan Snyder, have pointed to the play's duality of
modes, and the way it not only begins in comedy, but also
accommodates a comic vision of life (Snyder, 1979).

The formal qualities of the text have received a good deal of
attention. M.M. Mahood's book *Shakespeare's Wordplay* (1957)
fostered a sense of the relationships between the various kinds of
verbal dexterity and serious meanings. Several commentators,
notably Gibbons and Levenson among the play's editors, have
dwelt on the prevalence and variety of the formal devices
associated with sonnet sequences – the situations and language
of Petrarchan poetry – and the counterpoint between these and
the challenging 'realism' provided by such figures as the Nurse and
Mercutio. The development of the action is dominated by what
Nicholas Brooke identifies as two major ceremonies, 'the dance
betrothal of Act I' and 'the wedding-funeral of Act III' (Brooke,
106). Stanley Wells, in an important essay on the 'challenges' of
Romeo and Juliet, illustrates the extent to which directors have
persisted in diminishing the rhetorical variety and richness of the
script by removing repetitions and developments of imagery, and
by letting tragic mode 'seep' into the comedy of the earlier scenes
where comedy should predominate (Wells, 1996). Anthony
Dawson, taking a similar line to Wells, pleads for acknowledgement
of the parallelisms inherent in the play's structure (including the
three appearances of the Prince, and the speeches of Benvolio
and the Friar, explaining and describing important action) as
well as the rhetoric of individual scenes and speeches. While
acknowledging the importance of capturing the energy and

vigour of the script, he admits ruefully that he should like 'some time to see a production that embraced the formality as well' (Dawson, 140).

In terms of theatrical interpretation since the middle of the twentieth century, Verona has become more of a living city and less of a Renaissance ideal, the bawdy humour has been given freer expression, and the lovers are now measured by the standards of modern young people rather than a poetic and artistic ideal. One stage production of the play in London, two successful films and a Broadway musical have been particularly influential.

The stage production, directed by Franco Zeffirelli at the Old Vic in 1960, became emblematic: it was soon being cited as marking a point of no return in dealings with the play. (Peter Brook's 1970 RSC production of *A Midsummer Night's Dream* has acquired a similar status.) Reviewing a production at the Young Vic in 1971, Benedict Nightingale wrote: 'Since Zeffirelli reclaimed the play for reality, Romeos and Juliets have been moving further and further from the precious, knowing 30-year olds of theatrical tradition' (*New States.*, 10 Dec). Zeffirelli's film of the play, released in 1968, brought the values of his production to a wider audience. It has a supercharged romantic realism, believably adolescent lovers (seen, tastefully, in bed together) and a powerful sense of youth struggling against an 'ancient' grudge for which its elders were to blame. The 'enemies to peace' in Verona have the bravado, stylish self-display and sexual aggression of modern street gangs. In 1996 Baz Luhrmann's *Romeo + Juliet* transposed the play to a vivid modern-day Latin-American world, shot and edited with the brilliance and rapidity of pop videos and setting ideal lovers against a caricatured older generation. That Romeo and Juliet should meet in fancy dress when he (Leonardo di Caprio) is a knight in shining armour, and she (Clare Danes) an angel, perpetuates an idealizing tradition even in the midst of a hyperactive new world. The 'balcony scene' becomes a swimming-pool scene, with a witty gesture towards tradition in Romeo's final, clumsy assault on a vine-clad balcony (hitherto unregarded, and after Juliet has joined him by and in the pool).

Among the mixture of styles and ideas contributing to Luhrmann's film were elements of *West Side Story*, the 1957 stage musical (made into a film in 1961) by Jerome Robbins and Leonard Bernstein. Although it is not a strictly 'faithful' rendition of the play into the contemporary context of rival gangs and ethnic groups in New York City, the book by Arthur Laurents and lyrics by Stephen Sondheim are filled with echoes of the play's ideas and language, and the main outlines of the story correspond (Garebian). The opening brawl, the dance at the gym, a fire-escape balcony scene and the final 'rumble' correspond to the play's principal events, even though the shape of the narrative differs in one vital respect: Tony (Romeo) dies in a fight, rather than by suicide, and Maria (Juliet) survives him. More important, the music and dance brilliantly convey a sense of vitality, barely suppressed anger and (in two numbers, 'America' and 'Gee, Officer Krupke') social satire. The musical's invaluable gift to subsequent productions of Shakespeare's play has been the readiness of audiences to see correspondences between Verona's streets and those of New York or London as a necessary and legitimate, rather than accidental or trivializing, feature of productions. Bernard Levin praised Peter Hall's 1961 Stratford production for achieving 'an exciting sense of family . . . a feeling that there are two real groups in one real city and that the star-crossed lovers' tragedy is real and springs from it' (*D. Express*). Even Kenneth MacMillan's 1965 Royal Ballet production of the ballet to Prokofiev's score, although necessarily more picturesque and stylized, has a strong element of 'realistic' street life. By the 1970s, it seemed odd *not* to be reminded of whatever happened to be the current fashion in gang warfare. Even if the sociological dimension of the play's dynastic rivalries is not strictly comparable to that of modern gangs, evoking them was now a requirement. 'A *dog* of the house of Montague moves me', says Sampson in the play's first scene (1.1.7; my italics), claiming the same comprehensive loyalty to his faction as the boys who sing of the enduring sense of belonging and the street supremacy that goes with being a 'Jet'.

The other major influence for change in attitudes, also reflected by Zeffirelli's film, was a readiness to afford the play's treatment of sexuality the new freedoms claimed by contemporary drama and cinema and, up to a point, television. This was the era of the so-called 'satire boom' represented by *Private Eye* and the short-lived but influential television programme *That Was The Week That Was*, of *Beyond the Fringe* and Joe Orton's plays. The unsuccessful prosecution of Penguin Books in 1960, for publishing an unexpurgated paperback edition of D.H. Lawrence's *Lady Chatterley's Lover*, was one of the many significant showdowns over public morality. In his opening address the prosecution's leading counsel asked the jury 'Is it a book you would ever wish your wife or your servants to read?' This famous question was an unwitting summary of the sexual and social attitudes whose obsolescence the trial proclaimed (Rolph, 17; see also Marwick, 1999, 145–6). The 'sexual revolution' of the 1960s was legislated for by the implementation or repeal of a series of Acts of Parliament, supported by the availability of oral contraception and not as yet overshadowed by the threat of AIDS. Its progress caused widespread indignation among the appointed and self-appointed guardians of morals. Symptomatic of this were the 'Dirty Plays' furore (led by a governor of the RSC) and the foundation of the reactionary National Viewers' and Listeners' Association (NVLA) led by Mrs Mary Whitehouse, with its ambition to 'clean up' the broadcast media. Much was said about the corruption of youth. Liberal commentators identified a source for the anxiety. 'The real crisis of teenage morals', Alex Comfort wrote in his influential *Sex in Society*, 'affects not the teenager but his elders, who find themselves increasingly defending an ethos which they are beginning to recognise as unworkable' (Comfort, 101). Teenagers could indeed seem to themselves to be a race apart, a tendency noted by such chroniclers of youth movements as Colin McInnes. In his novel *Absolute Beginners* (1959) the narrator's elder brother Vernon represents a generation that missed out on all this:

> Even today, of course, there are some like him, i.e., kids of the right age, between fifteen or so and twenty, that I wouldn't myself describe as teenagers; I mean not kiddos who dig the teenage *thing*, or are it. But in poor Vernon's era, the sad slob, there just weren't any: can you believe it? Not any authentic teenagers at all. In those days, it seems, you were just an over-grown boy, or an under-grown man, life didn't seem to cater for anything whatever else between.
>
> (McInnes, 1959, 39)

Teenage culture had arrived in Britain from America decisively with the increased affluence of the mid-1950s, and simultaneously with the comic and serious celebrations of 'anger'. In the persons of James Dean and Marlon Brando, it has been suggested, teenagers were offered role models who reflected what they already were, rather than what they might be when they grew up. The strong element of fatalism in rock 'n' roll also had an impact. Benny Green connects the early and accidental deaths of Dean and of Buddy Holly, and the lyrics of such songs as Ray Peterson's 1959 hit 'Tell Laura I Love Her'. As well as validating rebellion against an older, uncomprehending generation, the new 'young' music gave currency to a sense of sudden, young death as 'a pop happening because it prevents its victim from growing older' (Green, 35).

Neither teenage rebellion or gang warfare as such, nor an equivalent of the kind of sexual behaviour – extramarital promiscuity – that preoccupied moralists, nor the cult of early death, is represented in the script of Shakespeare's play. The 'houses' are not street gangs, and Romeo and Juliet rush to marriage before they go to bed together. Far from making some kind of suicide pact, neither of them wishes to die until it seems as though there is no hope left. However, the situations and behaviour of the protagonists can seem to echo modern preoccupations in ways that enliven and fuel performances and engage young audiences. The chapters dealing with the lovers (4 and 5) and Mercutio (3) reflect these matters directly. In

Mercutio's case, it is likely that interpretations have been affected by changes since the 1960s in the law concerning homosexual relations between consenting adult males. In a sense, the history of performances is a history of revisions in what successive generations have thought possible and desirable in realizing scripts. Quite apart from the 'teenage' phenomenon, the advent of the 'angry young man' has a specific bearing on Mercutio. Walter Allen's review of Kingsley Amis's novel *Lucky Jim* (1954) might be a description of some of the Mercutios seen at Stratford after 1958:

> A new hero has arisen among us. Is he the intellectual tough, or the tough intellectual? He is consciously, even conscientiously, graceless. His face, when not dead-pan, is set in a snarl of exasperation. He has one skin too few, but his is not the sensitiveness of the young man in early twentieth-century fiction: it is to the phoney that his nerve-ends are tremblingly exposed, and at the least suspicion of the phoney he goes tough.   (Bergonzi, 136)

One can almost hear Mercutio's contempt for the duellist Tybalt, one of 'these new tuners of accent' and 'fashion-mongers' (2.4.29, 33). In 1968 the end of theatrical censorship by the Lord Chamberlain's Office acknowledged the pressure for greater freedom of expression, in language as well as action. Readers born in the last three decades should remember that sexually explicit language and violent behaviour were a relative rarity in the public media before the 1960s, and that in the days before 'fuck' was habitually heard on television, the bawdy in Shakespeare existed largely in a vacuum, an oasis of archaic profanity in an otherwise chastely spoken theatre.

These shifts in attitude, and a willingness to see the modern world in the stage's Veronas, are also reflected in the programmes sold to the theatre's audiences. In the 1950s programmes at the Shakespeare Memorial Theatre were elegantly printed but austere, with the cast, credits ('Stockings by Kayser Bondor. Shoes by Anello and Davide'), and perhaps a summary of the play's action.

Souvenir books offered photographs of the cast, arranged hierarchically (full pages for the stars). In the mid-1960s the programmes became dossiers of material the director thought relevant (now a magic word) to the play: critical comments, perhaps the director's address to the cast on the first day of rehearsals, a few photographs of actors in rehearsal (day clothes more casual than in the 1950s) and notes on previous productions. At the same time a free cast list was provided. In 1970, for one season, programmes became dossiers in a literal sense: folders containing a few bound and some loose pages, with a poster and cast list. The programme was likely to proclaim the leading idea of the production ('These violent delights have violent ends' in 1973) or even indicate the open-mindedness of the company performing it. In 1976 the actors had been asked to respond to a short questionnaire: they were to remember 'the most extremely violent thing you have done in your life', describe their first adult sexual experience, and jot down what Renaissance Italy meant to them. It is hard to imagine such an exercise being carried out by a director like Glen Byam Shaw, let alone the results being published for the audience to digest.

Sometimes programmes have indicated that a production has espoused a particular critical viewpoint, or have included an essay commissioned from an academic, but it is not usually possible to trace such debts and the essays occasionally have little bearing on the production. Apart from a general indebtedness to such studies of wordplay as that by M.M. Mahood and the account of *Shakespeare's Bawdy* by Eric Partridge (revised edition, 1955), or to the information included in such editions as T.J.B. Spencer's New Penguin (1967) and Brian Gibbons's Arden (second series, 1980[7]), direct academic input has been rare. Such influential essays as Kahn's 'Coming of age in Verona' should probably be considered as parallel to contemporary theatrical productions, reflecting the same preoccupations rather than directly influencing the directors or actors. The RSC's directors have not been notable for their attention to (or indeed respect for) academic writing, although scrupulous attention to the text and the notes of editors has been normal, even when the script has been put together without adherence to any one edition. The promptbooks do reveal a readiness on the part of successive directors to adopt their predecessors' cuts to the full text, either consciously ('Let's see what Peter cut here') or by serendipity. Quite apart from the more important cuts that affect the script's internal economy (of which changes in the final scene are the most common) it should be noted that some lines in the play have hardly ever been spoken: Juliet's reference to rumours that 'the lark and the loathed toad change eyes' (3.5.31–4) is a great rarity. A whole sequence that has hardly ever been performed in anything like its full form is that involving Peter and the musicians hired to play for the wedding (4.5.96–141).

In one important respect, these changing productions have not reflected a change in society at large: men have directed them all. Very few women directed on the main stage at Stratford before the 1990s, and only a handful have done so since then – perhaps more by choice than by conspiracy. The need to give a popular play maximum box-office potential has resulted in its being given in the largest of the Stratford theatres on all but one of the occasions (in 1989) when it has figured in the main season's repertoire. (In 1984 and 1997 a touring production was being shown in Stratford.) Not every director has wanted to work on the main stage during the last decade and a half.

It is also the case that the vast majority of the reviews that give us access to their impact on audiences have been written by men: the number of women reviewing plays for the national press has increased since the 1950s, but little of the journalism cited in this book reflects this. In the early part of the period under discussion, male critics displayed a confidence in their knowledge of how young Italian women mature that few would hazard nowadays. For the most part these were the same critics who prized accomplished, 'classical' character drawing, elegance of movement and sublime effects in speaking.

To a considerable extent, this book is a study of changing critical fashions seen through the play's reception at the hands of reviewers: even when an archive video or sound recording is available, productions come and go while the written word has remained. I have tried to balance these responses with a sense of how the productions might seem to other viewers, but it is not possible to accept their evidence for what happened without taking on some of the interpretation that colours the reports. Without wishing to patronize such experienced playgoers, or to seem ungrateful for the evidence provided by their voices from the past, I have tried to get round behind them. Of the fifteen productions discussed, I myself saw seven. Where reviews are not cited for an element in the description of a performance, it can be attributed either to the evidence of the promptbook, or (from 1986) the Shakespeare Centre's archive video, or (in the case of productions since 1973) my own memories and notes. Prompt-book notations commonly indicate the position of characters on stage from the point of view of the actor. In this book, all such indications are given from the audience's point of view, as if the reader were sitting facing the stage.

One consequence of using reviews as a source should be emphasized. Most reviewers have usually written on the basis of one viewing of the production, at the press night (nowadays this follows several previews), and have been obliged to send in their copy either late the same night or early the next day. The exceptions are the weekly reviewers for newspapers and magazines, and those who write for such academic journals as *Shakespeare Survey* and *Shakespeare Quarterly*, who have usually been able to see performances later in the season and often more than once. Even so, the work of actors has usually been judged on the basis of one early performance in the nervous situation of an opening night. Many (though by no means all) of the less favourable comments quoted in this book might have been qualified by a sight of the same actor at his or her fiftieth performance. In some cases, the transfer of a production to London has allowed reviewers a second viewing, and these notices have also been cited where appropriate.

After Adrian Noble's 1995 *Romeo and Juliet*, Michael Billington wrote: 'the main conclusion to be drawn from this decorative, heat-drained, diluted Verdian production – Stratford's fourth in the past decade – is that Shakespeare's lovers are over-exposed and that they would benefit from a period of entombed silence' (*Guardian*). Two years later another production opened in the Swan, and three years after that another was seen in the main house: this book is written in what is unlikely to be more than a short lull in Veronese tragic business at Stratford. The play's popularity (enhanced by its presence in the film *Shakespeare in Love*) and its frequency as an element of school and examination syllabuses place it on the 'A' list of works that the RSC can bank on at the box office – so far as anything can ever be banked on there. But those with a professional obligation to see every production should always remember that most audience members do not see the play more than once and many will be seeing it for the first time. I also found the 1995 production wearisome, but at one performance a row of fifteen-year-olds in front of me, at first restive and excited mainly by being on an outing, were absorbed and attentive by the end and wildly enthusiastic at the curtain call. The play itself may seem jejune to some, and overfamiliar to other experienced playgoers, but its power and vitality can survive even misconceived or overelaborate performances. Passion lends it power, even after decades of change in the way we expect that passion to be expressed.

NOTES

1 Ivor Brown, 1955 souvenir book, p. 1 (unnumbered).
2 Anthony Quayle, 1952 souvenir book, pp. 2–33, reprinted from the *Sphere*, 8 March 1952.
3 *Shakespeare Memorial Theatre 1948–50. A Photographic Record with Forewords by Ivor Brown and Anthony Quayle. Photographs by Angus McBean* (London, 1951), 11.

4 Sydney Edwards, 'Not even Shakespeare escapes Mr Healey', *Shropshire Star* (Wellington), 7 April 1976.
5 'A recession for the arts?', *What's On* (Birmingham), 3 May 1980.
6 'A fight to the final curtain at the RSC', *Guardian*, 22 April 1989.
7 All references to the text of *Romeo and Juliet* are to this edition.

1

FAIR VERONA

What kind of place is the city in which Romeo and Juliet meet their fate? Matteo Bandello's story, as presented in the second volume of William Painter's *Palace of Pleasure* in 1567, describes the town's situation on a trade route and the 'fertile mountains and pleasant valleys' that surround it. Verona is remarkable for the 'great number of very clear and lively fountains that serve for the ease and commodity of the place', its four bridges, and 'an infinite number of other honourable antiquities daily apparent unto those that be curious to view and look upon them' (Spencer, 1968, 51–2). Arthur Brooke's poem *Romeus and Juliet* (1562) adds nothing to this information, and fails to mention the antiquities. Shakespeare seems to have felt little need to embellish this. We learn of a meeting place called 'old free-town', at least one rich family's house has an orchard with a high wall, and there is a grove of sycamore near the city. The most important aspect of the play's Verona is how its citizens behave: fencing, dancing, quarrelling, talking, loving and dying. As Jill L. Levenson observes, it is also a remarkably poetic city, in the sense that 'no one writes poetry . . . but everyone speaks it for better or for worse' (Levenson, 2000, 56).

Since the beginning of the nineteenth century a substantial pictorial tradition has accumulated round the play, accompanying the iconography of the lovers and their fate developed by painters and illustrators, from Royal Academicians to the designers of cigar labels. In the Victorian theatre 'authentic' representations of the city's architecture, appropriately impressive period costumes and atmospheric lighting and music were indispensable. The play was illuminated by – or bore the burden of – a demand for images evoking the high Renaissance style, and the desire for beakers full of the warm south. It had to satisfy the longing for a world that combined superlative artistic achievement and passion. The critic Clement Scott gave an admiring account of Henry Irving's production at the Lyceum Theatre in 1882, which served as an example for what could be achieved in this theatrical style. Irving, wrote Scott, 'put poetry into motion and action', and the speaking of the Prologue by an actor made up as Dante offered additional literary endorsement to the twenty-two changes of scene that followed. There was elaborate 'local colour' in the crowds of the opening, 'a vision of old Italian luxury' at Capulet's feast, and lavish architectural and horticultural riches in the balcony scene. The deaths of Mercutio and Tybalt took place outside the city walls: 'the glaring white heat of the city, the low avenue of cypress trees, the scattered roofs of the buildings, and the admirable effects of light, made this a picture in relief, that lingers pleasingly on the memory' (Scott, 233, 235). Such accounts make it clear that the very achievement of realizing these pictures on stage conferred on the modern theatre the dignity of the period shown. The ultimate authority claimed by these productions was that they gave to the dramatist's imaginings a life and completeness his own theatres could never have afforded.

Harley Granville-Barker's *Preface* to the play, published in 1930, includes no speculations as to the physical appearance of the city. This is an implicit reassertion of the work's integrity in terms of the Elizabethan stage: pictorial considerations simply do not count. In the early twentieth century a new movement in Shakespearean staging reacted against the pictorialism of the Victorian and Edwardian theatre, and rediscovered – even if it did not always imitate – the open Elizabethan stage. Few productions were in fact so austere as to offer no sense of the Italian milieu, but definitions of the story's period, and even of Italy itself, varied considerably. Versions of these constructs are identifiable even when (as in the 1976 and 1989 Stratford productions) the director and designer have worked with a bare platform stage. The 'landmark' British productions of the play during the first six decades of the twentieth century – John Gielgud's in 1935, Peter Brook's in 1947 and Franco Zeffirelli's in 1960 – each evoked different versions of the past, with varying degrees of emphasis on elegance, violence, dust and heat. Michael Bogdanov's aggressive and influential staging at Stratford in 1986 (like his 1978 *Taming of the Shrew*) moved the play out of the Renaissance, providing it with an up-to-date Italy of social and political corruption. Similar, though less socially specific, stagings such as Ron Daniels's (1980) seemed to take place in a fusion of 'ancient' and modern quarrelling that owed as much to Stanley Kubrick's film *A Clockwork Orange* (1971) as to any sense of theatrical tradition. (An even more direct influence of this film was present in Karin Beier's Düsseldorf production, seen at the Barbican in 1994.) At the same time, 'period' productions have often suggested analogies with modern urban violence and, in some cases, the distinct influence of *West Side Story* (1957). That this might happen even without any touch of modernity in costume is suggested in Clive Barnes's review of Prokofiev's ballet at the Royal Opera House in 1965, with Margot Fonteyn and Rudolf Nureyev as the lovers. Every now and then the performance aroused 'an intriguing suspicion that what [Kenneth] MacMillan has achieved is a modern dress Romeo without modern dress. The leading characters are perhaps more recognizably of our own day than of Shakespeare's' (*New States. & Nat.*, 19 Feb 1965). As it happens, the jeans and jackets in the stage production of *West Side Story* had been chosen and cut with a view to emulating the 'classical' outline of Italian Renaissance hose and tunics (Garebian, 54–6).

In the last analysis, 'Verona' in stage or screen productions of *Romeo and Juliet* is invariably a superimposition of images: a sense of how life is lived in the play, an appeal to the audience's sense of the period represented, and an element of allusion to the contemporary world. In the absence of more specific architectural and cultural details, reviewers have tended to assess productions according to their evocation of 'southern' qualities, particularly heat, both meteorological and human. Sometimes the desire for these has been very acute. The grim social, economic and meteorological context of Peter Brook's 1947 production has been referred to already (see p. 3). When it opened the Shakespeare Memorial Theatre's season on 5 April, W.A. Darlington praised the director's achievement of 'an air of excitement, colour and hot blood', and noted that Brook gave 'the quarrel between the families real venom, and the fights real hatred' (*D. Telegraph*). In other words, the heat came as much from the action as from any effects of setting and lighting. For most of the critics this was already a hallmark of Brook's style (thus the *Daily Herald*: 'a fine swirl of movement, making the most of the crowds and torchlit masque'). In the drab everyday world of Britain in the late 1940s such vividness was all the more appealing. Brook had staged the play 'in glorious Technicolor' (*E. Standard*). The director himself claimed that he had taken his cue from Benvolio's warning 'now these hot days is the mad blood stirring' (3.1.4). The *Daily Mail* noted that 'the hot colours of the market-place at Verona were a welcome change from the wet and windy streets of Stratford-upon-Avon'. 'This is no austerity production', observed the *Daily Worker*, 'It is a kaleidoscope of costume and colour into which the producer . . . has thrown everything except the grand piano' (8 Apr). The *Coventry Evening Telegraph* reported that Brook had been to Portugal 'to study the play in the summer heat of that country', and that Bernard Shaw, no less, had 'advised him to concentrate on youthful lovers and virile fights' (5 Apr). The 'Levantine' and picturesque crowd (including at least one carpet-seller) does not in itself seem far removed from similar effects in the older pictorial tradition, or the late flowering of the style in George Cukor's stately and elaborately picturesque MGM film, released in 1936. More than one reviewer of Brook's production mentioned such orientalizing shows of a past era as *Chu-Chin-Chow*. What was distinctive was the way Brook framed this crowd, his combination at that stage in his career of picturesqueness and sparse elegance (Figure 1).

These responses set the agenda for the productions that followed: crowds and movement, the sense of heat and passion, and a tension between these and the production's context, both inside and outside the theatre itself. The reservations expressed about this important post-war Stratford staging would also reappear. Like Brook, others would be accused of being more concerned 'to stage an exciting duel than to catch the lyric emotion of the tragedy' (*Times*). The *Manchester Guardian* distinguished between the 'warmth and colour' of the crowd scenes, and the stark treatment of the 'balcony' scene and Juliet's bed-chamber, 'hardly less gaunt and unsoftened than the Capulet tomb' (Figure 29). The *Daily Mail* compared Brook's methods to those of the ballet: 'alive with colour and movement. Indeed, it turns out to be a contest of ballet versus the Bard, with the Bard an easy loser.' In the *Evening Standard* Beverley Baxter, whose belief that no one so young should direct the 'balcony' scene has been quoted already (p. 4), invoked rival media: 'One feels that to [Brook] the stage is alternately a gallery in which to display his paintings, then a screen on which to outmove the movies.' In fact Brook deployed his crowd of 'extras' in a sparse, uncluttered setting, as though the kind of picturesque local colour perfected by Irving in the 1880s had been cut out and stuck onto a bare arena. Ivor Brown recognized what he took to be an intention to 'deromanticise the tragedy', but felt that the director had failed to achieve the context this required and commented that the 'vast, cold blue cyclorama, with fragmentary scenery in front', did

FIGURE 1 (*opposite*) The indigo sky and orange arena with its low, crenellated town wall in Peter Brook's 1947 production. The prince (Robert Harris) brings the rival factions to order after the brawl in 1.1. Some of the colourfully 'Levantine' extras can be seen among the liveried Montagues and Capulets.

nothing to suggest to him 'the slightest sense of earthy and domestic circumstances or of an Italian city' (*Observer*). Rolf Gérard's settings combined a brilliant cyclorama and an open arena with architectural units resembling those found in early Renaissance paintings. Photographs suggest painterly positioning of figures in a landscape, and even of stylized gesture reminiscent of Italian Renaissance images (Figures 8 and 39).

Like the question of southern locale, and indeed in counterpoint to it, recognition of a director's 'deromanticizing' recurs in subsequent years. Often the consequences in design terms did not generate the desired sense of warmth and passion. In 1951 the Festival of Britain had been staged as a celebration of the British national genius, balancing hopes for the future with celebrations of tradition and achievement. The exhibition on the South Bank was a showcase for modernity in design, from jet planes on display to the chairs in the refreshment rooms. Pale woods and veneers, clean structural lines and light furnishing fabrics were the way of the future. Motley's set for the 1954 Stratford *Romeo and Juliet* (Figure 35), directed by Glen Byam Shaw, with its 'background of light oak' struck the *Daily Worker* as being 'as modern as the Festival of Britain architecture'. It showed 'a Verona that seems almost cool in midsummer, and though the pace there has the appropriately ardent rapidity, the effect of the stage picture all through is one of pale neatness' (*FT*). The *Daily Telegraph*'s headline, 'Utility Set for Romeo', invoked the spare and elegant functionalism achieved in wartime mass-production furniture. Other reviewers supplied the same comparisons, with varying degrees of surprise or scorn. Patrick Gibbs suggested that the light, airy settings 'did nothing to foster a mood appropriate to tragedy' (*D. Telegraph*). There was general agreement that in this context the events of the play seemed too modern. 'An Unromantic Romeo. Stratford a Far Cry from Verona' announced the *Stage*, noting that 'the architecture of Capulet's house, the magical enclosure of the orchard walls, and the grey constriction of the Friar's cell' had all been 'left severely to the imagination'. Ivor

Brown felt as though he were 'cooling himself in a modern and logical Sweden rather than sweating in old and feud-fevered Verona' (*Observer*). Margaret Harris, the designer, reflected later that if she had been able to put touches of gold on the bare wood, she might have averted such criticisms (Mullin, 141).

For the *Daily Mail* these 'cold, bald but serviceable settings' suggested 'a production conceived in modern dress and played as an afterthought in period'. 'Too much in the first part', wrote Harold Conway in the *Daily Sketch*, 'bore a similar stamp to a carnival night at the *palais de danse*: a rowdy night, with the spivs in.' In fact neither the behaviour nor the costume of Glen Byam Shaw's brawlers resembled the flashy suits and ties of post-war street criminals and profiteers – the 'spivs' or 'wide boys' – still less the younger 'Teddy Boys' of the 1950s with their velvet-collared 'Edwardian' coats, drainpipe trousers, suede shoes and disposition to gang warfare with bike chains and razors – such things would come to Stratford later.

As if in response, Motley's designs for Byam Shaw's 1958 production (Figure 2) were reminiscent of their work for Gielgud in 1935: elegant and unequivocally of the Renaissance. Alan Dent observed: 'Motley this time has gone to a different painter, one of the school of Perugia, for the delightful staging and brilliant clothes' (*News Chron.*). In the *Daily Mail* Cecil Wilson hailed 'a sun-kissed, starlit, hot-blooded background to the bitter-sweet tragedy of suffocated young love'. The *Stratford-upon-Avon Herald* rejoiced at the succession of stage effects evoking Italian painting, including such touches as 'the silvered tree-tops of the orchard which we have seen before in pictures of the Virgin and Child' and 'the latticed tomb in which Juliet lies at last with all the delicate, Titian-haired radiance of a young Renaissance angel'. The composition of figures within the framework of the set's arcades and loggias was enhanced by such effects as the tableau formed around the supposedly dead Juliet, with Paris arriving on the steps balancing a bouquet with the studied grace of Albrecht visiting Giselle's grave in Adam's romantic ballet (Figure 3).

Unimpressed, Kenneth Tynan announced in the *Observer* that his ideal production would be 'a mingling of Peter Brook's torrid, swarming production of eleven years ago, and Claire Bloom's fast, reckless Juliet at the Old Vic in 1952'. Byam Shaw's effort 'shows few signs that the play has been either rethought or refelt. Everything is generalized and over-ardent.' Two years later, at the Old Vic, Zeffirelli's *Romeo and Juliet* was to provide exactly that revision, marking like Brook's a change of approach that no subsequent director could safely ignore. Tynan hailed it triumphantly. This was a challenge not only to received ideas of the play, but more generally to notions of what the endangered and essential 'Shakespearean' quality might be. In a genuinely realistic handling 'what gets lost is not Shakespeare but the formal, dehumanized stereotype that we have so often made of him'.

> The production evoked a whole town, a whole riotous manner of living: so abundant and compelling was the life on stage that I could not wait to find out what happened next . . . The sets are spaciously atmospheric, composed of peeling, flaking walls that serve equally well for interiors or exteriors. Children scuffle in the alleys and vendors bawl their wares. We are unmistakably in Verona, or anyway in Italy; the director has even taught his English cast how to shrug. (Tynan, 1967, 50)

The rival factions were 'gangs of dawdlers with time on their hands; captives of the streets, like the boys in Fellini's film *I Vitelloni*'. Many other features of this production were to prove influential, in particular its handling of the play's language, the

---

FIGURE 2 (*opposite*) The dance in Glen Byam Shaw's 1958 production. Juliet (Dorothy Tutin) raises a torch, watched by Romeo (Richard Johnson, cloaked, right). The busy stage picture, accurately reproduced in Angus McBean's photograph, includes musicians in the left-hand gallery, Capulet and his aged cousin (Mark Dignam and Donald Eccles) seated on the left. The watchful Nurse (Angela Baddeley) is directly upstage of Juliet. Paris (Michael Meacham, left) and Mercutio (Edward Woodward) kneel at the front of the stage. The loggias and arcades of the set are backed with a black velvet drop, and candelabra and torches have been flown in and set for this scene. (1.5)

FIGURE 3 A tableau formed round the unconscious Juliet in Glen Byam Shaw's 1958 production. Musicians and Paris (Michael Meacham) are on the stairs at the left, with the Friar (Cyril Luckham) at the centre. Lady Capulet (Rachel Kempson) and the Nurse (Angela Baddeley) support Juliet (Dorothy Tutin) in graceful posture, and Capulet (Mark Dignam) looks on. The stairs and the central platform have been trucked on between the lateral segments of Motley's set, which are concealed by a false proscenium and curtains. These also provide a picture frame for the action. (4.5)

simple, direct playing of the lovers by John Stride and Judi Dench and the treatment of the text in the final sequences. The impact on Stratford productions, and on reactions to them, is evident in the first *Romeo and Juliet* of the new decade.

Peter Hall's *Romeo and Juliet* opened at Stratford in August 1961, some ten months after Zeffirelli's, and while the Old Vic production was still in repertoire and on tour. It could hardly hope to avoid comparison. Hall made his own claim to neo-realism – of a kind that would be apparent three years later in *The Wars of the Roses*. The sets were a far cry from Motley's elegant picture frames and loggias: they were by Sean Kenny, already famous for his creations of overpowering, mobile and 'realistic' architectural elements. These were environments to act in (and on occasion avoid) rather than pictures to pose in front of (Figure 24). Not everyone was convinced. T.C. Worsley thought Hall had made 'a serious if somewhat heavy-handed attempt to let the play speak for itself without tricks or gimmicks', but contrasted its 'English traditional approach' with that of the Italian director (*FT*). Robert Muller in the *Daily Mail* ('Hall Squeezes the Life from Romeo') longed to get back to Zeffirelli's Verona. Sean Kenny's design was 'strangely disappointing . . . an unwieldy clutter of columns and arches and windows, built on a revolving stage, dominated by a great timbered staircase that is negotiable only by lumbering up and thumping down'. Worse, the supposedly realistic acting carried none of the conviction of Zeffirelli's shoulder-shrugging youths. 'For here we are back among actors: actors attitudinizing, actors slapping their thighs, actors yoo-hooing, actors wearing masks and holding torches aloft.' For better-disposed reviewers, Hall's management of the crowds achieved the appropriate effect. 'The first meeting of the Montagues and Capulets is literally a dust-up, in which the air is filled with feathers from a servant's basket' (*Birm. Mail*), and 'even the Bolshoi [Ballet] would have been hard put to it to beat the athleticism of the swirling swordplay' (*Glos. Echo*). Desmond Heeley's costumes were praised in the *Stage* for seeming to be what these figures might wear for ordinary purposes rather than images designed to evoke a period in art. These were signs of a trend that was soon to dominate British Shakespeare productions. The feathers scattered from a servant's basket in 1961 were importing the clutter of such comedy productions as Peter Hall and John Barton's 1960 *The Taming of the Shrew* into the tragic arena of another Italian town, and bringing it down to earth. A degree of social realism would replace local colour, and the familial and social identities of characters would be registered.

The production by the Greek director Karolos Koun (1967) was taken as a refusal to 'out-Zeffirelli Zeffirelli' with impressions of heat and Mediterranean sunlight. Instead the designer Timothy O'Brien had created 'a city of cool, flat, geometric shapes in front of which actors and supers circulated with a tepidness that pushed the emotional temperature barely beyond freezing point' (*Plays & P.*). There was 'no hint of sunny Verona' (*E. Standard*), and the colours of the actors' costumes (with a preponderance of reds) made them stand out against 'the movable grey shapes against a grey background' (*D. Mail*) that shifted noiselessly into place for each new scene and seemed at times 'like a gigantic trap' (*Guardian*). Despite this classical restraint and intensity, Koun's production was consistent with RSC policy in focusing on the family, creating a strong sense of family ties and identities and making Lady Capulet and the Nurse (Figure 11) relatively youthful. The 'tense, narrow, doom-laden production' was acknowledged to be the work of a director with 'a Mediterranean eye for the tyranny of sexual passion and the brief glory of the flesh' (*Birm. Post*). This was a 'southern' view of the play quite different in emphasis from Zeffirelli's. Irving Wardle suggested that, whereas Zeffirelli's 'coltish' young lovers might have been saved by some fresh turn of events, in Koun's production Estelle Kohler and Ian Holm were 'firmly locked into an implacable pattern' (*Times*). From the opening, as the cast assembled slowly on stage for the Prologue, the citizenry of Verona were employed as a mute chorus, to 'loom over the proceedings' (*FT*), and the fighting in the streets was 'sullenly rather than blazingly angry' (*Birm. Post*). Verona had become 'a city ruined by hate', and Harold Hobson was fascinated by the relentless exploration and illustration of sexual word-play, along with a lack of 'chivalry' in the fights. The 'sword points thrusting into private parts' were 'a savage parody on Verona's degradation of love' (*S. Times*).

Explicit performance of the play's rich vein of bawdy had become an established feature of Stratford's dealings with *Romeo and Juliet*. The abolition in 1968 of pre-censorship of the drama by the Lord Chamberlain's office finally removed an absurd restriction on the work of dramatists who were already pushing against the boundaries of 'good taste' and traditional pieties. By 1973, when Terry Hands directed *Romeo and Juliet* at Stratford, the RSC had staged such iconoclastic works as Peter Weiss's *Marat/Sade* (Aldwych, 1964, directed by Peter Brook) and Jean Genet's *The Balcony* (Aldwych, 1972, directed by Hands). The new *Romeo and Juliet* underlined 'all that is harsh and violent in the play', in a permanent set by Farrah that seemed to transport the action to 'a shipyard or the cage of a service lift' (*Times*).

Against a black background, lit sometimes by flickering gas torches and flares (including one in the centre of the stage), the iron grilles and stairs of the set evoked the fire escapes of *West Side Story* without any of the musical's wistful urban romance (Figure 33). 'There is no suggestion of Italy, of over-powering heat, of daylight even', complained the *Guardian*, adding that Hands's recent work on Genet seemed to have left its mark. The 'great rich Capulet' and his family seemed to have been taken down a peg or two: masters and servants wore similar homespun breeches and shirts. The more upmarket 'county' Paris, played by Anthony Pedley, was distinguished by a bulky jacket in what seemed like the then fashionable 'fun fur'. A washing line hung across the street at the beginning of the play, suggesting a back street rather than a grand thoroughfare: in keeping with the company's current leaning towards symbolism, the laundry was vivid red. Richard David noted that (except for the 'balcony' scene and their farewell at dawn) the lovers' scenes were played downstage 'not only on the lowest level but very much within the living circle of the audience', while events that influenced their destiny took place predominantly above (David, 107). The fighting was brutal and unceremonious, David Suchet's close-cropped Tybalt resembled a 'skinhead', and Bernard Lloyd was a savage and sexually obsessed Mercutio (see pp. 103–4). In the *Sunday Telegraph* Frank Marcus suggested that Hands had substituted 'the sombre, doom-laden atmosphere of a Jacobean revenge melodrama for the poignant ecstasies of young love'. 'The aghast clucking over the gin-and-tonics in the interval' provoked Benedict Nightingale in the *New Statesman* to ask what kind of performance the audience and many of his colleagues would prefer. To his mind this was in fact an 'original and arresting' production. Under the title 'Angry Brigade' – referring to a violent anarchist group – he identified 'seething, unsightly anger' as the predominant passion in Hands's Verona, and sketched a 'traditional' *Romeo and Juliet*.

> Mercutio should have been the ebullient wag of theatrical tradition
> . . . The nurse should have been something more comfy and folksy . . .
> Juliet should neither have been so flauntingly interested in sex
> before meeting Romeo, nor thrown herself at him quite so recklessly
> . . . Romeo, similarly, should have loved, died, and even killed like
> the Renaissance Mr. Right he is.

In general, 'The fights should have been more gentlemanly, the deaths less bloody.' The defiant lack of picturesque 'local colour' was accompanied by an insistence on the symbolic dimension of the play. A naked flame represented the Capulet hearth and a maypole rose from the floor to provide a focus for the dancers. Juliet's garlanded bridal bed was stripped of its pink festoons as Capulet solemnly proclaimed 'All things that we ordained festival / Turn from their office to black funeral' (4.5.84–5). A mysterious hooded figure appeared on the top gallery during the Prologue, which was spoken by the actor who played the Prince, as the cast assembled in two lines on stage and faced the audience. The figure reappeared during the brawl in 2.1 and at other 'fateful' moments, and was later revealed to be the Apothecary. Such devices constituted a physical accompaniment to the element of rhetorical stylization in the text itself, and were typical of much RSC work in the late 1960s and early 1970s.

Trevor Nunn and Barry Kyle, in 1976, offered theatrical radicalism of a different kind with a bare permanent setting (Figure 30). It evoked the Elizabethan theatre under almost unrelieved bright lighting that allowed no opportunity for doom-laden atmospherics or, in fact, sun-baked piazzas. To a degree this was yet another indication of the struggle between Shakespeare's plays and the Stratford theatre that had been going on since the 1930s. Tanya Moiseiwitsch had designed a permanent wooden structure of stairs, balconies and platforms for the 1951 season of history plays, and several subsequent productions had effectively placed a pseudo-Elizabethan acting space on the stage of the main house. In 1976 the illusion of a Shakespearean theatre was more complete, although in fact it could never be either 'in the round' (as one headline proclaimed) or even a proper thrust. There were spectators in two rows of gallery seats at the back of the stage, but they were hardly ever addressed by the actors, and some reviewers found their presence distracting. In any case, as Gareth Lloyd Evans observed, there was little evidence that Elizabethan public playhouses ever had more than a few audience members in that position (*SA Herald*). This was 'a cool, dry, indoor world' (*Guardian*), and for all the boisterousness of much of the action, the production failed to create a sense of civic strife or passion. Romeo's costume was 'as near as you can get near to blue jeans in a seventeenth-century ambience' (*FT*). The performance began with actors limbering up and practising fencing moves, and, in a decision that recalled the Chorus in the previous season's *Henry V*, Nunn had the Prologue spoken by an actor in modern-dress denims, who later appropriated some of the Prince's concluding lines.

In Ron Daniels's 1980 production the action unfolded in 'an intimidatingly stylised urban jungle' (*Observer*). Ralph Koltai's design was dominated by peeling stucco walls, famously a feature of Zeffirelli's Verona but here reduced to movable screens manoeuvred into position by stage staff (Figure 32). The street violence that seemed partly of the past, partly of the future, and the zippered leather jackets and breeches that Nadine Baylis had given the youths recalled both Marlon Brando as a motorcyclist in *The Wild One* (1954) and the neatly stylish devotees of 'ultra-violence' in the film *A Clockwork Orange*. Stephen Oliver's eclectic, jazzy, score and the choreography of David Toguri helped to generate 'a quality of spontaneous sexual combustion' (*Guardian*), but an uncompromisingly modern setting put a strain on some of the social relationships. Why wouldn't such a resourceful and feisty Juliet as Judy Buxton's simply leave home? Roger Warren found this 'a remorselessly blank view, a faceless precinct for urban violence, where rival gangs lounged, hands in pockets'. Such a 'modern urban world' might give a context to Anton Lesser's Romeo but 'had no place for great houses and so tended to deprive Juliet of *her* context' (Warren, 1981, 152). Michael Bogdanov's 1986 production took the process a stage further, being set in 'a modern north Italian city, all brass and marble, sports cars, motor bikes, cycling clerics and hard-faced, swanky teenagers' (*S. Times*). Capulet (Richard Moore) had become a self-made tycoon and the Prince a sinister, trench-coated figure in dark glasses and accompanied by minders (Figure 4). It was implied that political and financial corruption were rife, but this vivid cartoon-like political social message also made it easier to believe that Juliet couldn't simply make an escape and marry whom she liked. As Niamh Cusack, who played Juliet, explained:

> She has been brought up in this environment and knows no other; protected but without friends; no-one to go out and meet on the piazza, no motor-scooter like all the boys seem to have; no one to compare notes with. A limo takes her here, there, and everywhere; life is organized for her and very sheltered.   (Cusack, 125)

FIGURE 4 (*opposite*) The Prince (David Glover) with Paris (Robert Morgan) at his side, harangues the families from the staircase landing at the end of 1.1. Chris Dyer's 1986 set offers an open white stage, with a staircase tower mounted on the revolve. Black-and-white photographic slides – not visible here – were projected on the back wall to help set the scene or provide ironic commentary. The balcony for 2.2 is on the right, in front of the proscenium arch.

With the Montagues and Capulets locked in a Mafia-style rivalry, their children were at once privileged and confined in a manner that suits the play: ten years later Baz Luhrmann's film would use a similar social framework.

In the *Guardian* Michael Billington acknowledged that Bogdanov had created 'a complete society in which everyone has a defined place'. It was a world 'of rich kids, fixed marriages and tough deals'. In this respect it engaged directly with current political and social preoccupations: Margaret Thatcher's government was supposedly leading the way to a classless, remorselessly upwardly mobile Britain, stripped of collective responsibilities and giving free reign to the generation of wealth. In fact Thatcher even went so far as to claim that there was no such thing as 'society'. The production was identified as 'a cross between *Absolute Beginners* and *West Side Story*, with a dash of *La Dolce Vita*' (*FT*). Conservative reviewers had no wish to linger in this city – 'Not much like the Verona I knew in 1981', complained J.C. Trewin (*Birm. Post*) – and there were complaints that the language was often at odds with the setting (*D. Telegraph*), and that the new context 'weakened the force' of the play's poetry (*SA Herald*). *Punch* expressed the most interesting reservations: Verona had been sited too far north, its sparse street life could not 'altogether symbolize a sun-baked community of seething sexual activity'. The Verona that Sheridan Morley missed was not exactly that known to Trewin. He sympathized with the desire to transpose the play into a modern setting, but this one had simply not succeeded as well as *West Side Story* or Jonathan Miller's recent 'Mafia' *Rigoletto* for English National Opera.

Two productions outside the main house, John Caird's at The Other Place in 1984 and Terry Hands's at the Swan in 1989, showed what might be achieved with more intimate staging. Caird's compact touring production – which used an unusually full text – played with the audience on three sides of a flat stage. Along the back wall of beaten metal that ran along the lower level of the theatre, death masks were let into niches (Figure 5). A small

FIGURE 5 Mercutio (Roger Allam, left) is outraged by the treatment of
Romeo by Tybalt (Andrew Hall, right). Benvolio (James Simmons) looks
on. Let into the back wall of the simple permanent set for this touring
production, seen at The Other Place in 1984, are death masks and, on the
right, a small shrine. The leather costumes suggest modern bikers
(compare Figure 25), but with such 'Renaissance' details as the slit sleeves
and white shirt worn by Tybalt. (3.1)

hanging representing Christ's face – rather like an icon – served as
masking on the upper level at the right-hand side: together with
the burnished metal of the set and the death masks, it enhanced
the sense of the play's religious element. (The Friar not only
presided over the opening funeral, but also spoke both Prologue
and Epilogue.) The lighting by Brian Harris was darkly atmospheric.
In the studio space the proximity of the actors helped to sustain
the play's energy and momentum, and Harris varied the general
darkness with such effects as a dappled garden for Juliet's first
scene with her mother and the Nurse, a soft morning light
(birdsong was heard) for the Friar's botanizing expedition, and a
blazing hot midday for the fateful combat. Jean Fuzier noted how
'the rhythm of the brawls, fast, taking up all of the playing area,

threaten[ed] the audience's own space', turning the front-row spectators into 'innocent bystanders about to be engulfed in the violence on Verona's main square' (*Cahiers Elis.*). Hands's return to the play reverted to 'period' costume and a bare stage. It achieved a sense of heat and sunlight (with such details as the young men mopping their brows with wet cloths at the beginning of 3.1) but did little to characterize the city. Apart from the warm wood of the flooring and galleries and the costumes in shades of buff and cream, the only conspicuous local colour was the green of willow fronds that hung behind the right-hand side of the balcony to represent the orchard (Figure 6).

The two main-house productions staged in the next decade seemed to have problems with the need to fill the high and deep stage space with scenery. Unfortunately, they were notably deficient in light and heat, and seemed to unfold in an elaborately realized world that was nonetheless remote from that of the spectators. In 1991 David Leveaux and his designer Alison Chitty presented a vast grey box divided up and screened off with panels that seemed to be fragments of Renaissance painting: praying and reaching hands, bits of landscape, angels. The liturgical music incorporated in Ilona Sekacz's sound design, and the unremittingly sombre lighting gave even the outdoor scenes 'a churchy, dark, sepulchral feel' (*Independent*). To one critic there was a discernible symbolism, with images of hands reaching and touching in panels but never meeting (*SA Herald*). Leveaux, an exciting and versatile director, had not staged Shakespeare on this scale before, and there were complaints that the new policy of guest directors (the established 'associate director' group had been disbanded) was allowing newcomers to learn on the job at the audience's expense. The actors seemed to be posed in beautiful but time-consuming tableaux. The performance proceeded at a stately pace, coming in at just under four hours and making the Chorus's promise of two hours' traffic all the more annoying. Although the pictorial effects alluded to Renaissance art, the men's costumes tended once again to suggest a more contemporary leather look. In this, as well as its

FIGURE 6 The Swan's platform stage and wooden galleries in 1989, with gates set across the back for the final scene. Juliet's balcony, backed by green fronds, is on the top level at the right. (On a structure with so many potential balconies, the 'orchard' vegetation helps to identify it.)

sombre setting, Leveaux's production resembled that of Caird at The Other Place in 1984. On the vast main-house stage, Leveaux could not bring sufficient life force to a Verona that, in the words of Paul Taylor, 'boasted all the holiday attractions of a sepulchre, well before the tomb scene' (*Independent*). Life in this city was nasty and brutish, but not, alas, short. Tim McInnerny's Mercutio was obsessively violent and even the normally pacific Benvolio showed signs of aggression. The smoky, doom-laden atmosphere complemented the performance of the two lovers, in particular Michael Maloney as Romeo. The Prince, played by Julian Glover, was a harsh, menacing presence. At least one reviewer thought this was more the tragedy of a city whose autocratic ruler could not keep the peace, than of a pair of star-crossed lovers (*Cahiers Elis.*).

Leveaux's Verona self-consciously evoked Renaissance art, peopled by figures given to formal, choreographed movement. Like the choric crowd in 1967, the citizens in 1991 tended to loom. In the first scene, as Benvolio and Tybalt clashed, they rushed on and gathered in a knot at the centre. Twice the combat shifted into slow motion, accompanied by what sounded like an amplified heartbeat. Suddenly a mêlée developed, with the onlookers swirling slowly across the stage, until on the Prince's entrance the combat reverted to full speed. The 1995 production directed by Adrian Noble was no less self-conscious in its allusions to an artistic past, but lacked the element of stylization. The settings and costumes by Kendra Ullyart evoked the Italy of the Risorgimento. (Strains of the *brindisi* from Verdi's *La Traviata* were even heard during what seemed to be Juliet's coming-out party.) The play was filled with domestic detail. As in Bogdanov's 1986 staging, life on the piazza revolved round a café where coffee was drunk, newspapers were read and tips left for waiters. There were some odd inconsistencies: one wondered why washing lines should hang across the street outside the grand gates of the Capulet residence, and the dapper, uniformed prince and the riflemen who halted the fray with a whiff of grapeshot over the heads of the crowd seemed to have wandered in from a comic opera (Figure 34). At the same time, the set and the lighting emphasized the doom that hung over the star-crossed lovers. One reviewer identified the narrow, high-walled streets with 'towering cold authoritarianism' and the blind alleys and enclosed courtyards with 'forcefully channelled, short lives' (*TLS*). In the *Independent*, Paul Taylor welcomed Noble's achievement of a 'plausible social context' for the feud, in a world that had 'certain cultural links' with Francis Ford Copolla's *Godfather* films. This may have been true of moments in the action, such as Tybalt's being handed a sword hidden under a coat on the arm of one of the henchmen who attended him, but there was little chance for any suggestion of organized crime and dynastic power – nor was the period appropriate. Despite the brooding intensity of the stage pictures and the music, the lovers themselves, played by Zubin Varla and Lucy Whybrow, were fatally underpowered.

A far more effective and fully realized evocation of Italy was achieved by Michael Attenborough, whose touring production visited the Swan Theatre in the autumn of 1997. Here the period was around 1910, the city was much more rural, and the families prosperous but neither great nor rich – one wondered how they would find the funds for those golden statues of the lovers. The director wanted to 'strip the play of its economic grandeur and find the sheer scale of the passions' (*SA Standard*). Although reviewers were not sure whether they were in Sicily or a more appropriately northern region, it was generally agreed that the concentration, simplicity and realism of the setting was an advantage: 'men with grimy vests, period caps and scuffed shoes wander around the decaying city-square stonework' (*Times*).

The last Stratford *Romeo and Juliet* of the twentieth century (or the first of the twenty-first) was performed in the main house during the 'summer festival season' of 2000. The director was Michael Boyd, whose recent work at Stratford had included *Much Ado About Nothing* (1997) and *A Midsummer Night's Dream* (1999). Both productions had shown a disposition for the darker side of comedy, dislocating and ironizing social and sexual relationships. Collaborating again with the designer Tom Piper, Boyd placed the tragedy of love in a hostile environment, a bare platform with a runway down through the auditorium and two walls of plain wood curving into a 'blind' exit at the back of the stage. The play began with a chair hurled onto the stage, followed by Samson and Gregory, and in the brawl that followed Samson's face was smashed against the wall: the large bloodstain this made remained throughout the play. Although the costumes were of the sixteenth century, the set reminded some reviewers of such examples of modern urban brutalism as an airport departure lounge (*D. Express*) or 'a hostile, inner-city multi-storey car-park' (*Mail Sun.*). For others it was more abstract, a 'harsh arena' (*Observer*) or 'a Samuel Beckett nightclub' (*E. Standard*). Once again, the play's street violence evoked interesting comparisons. Robert Gore-Langton, who thought 'the air of loutishness' reminiscent of 'English fans abroad' (D. Express), was one of a number of reviewers who mentioned recent riots by 'supporters' of the English team in the Euro-2000 soccer tournament. Benedict Nightingale, mindful of the director's career at the Tron theatre in Glasgow, felt that he had little time for 'southern softness' and had created 'something close to a Gorbals Romeo and Juliet' (Times). Robert Hewison echoed responses to Terry Hands's 1973 production by suggesting that Boyd was 'determined to roughen up the text and make it more like a Jacobean tragedy than an Elizabethan romance' (S. Times). Romeo emerged from among the fighters to deliver the prologue, Tybalt and Mercutio came back from the dead to watch the final scenes, and the lovers left their grave and walked off through the audience at the end (Figure 44). Such devices qualified the touches of domestic realism – familiar, ordinary behaviour – that also characterized his production. The music that accompanied and punctuated the action from offstage consisted mainly of plangent chords and broken elegiac phrases from musicians placed in view of the auditorium. An onstage chorus of servants and musicians watched the action sardonically, occasionally contributing sour vocal and musical accompaniment. The lighting was expressive rather than realistic: washes of red or violet light shone up the white walls to emphasize moments of passion and foreboding. In this society 'grace' had little chance against the power of 'rude will'. The ineffective Prince, played by Alfred Burke, was an aged man in the doublet and hose of an earlier generation, barely able to walk, despite the aid of two walking sticks. Paris seemed to be in charge of the local militia (who were threatening, but hardly effective) and the brutality of Juliet's father seemed entirely credible. The new century was beginning with the bleakest vision of Verona yet seen at Stratford.

Consideration of the ways in which Verona has been characterized allows an overview of the play's Stratford career since 1947. The fifteen productions of Romeo and Juliet break down into two groups. In the three before 1961, reviewers tended to discuss the degree of success with which the romance of the play and an idealized vision of its lovers and their fate had been achieved. From 1967 onwards, productions offered a franker representation of sexuality, both in the lovers and in the society around them. There have been considerable variations in the sense of social class and gender identity, as will become especially evident in discussion of the two lovers and of Mercutio. So far as 'Fair Verona' is concerned, direction and design have suggested increasingly conscious and worked-out analogies between the violent feud and its modern equivalents. Even when there is no strict equivalence between the terms of the family feud and those of inner-city race riots or gang warfare, the images of violence have been too immediate to be picturesque or remote. Interestingly, none of the Stratford productions has attempted to suggest analogies with conflict in Northern Ireland, or the racial tensions on the British mainland, which came to a flash point in the inner-city riots of the mid-1980s. Colour-blind casting has sometimes been practised, but not in order to make direct and consistent comparisons possible: in 1986 Hugh Quarshie played Tybalt and in 1997 Ray Fearon was Romeo, but the fact that both actors are black had no particular significance and went unmentioned in most reviews. Domestic realism, either in the marketplace or at home (laundry, carpet-beating, cooking), has predominated in some productions, being balanced in others by a degree of stylization.

When the Italian Renaissance has been evoked, it has not necessarily been characterized as serene or elegant. As well as complete transpositions to more recent periods (in 1986, 1995 and 1997), most 'period' productions have combined elements of modern dress with those of the sixteenth or seventeenth centuries (in 1973, 1976, 1980, 1991 and 2000). Even in 1967, with Romeo and the men in hose and jerkin, the materials (ribbed tights, rough fabrics) did not suggest anything like the classical beauty of line provided in 1954 and 1958 by Motley. Juliet's costume for the

FIGURE 7 Estelle Kohler and Ian Holm in the 'balcony' scene (2.2) in 1967. *West Side Story* is evoked by the photographer's choice of angle and the metal rail of the balcony, which resembles a fire escape.

dance had the 'op art' appliqué swirls of contemporary fashion, and the balcony scene, in particular, was thought to evoke the ever-recurrent *West Side Story* (Figure 7). In fact, the musical has kept turning up in responses to the play. In 2000, thirty-three years after its première, one critic asked 'Has *Romeo and Juliet* ever recovered from *West Side Story*?' (*Spectator*). 'I don't know about you', another remarked, 'but I've always preferred *West Side Story* to this play' (*D. Express*).

2

TWO
HOUSEHOLDS

STATUS AND PASSION

The play begins with two Capulet servants, Samson and Gregory, picking a quarrel with their opposite numbers from the Montague household. Even though the origin of the 'ancient grudge' is never revealed, its expression is in terms of sexual and verbal aggression that quickly takes bawdy talk (which the play is rich in) to potentially murderous lengths. Benvolio, a Montague, tries to stop them, and the Capulet Tybalt insults and attacks him. The ensuing brawl is joined by the heads of both houses, weighing in with antique weapons ('Give me my long sword, ho!', 1.1.73) in comic 'old man' mode while their wives try to restrain them. After the Prince has quelled the riot and dismissed the participants, Montague and his wife remain on stage and quiz Benvolio about their son's worrying state of mind. He ushers them off the stage so that he can accost Romeo, and that is the last we see of the Montagues until the aftermath of the fight that kills Tybalt and Mercutio and sends Romeo into banishment. Lady Montague, we learn in the final scene of the play, has died on the same night as her son and his secret bride. Up to the end of 3.1 Romeo is associated with Benvolio: in Mantua and at the Capulet tomb he is accompanied by Balthasar, who seems to be the 'man' whose confidentiality the Nurse is anxious to establish in 2.4.

By contrast, the Capulet household is more populous: in addition to Juliet, her parents and Tybalt, there are the Nurse and Peter, who as well as his barely competent discharge of message-carrying duties is sent with her as an ineffectual bodyguard. At his 'old accustom'd feast' (1.2.20) Capulet reminisces with an aged 'cousin', and a handful of servants are available to make preparations for the feast and, later, the intended wedding with Paris. Capulet is referred to as relatively old (for example, in the Prince's rebuke at 1.1.87–95), and his wife tells Juliet that she herself was married 'much upon' her years (1.3.72). This has sometimes been put together with Capulet's reply to Paris's argument that 'Younger than she are happy mothers made' – 'And too soon marr'd are those so early made' (1.2.12–13) – to deduce that a difference in their ages causes difficulties in the Capulets' marriage.

Whatever balance is struck between the comic and threatening in the first exchanges of the play, the households are introduced at a below-stairs level that recurs throughout. Since the 1950s, productions have usually lacked the number of actors needed to provide many innocent bystanders, and Verona has often seemed to be populated only by the principal members of the rival factions. In 2000 the opening dialogue was played directly to the audience, as though it were they who were being challenged to belittle Sampson's sexual prowess. The first view of the heads of the two households has invariably been undignified, but their status has usually been much higher than that of the servants. In Terry Hands's 1973 production Benvolio and Tybalt were not sharply distinguished from the servants by the cut of their costumes, but the materials used were more costly. Indeed, with the notable exception of Michael Attenborough's 1997 production, with its small-town setting, the social status of the two households has been high, taking up the 'dignity' referred to by the opening chorus, and endorsing Peter's boastful reference to 'the great rich Capulet' (1.2.81) and the Nurse's promise that he that marries Juliet 'shall have the chinks' (1.5.116). (Attenborough's revised script made most of the servants into 'friends' or relatives of the principals, Paris lost his 'County' and the programme listed 'Capulet's wife' rather than 'Lady Capulet'.) Sometimes Paris has been represented as a gilded youth, with the implication that Capulet seeks advancement through his daughter's marriage with an aristocratic relative of the Prince, while Paris is in quest of a profitable marriage with the daughter of a rich bourgeois family. In Michael Bogdanov's production (1986) Richard Moore's northern accent suggested a self-made man (even though the setting was emphatically Italian), and his wife's smart suits and elegant ball gown were echoed further down the scale by the Nurse's similarly well-chosen wardrobe.

The Capulet household has more than its fair share of passionate feeling. Tybalt is established as a hothead, indoors as well as out, who has to be restrained by his uncle from spoiling the feast by attacking Romeo, but he is also the focus of affection. Juliet and the Nurse seem genuinely distraught by the news of his death, as well as by Romeo's banishment. Capulet's wife grieves eloquently for him. She has occasionally been represented as having an affair with Tybalt, made apparent during the confrontation with his uncle in 1.5. In 1986 Anna Nygh, as Lady Capulet, had perched near Hugh Quarshie on the stairs during the party, joining him for a slow dance while her husband fussed about the other guests. Both seemed a good ten years younger than Capulet, and she wore a figure-hugging ball gown that was slit up the side. Tybalt turned to her, rather than her husband, with 'This by his voice should be a Montague' (1.5.53ff.) before moving threateningly towards Romeo. Capulet stopped his nephew at the centre of the stage, and his wife watched disdainfully as he restrained him. Tybalt then harangued Capulet with 'Patience perforce with wilful choler meeting . . . ' (88), before stalking off upstage. After a withering look at her husband, Lady Capulet followed Tybalt. In 1989 Terry Hands shifted the focus briefly onto Juliet. Capulet slapped Tybalt's face and the dance suddenly stopped. Capulet moved upstage to cheer on the guests, leaving Tybalt downstage. He addressed his ominous 'Patience' lines directly to the audience before making to leave: as he moved upstage, Juliet was about to follow him when Romeo pulled her back by the hand. Similar but more violent business, in keeping with the rest of the production, was used in 1991, when Capulet not only slapped Tybalt as he insisted 'He *shall* be endur'd' (75; my italics) but also threw him to the floor. Again, Tybalt's parting lines were spoken to the audience. In the more bourgeois setting of 1995, Capulet's remonstrations were relatively subdued, and no violence was used. This time Tybalt's final lines were addressed more to himself than directly to the audience.

Bogdanov took the Tybalt/Capulet's wife story further in the aftermath of the fight in 3.1. Capulet slapped his wife's face after she had knelt to make her impassioned plea to the Prince. In a scene of high feelings, Lady Montague was heard to shout 'No!' as sentence was pronounced, motivating the Prince's 'I will be deaf to pleading and excuses' (194). Subsequently, in 3.4 when Capulet told Paris that Juliet 'lov'd her kinsman Tybalt dearly', he embraced his wife with 'And so did I' (3–4), but she turned away from him. As he discussed marriage plans with Paris she listened coldly, and at the end of the scene, Capulet opened his arms to her but she walked off on the opposite side of the stage. Hands, in 1989, conveyed a sense that Capulet's schemes did not altogether please his wife, who clearly felt that more explanation should have been forthcoming, and disliked the haste of the arrangements. But it did not seem part of a larger pattern of estrangement: she had, after all, been given an unwelcome task in broaching the marriage plan. In 1991 David Leveaux made the same point even more forcefully. Lady Capulet clearly needed some persuading, and her husband was pushing matters a long way as he kissed Paris on both cheeks and told her to tell Juliet of 'my son Paris' love' (16). She seemed to want an explanation, but Capulet went off upstage to the right. She paused for a moment, then left in the opposite direction.

Even if the Capulets are not, as a reviewer remarked of Brenda Bruce and Jeffery Dench in 1973, 'on the brink of divorce' (*Times*),

the whole household is under considerable strain. So far as
Capulet's temperament and his relationship with his household
are concerned, the major crisis comes in the latter part of 3.5,
when Juliet refuses to marry Paris. As Jill L. Levenson observes,
this long sequence dramatizes the obduracy in social and
economic terms which the lovers face (Levenson, 2000, 21). The
father begins by comforting Juliet, then the meaning of her
'chopp'd logic' (149) finally gets through to him, and he ends by
threatening her and insulting the Nurse. How violent does he
become? For the modern actor this is a difficult scene, involving as
it does a degree of passion directed at three women. From being
fussy and over-anxious, more a comic paterfamilias than a tyrant,
Capulet is suddenly precipitated into behaviour that audiences
find especially reprehensible. Up to the middle of the last century
it might also have been construed in class terms: gentlemen did
not hit their womenfolk. Often, as in 1991, the disposition of the
actors on the stage has placed Capulet in the centre with Juliet
and the Nurse and his wife at either side: a formation display of
male anger. 'My fingers itch' (164) has often been treated as an
indication that he is perilously close to striking his daughter, but
some productions have made Capulet more violent before this
point. For most directors, the principle seems to have been that a
little physical action goes a long way, the language being harsh
enough. In 1947 Capulet threw Juliet to the ground on 'Hang thee
young baggage, disobedient wretch!' (160) and in 1954 he threw
her down twice. John Woodvine (1976), 'a creature of ice-cold
fury', shook Juliet like a rag doll and flung her to the floor
(*Guardian*). Bogdanov (1986) allowed for tenderness at first, with
Capulet kissing Juliet's hair when he came in, but throwing her
down on 'Out, you baggage!' (156) and swinging her onto the bed
with 'Speak not, reply not, do not answer me' before the
threatening 'My fingers itch' (163–4). In 1995 Capulet's 'How
now, how, now? [*sic*] Chopp'd logic?' (149ff.) was at first genuinely
puzzled, and Juliet clung to him until, realizing what she meant,
he pushed her away. He threw her onto the bed and she hid under

the sheets, which he then pulled off. The extremity of his rejection – 'Hang! Beg! Starve! Die in the streets!' (192) – was marked by the Nurse crossing herself. In 1997 Capulet grabbed Juliet's face with his final line, 'Trust to't, bethink you. I'll not be forsworn' (195). In 1991 Capulet had embraced Juliet warmly with 'How now, a conduit girl?' (129) but her equivocation soon made him very angry. With the first 'How now' he at once threw her to the floor, and he turned on his wife – 'God's bread, it makes me mad' – when she rebuked him with 'You are too hot' (176, 175). By now he was at the centre with the women around him. At 'I do not use to jest' (189) Juliet knelt and held on to his leg, but he lifted her off and pushed her away. Juliet then kneeled in vain to her mother as she left.

One of the most extreme versions of the scene was that of Hands in 1989, when Bernard Horsfall's Capulet, 'hilariously choleric and cranky' (*Independent*), moved from great tenderness to a demeaning assault. When he came in he embraced Juliet lovingly, centre stage. The lines comparing her to a 'bark' tossed by a storm, usually omitted (116–18), were spoken soothingly as though calming her. When Capulet's anger began to mount, however, Juliet ran round the stage to escape him, eventually falling to her knees and clinging to his robe. The Nurse did her best to protect Juliet, who ran upstage to escape, but Capulet dragged her back, lifted her up and spanked her, despite his wife's attempts to restrain him.

Lady Capulet refuses to give any comfort to her daughter, which has often been consistent with a 'chilly' reading of the part: Cherry Morris (1961) was 'a thin, pale Lady Capulet, from whom the last spark of humanity ha[d] been extracted' (*Punch*), Linda Spurrier (1989) 'icily unmaternal' (*Independent*) and Celia Gregory (1991) 'as remote from her daughter's predicament as a statue in a square from the people hurrying through' (*SA Herald*). Sheila Allen (1967) was 'an opulent young matron' just about twice her daughter's age, with 'an air of rather fancying Paris for herself' (*S. Telegraph*), which may have contributed to her impatience with the Juliet's lack of enthusiasm for this grand matrimonial prize.

Juliet's contrite return and the hastening of preparations for the wedding (4.2) is usually dealt with simply, though there have been variations in the degree of her self-abasement. In 1954, for example, Juliet knelt to her father, who kissed her, and in 1989 she prostrated herself. In 1986 Richard Moore hugged Niamh Cusack and whirled her round gleefully. Bogdanov used the occasion to indicate the widening gulf between her parents. Capulet was at his desk, giving instructions with typical imperious enthusiasm to his hard-pressed aide ('So many guests invite as here are writ', 1), while his wife stood at some distance upstage with papers in her hand. Juliet came in and knelt by the desk to beg forgiveness. Newly energized, Capulet tried to buzz servants on his intercom, but no one answered. As his wife was about to speak to him, he cut her off with 'I'll not to bed tonight, let me alone' (42). She crumpled her papers, threw them at him and walked off, leaving him to his phone calls. Leveaux (1991) made a similar point. Juliet prostrated herself full length on stage, and the blocking replicated that of 3.2: a triangular composition with Capulet at the centre and the Nurse and his wife on either side. Her mother stayed in one place throughout the scene then moved up to a door on the right-hand side. After Capulet's declaration 'My heart is wondrous light / Since this same wayward girl is so reclaim'd' (46–7) she paused for a moment then exited, leaving him alone in the centre of the forestage.

The grieving of the Capulet family when Juliet is discovered, seemingly dead, in 4.5, is discussed in chapter 5. In this context it is worth noting that the scene brings together the whole household for the last time, with the Friar as a source of counsel and, often, as the strong upstage focus of the stage picture. Like the scenes in which the Prince commands attention – often from the same position – over an onstage crowd and the watching spectators, it offers yet another variation on the series of 'family portraits' in the play. In this instance, Laurence effectively takes over from Capulet.

THE NURSE

How old is the Nurse? If Juliet is fourteen, and was breast-fed by her, she is likely to be no older than fifty, but a tradition had long existed of playing her as a person of very advanced years. As Peter Holding observes, the character helps to convey 'the contrast between an extended past and the terrible brevity of the play's action' (Holding, 25). Edith Evans, playing the part in Gielgud's 1935 production when she was in her forties, had delivered one of the most memorable 'character' performances of the century. The traditional costuming consisted of a voluminous gown and a white or cream-coloured wimple, which had the additional advantage of making it unnecessary to make up the neck. In Peter Brook's 1947 production Beatrix Lehmann, who was in her mid-forties, wore an unconventional costume more in keeping with the high-waisted early Italian line adopted by the designer, but still 'aged up' for the part (Figure 8). The *Times* thought she looked like 'a Tenniel drawing' and the *Stage* noticed the same reminiscence of *Through the Looking Glass*: 'something between the Red Queen and a Piccadilly flower-woman, a dry, rheumatic creature, not as earthy as tradition would have her'. To Harold Hobson she was 'crack-voiced' and had a 'shuffling, rheumatic walk' (*S. Times*). Alan Dent, who found nothing much to enjoy in the whole production ('The Bard Betrayed' was his headline), thought this Nurse 'the most frightening and least funny I ever hope to see'. She evoked Hieronymus Bosch rather than Sir John Tenniel, and seemed 'racked by every ailment known to pathology, from dropsy downwards'. A problem specific to an 'aged' Nurse was hinted at in his conclusion that 'The Capulets would have pensioned off such a hag long before Juliet was even weaned' (*News Chron.*). The conventionally swathed and wimpled Nurse in Byam Shaw's 1954 production was Rosalind Atkinson (aged thirty), whom the *Liverpool Post* admonished in somewhat headmasterly 'Must try harder' style: 'she will have to make up her mind whether she is middle-aged or decrepit, she must not

FIGURE 8 1947: Lady Capulet (Muriel Davidson), Juliet (Daphne Slater) and the Nurse (Beatrix Lehmann) in 1.3. The vivid stylized dresses and headgear of the two older women contrast with Juliet's simple, demurely enveloping gown and 'natural' hair. The group is set against the empty space of the stage, with a canopy apparently hovering in the air above them.

alternate the two'. The *News Chronicle* noted that she had taken too literally the Nurse's claim to have only four teeth. The *Daily Mail* complained that she 'waddle[d], cackle[d] and croak[ed] her way too grotesquely through the comedy', and entered into the plan for the secret marriage 'with a gusto that hardly befit[ted] the trusted family retainer'. She did, however, discover 'a new dignity in the final grief'. Angela Baddeley was 'dry' and 'consequential' in

FIGURE 9 The Nurse (Angela Baddeley), Juliet (Dorothy Tutin) and Lady Capulet (Rachel Kempson) in 1.3, in Glen Byam Shaw's 1958 production. This is a 'traditional' older Nurse, with a haughtily patrician Lady Capulet. Tutin's vivid red hair and the design of her dress (emphasizing the line of her neck) suggest Renaissance style filtered through Pre-Raphaelite painting. The photograph, though posed, seems to give a fair representation of the staging.

Byam Shaw's 1958 production (*Times*). Rosemary Anne Sisson, who thought her 'immensely funny' in the anecdote about her husband and in her encounter with Mercutio, admired Baddeley's progression from 'the warm, Nursery intimacy of her first scene with Juliet' (Figure 9) to the 'fearfully well-intentioned lack of comprehension' and the 'stony bitterness' of Juliet's 'Amen' when

FIGURE 10 1961: Juliet (Dorothy Tutin) and the Nurse (Edith Evans) with the rope ladder, in 3.5.

the Nurse insists with an oath – 'And from my soul too, else beshrew them both' (3.5.227) – that she has spoken from the heart in urging marriage with Paris (*SA Herald*).

Dame Edith Evans, in Peter Hall's 1961 production, delivered the kind of performance for which 'definitive', a word already going out of fashion, might have been coined (Figure 10). Those who recalled her 1935 performance claimed that her Nurse had softened: 'she is sweeter, more mellow, but just as fond of the sound of her own voice, just as unconsciously funny, just as much of a wicked old tease' (*Western Ind.*). Others reached for painterly analogies. She had 'the detailed solidity of a Dürer drawing' (*Punch*) and was a portrait 'that Vermeer would not have been ashamed to sign' (*Observer*). T.C. Worsley was one of a number of critics who hailed a textbook example of technique, 'a master-piece in the great classical manner, with every phrase relished on the tongue and acted with the most marvellous economy, in which even the slightest movement is calculated to produce the maximum of effect' (*FT*). Although Evans seemed to have 'not yet completely chosen her accent', Welsh prevailed, as it does on the studio recording of the play made for Caedmon Records at the time of Hall's production. (Claire Bloom plays Juliet, with Albert Finney as Romeo.) The qualities enumerated by reviewers suggest a dynamic as well as multifaceted characterization: 'immense authority, a wealth of common sense and an overwhelming degree of motherliness' (*Stage*); 'warmth and gentleness . . . bewilderment and pathos' (*D. Express*); 'half sycophant, half termagant' (*S. Telegraph*). Despite her age, this Nurse seemed vital and determined to participate fully in life: 'a picture of age embracing life and loving it to the last memory' (*SA Herald*). Consequently, her last exit took on tragic dimensions, 'when the old Nurse, after weeping her heart out by Juliet's bed, lumbers away up the steps and out of our sight, though she must stay for ever in the memory' (*Birm. Post*). Trewin's account also reflects the critic's elegiac sense of the evanescent nature of the actor's art.

Edith Evans was not quite the last of the 'ancient' Nurses. In 1973 Beatrix Lehmann returned to the role she had played in 1947, appearing now as a hatchet-faced, lugubrious-eyed figure dressed with extravagant bad taste, even by the standards of Farrah's violent Verona: she tottered on in wooden pattens, a lemon-yellow skirt billowing behind her like a sail, in 2.4. Richard David missed the 'glorious expansiveness' and 'relaxed warmth' that should characterize her recollections of Juliet's childhood in 1.3, but found the later scenes 'superb' (David, 109–10). Six years before this, Elizabeth Spriggs had shared in the general revision of characterizations that marked Karolos Koun's production: 'not the usual vulgar old gossip, but a shrewd nun-like figure who competes with Romeo for Juliet's love' (*Times*). This bespectacled, benign Nurse (Figure 11) might well be only a few years older than Lady Capulet, played by Sheila Allen as an attractive woman in her early thirties. A similarly youthful mother and Nurse

FIGURE 11 Estelle Kohler and Elizabeth Spriggs as Juliet and the Nurse in 1967 (2.5). Juliet's hair, make-up (with pale lipstick) and dress reflect contemporary fashion. The Nurse is relatively youthful, though the spectacles (which here she holds in her left hand) enable her to adopt a slightly older persona. The plain grey screens of Timothy O'Brien's set are visible behind.

accompanied Amanda Root's convincingly early adolescent Juliet in 1984 (Figure 12). Just as the *grande dame* demeanour usually assumed by Lady Capulet had been abandoned, the Nurse now seemed far less remote in age and experience from her charge. Marie Kean (1976), again middle-aged, had 'the warm voice of the O'Casey tenements' (*Birm. Post*) and was agreed by reviewers to be credible, if not especially surprising. Far from boring Juliet and her

FIGURE 12 Lady Capulet (Penny Downie), the Nurse (Polly James) and Juliet (Amanda Root) at The Other Place in 1984. The Nurse and mother are young, and Lady Capulet's costume is rich and 'authentic', with her hair dressed in a net. Juliet wears a less sophisticated dress and her natural-looking curls escape from a small skullcap worn on the back of the head. (1.3)

mother or providing evidence of senility, her garrulous jokes sent them into 'increasing tucks of laughter' (*Times*).

The process of rejuvenating the Nurse was taken a stage further in 1980 with the aid of modern dress (Figure 13). At the same time, the element of class distinction was diminished. Brenda Bruce played 'a woman in early middle age, by turns teasing, testy, consequential, affectionate and timeserving' (*Birm. Post*). This 'pugnacious menial given to slapping her own hand whenever she speaks out of turn' (*Times*) was conceived as a surrogate mother for Juliet – or, to be precise, Juliet was seen by the Nurse as a substitute for the family she had lost (Susan, 'of an age' with Juliet, and the 'merry' husband). Bruce has described how this relationship affected her understanding – as Nurse – of every scene she appeared in. Reviewers were unanimous in praise for the vigour

FIGURE 13 The Nurse (Brenda Bruce), Juliet (Judy Buxton) and Lady Capulet (Barbara Kinghorn) in 1.3. The costumes of the Nurse and Lady Capulet are of woven silk, in warm reds and browns, while Juliet wears a simple shift, gathered under the bust in a casual approximation of Empire Style. The period evoked in this 1980 production is uncertain, but with strong hints (especially in hairstyles) of the present day.

and sense of reality she conveyed, from the first scene where she was able to handle Juliet 'as unceremoniously as an infant' (*Times*) to the agony of discovering that her 'daughter' is dead. J.C. Trewin, dismissive of much else in Ron Daniels's production, welcomed the absence of 'the routine wheeze-and-grate' (*Birm. Post*). No cliché about the character was allowed to pass unexamined. Bruce found to her delight that Nadine Baylis's costume designs respected her relative youthfulness, providing her with simple, bright-coloured and fashionable gowns in woven silk.

> If I had found myself weighed down with layers of heavy woollen skirts, my face and head half hidden in a wimple, the feeling of lightness and delight I was hoping to achieve in the first scene would have been a much more difficult task.   (Bruce, 97)

For her hair, she chose a red bubble-cut. The sense of a generation gap was greatly diminished, and she seemed to share the fashion sense of her mistress. The same might be said of Dilys Laye, in 1986, who affected a not-quite-posh accent and wore designer clothes. She trilled happy little songs to herself, and her poise was too clearly put on. Bruce, although fashionably dressed, seemed without affectation. With both performances, the shift of period made Capulet's verbal onslaught in 3.5 ('And why, my Lady Wisdom? Hold your tongue . . . ', 170ff.) especially shocking. He was attacking a well-dressed, intimate family member rather than a menial, and reminding her she was 'only a servant'.

Margaret Courtenay (1989) was voluminously swathed in a more traditional manner, but was capable of energetic movement. She used a 'rustic burr', which Michael Coveney considered the all-purpose stage-rural accent known as 'Mummersetshire' (*FT*). Irving Wardle thought her 'near vaudeville', but she did manage to achieve a certain dignity (*Times*). To Michael Billington her reaction to Mercutio – 'I am none of his flirt-gills' (2.4.150) – sounded like 'a duchess disdaining a pass by the footman' (*Guardian*). Sheila Reid had an Irish accent in Stratford, but mutated to Scottish for the Barbican transfer of Leveaux's 1991 production. To an English audience these Celtic accents did not seem distinctly rural. Like Marie Kean's Nurse from an 'O'Casey tenement' in 1976 and Eileen McCallum's urban Scot in 2000 (Figure 14), the associations were of canniness and kindly realism. In McCallum's case, the effect was not altogether winning. She was 'a salty Scot who never tires of her own banal opinions' (*Mail Sun.*), 'a self-absorbed Scots motormouth . . . who projects just the right mix of garrulous warmth and unsettling moral irresponsibility' (*Independent*). Aqua vitae obviously helped her through the day, and the draughts from her pocket flask became more frequent as the play went on. McCallum also holds the distinction of being the first performer of the role at Stratford to have farted audibly (and regularly, on cue) in the middle of one of her speeches.

The Nurse's first appearance, in 1.3, can establish a great deal about life in the Capulet household. Productions have varied in the extent to which Juliet and her mother indulge her in the extraordinary and well-nigh unstoppable flow of her principal speech. As Stanley Wells points out, 'the information she has to convey . . . is entirely contained in its second line – "Come Lammas Eve at night she shall be fourteen"' (1.3.17) (Wells, 1993, 199–200). Lady Capulet's nervousness in raising the topic of marriage, and her initial uncertainty about including the Nurse in the conversation, have sometimes reflected a lack of warmth in the mother–daughter relationship. The Nurse's behaviour has usually made up abundantly for this by including a good deal of easy physical intimacy. In 1947 Beatrix Lehmann pulled Juliet to the floor as she got into her reminiscing stride with 'I never shall forget it' (24) and drew her to her knee with 'Were not I thine only Nurse / I would say thou hadst suck'd wisdom from my teat' (67–8). In 1976 Juliet's 'affectionate enjoyment, bursting with suppressed laughter, of her Nurse's tale was endearing, and a nice counterpoint to her mother's obvious impatience' (David, 118). In 1989 Margaret Courtenay embraced Juliet, and the two of them stayed close together enjoying the 'falling backwards' jest: it failed to amuse Lady Capulet. Eventually the Nurse held her peace, but only for a few moments, and both she and Juliet began laughing again. In a simple, motherly gesture the Nurse took off Juliet's apron as the marriage issue was raised. Her glee at the prospect of Paris ('He's a flower, in faith a very flower', 78) contrasted with the continuing awkwardness of Lady Capulet, who spelled out her elaborate explanation about Paris – 'Read o'er the volume of young Paris' face' (81) – and had to reach for the working out of the metaphor: 'this – unbound lover' (87). Juliet for her part seemed to need to be told all this, and was genuinely attentive. The Nurse was not the only trusted servant to enjoy a simple, warm relationship with Juliet: when Peter came on he picked Juliet up and swung her around.

A different inflection of the scene, much less hard on Lady Capulet, was achieved in 1991. A cloth with herbs and flowers was brought on, and the three women knelt down on the floor to sort them out. Juliet put on her shoes while the Nurse rattled on about her husband's mildly bawdy prophecy, and she leaned lovingly against her mother, enjoying the story. An element of domestic activity helps to focus the scene: in 1995 Juliet was already getting ready for the party. The Nurse entered carrying a crinoline, which was subsequently tied round Juliet's waist as her mother expatiated on Paris's virtues. During the Nurse's tale she fell back on the bed in comic boredom and exasperation. After 'Susan and she – God rest all Christian souls – / Were of an age' (18–19) the Nurse tickled Juliet, taking her in her arms, and cradling her. Meanwhile Lady Capulet, like a good nineteenth-century mother (even in Italy), was not keen to hear talk of wormwood and dugs (26). (The line itself was cut in 1986, possibly as inappropriate to Dilys Laye's genteel Nurse.) Juliet and the Nurse, together on the bed, were in their own world. 'To see now how a jest shall come about' (45) was tender, and she stroked the spot on Juliet's brow where one might suppose the famous lump to have appeared.

Attenborough's 1997 production made a great show of domesticity in this scene, as elsewhere in the play. The props list included 'worktop, dough and flour, bowl and cloth, bottle and glass, pot of sauce, spoon, knife, four bottles'. Juliet was chopping herbs for the pot of *ragù* later offered at the homely feast. Again the Nurse hugged Juliet, and tickled her on 'No less, nay, bigger. Women grow by men' (95). Alexandra Gilbreath (2000) gave the Nurse a playful slap on the behind as she urged her to 'stint' her tale (58), while Lady Capulet watched from the side of the stage, barely suppressing her impatience. Routine but by no means insincere piety also figures in the scheme of things. (Going to confession has an important place in the story, after all.) Often the thought of her dead husband and daughter, Susan, has been marked by a momentary pause on 'God rest all Christian souls' (18) and 'God be with his soul' (39). More often than not (as in 1986, 1991, 1995 and 1997) it has been emphasized by the Nurse crossing herself.

At the party the Nurse has sometimes been included in the general merriment: in 1976 Tybalt made a point of dancing with her, which supported her subsequent claim that he was the best friend she ever had (3.2.61). But her presence is really functional, providing the lovers with vital information about each other. Her reaction to the taunting she encounters in 2.4, when she goes to carry Juliet's message to Romeo, is discussed below, in connection with Mercutio (pp. 107–8). Often the last section of the scene, with the play on the letter 'R' (202–9), has been omitted, but the lines before it have usually been kept in: they are an opportunity to let Romeo know he isn't the only contender, whilst showing that she is on his side and underlining her confidential relationship with her young mistress. As Brenda Bruce observed, the Nurse is 'as severe in her interviewing of Romeo as a possible suitor as Capulet is in his interviewing of Paris' (Bruce, 97). After what she takes to be his 'gentlemanlike offer' (175) it is as though he has suddenly passed the test. Sandra Voe (1997) was 'blearily flirtatious, maddeningly slow in getting to the nub of things' (*Times*). She hugged Romeo before he could finish the rather formal sentence with which he was trying to assure her, 'Nurse, commend me to thy lady and mistress. I protest unto thee – ' with 'Good heart, and i'faith I will tell her as much' (169–70). Clearly he was already part of her mistress's life. The dialogue that follows also allows her to make a play of refusing and then accepting a tip (at 180: 'No truly, sir; not a penny'). In 1986 Sean Bean offered Dilys Laye a banknote, which she first refused then grabbed with practised dispatch. This Nurse might have seemed spontaneous – she even started to tell the 'falling backwards' story again but stopped and crossed herself – but she was very strategic in her teasing.

Physical intimacy is written into the next scene, when the Nurse reports to Juliet, demanding that her aching back and head receive their proper due before she delivers the all-important message. Zena Walker (1954) had to stand in front of the Nurse to stop her leaving in mock indignation, and in 1973 Estelle Kohler's relationship with Beatrix Lehmann was 'tense and twanging' (David, 110). Sometimes the Nurse's behaviour has not been easy to read: in 1976 the *Stage* insisted that Marie Kean (otherwise considered warm and motherly) was sadistic in keeping the news back from Juliet, but there has usually been some equivalent of Edith Evans's reassuring 'sly smile aside' (*Leam. Spa Cour.*, 1961).

In Bogdanov's production (1986) Niamh Cusack was sitting on the steps of the set's central tower as the scene began and the clock struck nine. At the end of her speech the Nurse's tricycle horn was heard offstage. The Nurse, partial to her liquor throughout, was going to take a drink from her flask when the exasperated Juliet snatched it away, insisting on knowing whether the news was good or bad: 'Say either, and I'll stay the circumstance. / Let me be satisfied: is't good or bad?' (2.5.36–7).

Claire Holman (1991) excelled in caring behaviour under trying circumstances: she ran downstage with a chair and set it on the forestage as the Nurse came in. Going beyond treatment for her aching back and head, the Nurse took off her shoes for Juliet to massage her feet. Juliet, coaxing rather than rampantly impatient, kissed her hand on 'Sweet, sweet, sweet Nurse' (55), and was so rapt in contemplation of the marvellous news that the Nurse needed to gesture to her to get a move on before she rushed off to Friar Laurence's cell. Lucy Whybrow (1995), who had been oddly matter of fact in the scene's opening speech, continued her 'child-like' performance by being cradled in the Nurse's arms.

The Nurse's next scene (3.2) also involves the bringing of news, this time desperately bad. Once again, Juliet and the Nurse seem to be on different wavelengths – though not exactly at cross-purposes. Brenda Bruce suggests that the Nurse is in a state of shock, and that the realization of the darker side of human nature is something she finds difficult to take in. At 3.2.88 she cut 'Give me some aqua vitae', using 'Ah, where's my man?' as a cry for her dead husband, 'someone of my own to help my anguish' (Bruce, 97). Productions have usually cut about twenty lines, removing some of the elaborations of imagery and rhetorical figures, specifically 'I am not I if there be such an "I"' and the following three lines (48–51); some of the oxymora that follow 'O serpent heart, hid with a flowering face' (73ff.); and the lines near the end of the scene which recapitulate the theme of utterance (from 116 to 120 or 124). In 1989 Juliet ran on as a bell chimed, reminding the audience of the parallel scene before her marriage. In the Swan, Georgia Slowe was able to use direct address to the audience to mark the argument of the speech beginning 'Shall I speak ill of him that is my husband?' (97ff.). This is a passage where the Nurse is often set apart, absorbed in her own grief ('There's no trust / No faith, no honesty in men', 85–6). Claire Holman (1991) collapsed on the floor when she thought that Romeo had been killed ('O, break my heart. Poor bankrupt, break at once', 57) but got up when the Nurse mentioned Tybalt. The split between the two was clear: the Nurse was lecturing Juliet with 'There's no trust / No faith, no honesty' and after 'Blister'd be thy tongue' (90) Juliet pushed her away by pressing her forehead with 'Upon his brow shame is asham'd to sit' (92). Juliet came to the centre of the stage and fell to her knees for what now became a soliloquy (97ff.), at the end of which the Nurse came to her. With 'Where is my father and my mother, Nurse?' (127) Juliet took the Nurse's hand and the cords. Brenda Bruce (1980) felt that taking Juliet in her arms and promising to bring the couple together was a victory of her affection for Juliet over the sense of 'bitterness and loss and waste' that had so shocked her (Bruce, 98).

Bruce carried this idea through to the scene with Romeo in Friar Laurence's cell (3.3), where she knelt by Anton Lesser, comforting him as if he were a weeping child ('Why should you fall into so deep an O?', 90). She was not the first Nurse to yield to this motherly impulse: in 1954 Romeo put his head on the Nurse's lap when he asked 'what says / My conceal'd lady to our cancell'd love?' (96–7). In 1991 Sheila Reid's 'Stand up' (88) was soft, as if coaxing a child: Romeo embraced the Nurse and she comforted him. As Romeo gets more hysterical and draws a knife many productions have followed the Q1 stage direction: '*He offers to stab himself, and Nurse snatches the dagger away'* (107). Reid wrestled Michael Maloney to the floor to disarm him, and in 1989 the Friar and the Nurse collaborated in dragging Romeo away from the dagger's point. Dilys Laye, in 1986, left the strong-arm stuff to Robert Demeger's streetwise Friar, and fortified herself with another swig from her flask. The Nurse's lines as she begins to take her leave usually get a laugh:

> O lord, I could have stay'd here all the night
> To hear good counsel. O, What learning is!
>
> (158–9)

They are also her last entirely comic moment in the play. She is about to find herself in the centre of a violent family dispute, at the end of which she will have betrayed Juliet. Praising Paris will no longer be a matter of good-humoured worldliness.

Her last physical contact with a conscious Juliet can recall the earlier scenes of comfort and affection. In 1947 Beatrix Lehmann took Juliet on her knee in response to 'Comfort me, counsel me' (3.5.208) and in 1954 Rosalind Atkinson half-lifted Zena Walker up, taking her on her knee to give her the fatal advice. Elizabeth Spriggs (1967) attempted to convey that the Nurse knows her suggestion is a betrayal, but makes it after a struggle with her conscience in an attempt to do what is best for Juliet – a tactic Stanley Wells found unconvincing (Wells, 1996, 13). Brenda Bruce (1980) made the advice to marry Paris 'sound the most logical thing in the world' (*S. Telegraph*). In the actress's view, the speech must be delivered without any attempt at comforting, and simply as a statement of the situation (Bruce, 99–100). In 1986 Niamh Cusack lay with her head in Dilys Laye's lap until 'Romeo's a dishclout to him' (219), where the pragmatism has begun to turn into real betrayal of Romeo's person as well as a rationalization of bigamy. It is also the moment when the Nurse's materialistic view of the world comes to the fore, together with her self-interest in promoting the Capulet family's advancement through alliance to a nobleman. Bruce was particularly anxious not to get a laugh on this line – she wanted the audience to be shocked by it. After the speech she fussed about, making the bed 'in an attempt to make the advice acceptable' (Bruce, 100). Claire Holman (1991) embraced the Nurse to ask for comfort, and Sandra Voe (1997) folded Juliet in her cloak, stroking her. There was a sense that the Nurse was trying to convince herself, and she even turned downstage and away from Juliet, as if absorbed in her own argument. At the end, rejection was simple and clear: now the Nurse moved towards Juliet and Juliet turned away from her. Beatrix Lehmann in 1947 seemed unaware of the difficulty: on her exit line, 'Marry, I will; and this is wisely done' (234), she rose and crossed to Juliet's right, patting her face as she went. In 1973 Estelle Kohler paused after the Nurse's advice, then spoke the rest of her lines abstractedly in a flat tone, almost as if lost in an interior monologue. In 1976 the scene was 'a study in stillness'. Richard David describes how Juliet's gradual awareness of the meaning of the Nurse's advice was marked by 'a series of significant withdrawals so that from nestling in the Nurse's lap she came to be completely separated from her on an isolated stool centre stage' (David, 118). Most performers of the part have been anxious to show that the Nurse has at least an inkling of what is going on: in 1989 Margaret Courtenay came in quickly and suspiciously with 'What?' to Juliet's 'Amen' after 'else beshrew them both' (227).

Brenda Bruce observes that from now on the Nurse probably watches Juliet very carefully: hence the observation 'See where she comes from shrift with merry look' as Juliet returns from the Friar's cell at 4.2.15. Both Dilys Laye and Margaret Courtenay seemed to take the apparent change of heart at face value, and went off happily singing *sotto voce* as Juliet prepared to go to bed. The discovery of Juliet's drugged body is a demanding scene for the Nurse, and combines the last instalment of her fund of sexual humour together with a final moment of closeness to her mistress – but it has produced little by way of variations in business and interpretation. The sequence has been mainly a matter of timing

FIGURE 14 Leaning against the headboard of her mistress's bed, the Nurse (Eileen McCallum) savours a bawdy thought before trying to wake up Juliet in Michael Boyd's 2000 production. (4.5)

and strategy on the performer's part, indicated by pauses but little else in the written records, and reviewers have usually commented on it only in the most general terms. Beatrix Lehmann, in 1973, felt Juliet's feet to see whether or not they were cold, a testimony to the deceptive power of the drugs. The Nurse, of course, does not know of the plan involving the sleeping potion, feigned death and burial. In 1980 Brenda Bruce took care to dispose of the empty vial 'as incriminating evidence dangerous to herself' (*Cahiers Elis.*). Eileen McCallum's Nurse, in 2000 (Figure 14), leaned at first against the bed-head, refreshing herself from her hip flask, and played the whole sequence as broad, raucous comedy up to the final 'lady', when she turned Juliet over.

The Nurse is Juliet's last hope for sympathetic counsel within the immediate family circle. Once she has shown her limitations, the Friar becomes the only source of support. As Coppélia Kahn observes, the Nurse's advice at the end of 3.5 is part of her complete involvement in the patriarchal system from which Juliet must free herself to come of age. She 'cannot comprehend a loyalty to Romeo that would involve opposing Capulet' and for her 'affection and submission have always been one' (Kahn, 185). Whereas the Nurse's world is bound in by material considerations, the Friar's is announced on his first appearance as taking in a comprehensive view of the processes of Nature as well as spirituality.

GHOSTLY SIRE, GALLANT SPIRIT

Together with the Nurse, Friar Laurence and Mercutio are the figures in the play who are closest to the lovers, and have some status as authorities in relation to their emotional and spiritual consciousness. They stand in contrast to the more remote, 'official' authorities vested in the Prince and, tellingly, Juliet's parents. Laurence has access to a spiritual vision unavailable to the Nurse, but at the same time concerns himself energetically with earthly matters. Mercutio, it can be argued, has a similar mediatory function. In Romeo's liminal state of adolescence, both are offered as prospective guides across a threshold, although Mercutio's notion of the mature life seems limited to the satisfaction of appetite and the pleasures of wit. The play's outcome works ironically against him: he dies knowing nothing of Romeo's relationship with Juliet, which is the real reason for his accidental death (in so far as Romeo's refusal to fight his unwitting kinsman Tybalt provokes Mercutio to challenge the latter). The Friar is the last of the supportive friends to desert Romeo and Juliet, and that only after he has provided them with conduct not into life but (literally) into the tomb. In this connection, the parallel between the Friar and his fellow druggist the Apothecary has not gone unnoticed.

FRIAR LAURENCE

The Friar's independence and confidentiality are confirmed by his standing as confessor to both protagonists, and he first appears in 2.3 immediately after Romeo has announced his resolve to 'crave' his help and recount the 'dear hap' of his encounter with Juliet (2.2.193). In this, the first reference to Laurence in the play, the second and subsequent Quarto editions have Romeo speak of his 'Ghostly Friers close cell' at 192–3, while the First Folio has 'Fries' and the First Quarto 'fathers'. This has led some editors, including Brian Gibbons in the Arden edition, to prefer the conjectural 'Ghostly Sire's', which registers the spiritual and quasi-paternal aspects of his function in Romeo's life. Like the Nurse, he is a surrogate parent, and unlike her he is one with a sense of responsibility towards the city as well as the lovers: the marriage will help to promote peace between the families. Unfortunately, like the Nurse, Laurence ultimately fails. He dispenses theoretical and practical wisdom, and aids and abets the lovers, but is defeated by the force of circumstance, society or destiny, depending how one interprets the 'misadventured, piteous overthrows' (Prologue 7) of the play's final movement. In counselling Romeo and Juliet both before and after the fatal brawl of 3.1, and up to the moment when he flees from the tomb ('I dare no longer stay', 5.3.159), Laurence seems a model of dependable good sense and pragmatism. Many actors have also found a degree of passionate commitment that rises to the challenge of Romeo's hysteria in 3.3. Unlike the Nurse, he never offers advice that is self-serving or insensitive. Nothing in the dialogue of the final scene acknowledges the kind of dissatisfaction his desertion of Juliet has caused to many readers and audiences. The Prince's 'We still have known thee for a holy man' (5.3.269) appears to accept his account of the stratagems and mischances and implicitly reject the need for him to suffer 'the rigour of severest law' (268). Directors and actors have often managed to indicate something of this, although the full extent of Laurence's explanation has rarely been heard.

The pressure of space has usually led newspaper reviewers to deal summarily with performances of the role, except for unusual circumstances (such as at least one account of the 2000 production where a critic found the Friar the most interesting figure in the production). Most Friars have merited no more than a telling sentence or phrase – often little more than an adjective or two in a concluding paragraph. Nevertheless, we can obtain a sense of some general tendencies. Leo McKern (1954) was thought to have given the Friar 'unusual substance' (*S. Times*) by emphasizing 'the human rather than the priestly side' (*Stage*). One response to his interpretation indicates the kind of routine holiness expected: the *Liverpool Daily Post* suggested that a Friar 'portrayed . . . with lively human business rather than piety' was 'not Shakespeare's conception', and threw into relief 'the futility of that cleric's machinations'. In other words, a more piously remote Laurence might more easily be disconnected from contaminating involvement in the mundane failures that destroy his plans. In fact, down-to-earth good sense combined with passionate involvement have been the keynotes of most performances of the role since the 1960s, notably those by Sebastian Shaw (1967), Tony Church (1973), David Waller (1976), Robert Demeger (1986), Julian Glover (1995), Richard Cordery (1997) and Des McAleer (2000). An element of rigour has often been found valuable, although occasionally it has been pushed towards aggression, as with David Waller's 'robust, rustic presence' (*Coventry E. Tel.*), or Robert Demeger (Figure 15), who manhandled Romeo and even petulantly struck Friar John to emphasize that the undelivered letter was of grave importance. Demeger, closer to Romeo in age and background (both had northern accents), did not hesitate to hit him. Roger Warren suggested this 'young, tough, no-nonsense parish priest' offered 'a convincingly contemporary image for the church' and that their relationship might even account for Romeo's belief in the sacraments, otherwise surprising in the materialistic world of Bogdanov's production (Warren, 1987, 85). Julian Glover (1995),

FIGURE 15 Juliet (Niamh Cusack) and Romeo (Sean Bean) with Robert Demeger's street-wise Friar in 2.6, in Michael Bogdanov's 1986 production.

confronted in his cell with an unusually hysterical Romeo, was 'animated, affectionately exasperated' (*TLS*) and seemed ready to slap the young whiner's face. Richard Cordery (1997) was 'a robust priest rather than the usual dreamy allotment-holder' (*Times*). Des McAleer, in the stark 2000 production, did not please every critic ('a Friar Laurence you wouldn't trust with your watch, let alone your life' wrote Lyn Gardner in the *Guardian*), but was generally considered 'authoritative and movingly humane' (*D. Telegraph*) – and he would not take any nonsense from his spiritual charges. One reviewer even suggested that he was 'a sort of Franciscan Puritan, the sort one would almost imagine chaining up Verona's playground swings on the Lord's day' (FT).

The sense of a sensitive, principled and loving man shockingly defeated has sometimes been made especially poignant. Sebastian Shaw (1967) (Figure 16) was 'strong' and 'dangerously over-confident' (Birm. Post). At the end he was left kneeling apart from the mourners, 'chastened by the defeat of reason' (New States.). As he entered the tomb Tony Church's 'lurching realization' of what had taken place (1973) seemed 'by far the most moving moment in the play' (Plays & P.). A sense that Friar Laurence has a problem with sex has occasionally been hinted at. Michael Billington, for example, described Edwin Richfield (1980) as 'a ravaged and embittered celibate' (Guardian). The most benignly patrician Laurence was Max Adrian (1961), a 'straight-backed priest in his prime' (Birm. Mail) with an element of wit and sophistication that suggested a much higher status than McKern's homely bustler or the bicycling streetwise cleric of Demeger. Adrian, 'spry and rightly punning' (Man. Guardian), 'enter[ed] joyfully into the lovers' conspiracy, being entirely on their side from the beginning' (Stage). It may be that his performance took up the tone of Dorothy Tutin and Edith Evans: like him, both were accomplished 'high comedy' performers.

The Friar's first speech establishes him as a moralist as well as a herbalist, setting up another of the binary oppositions that dominate the play – 'grace and rude will' (2.3.24) – and then providing an example for immediate examination in the shape of the allegedly reformed Romeo. Roger Warren admired the way in which David Waller (1976), 'not the usual pious contemplative, but a vigorously earthy man, and an enthusiastic seeker after the "virtues excellent" in the world of nature', conveyed his enthusiasm in 'the punch and committed force' with which he spoke of the twofold power, poisonous and medicinal, of the 'weak flower' (19) (Warren, 1977, 170). Other actors – notably

FIGURE 16 Romeo (Ian Holm) and Juliet (Estelle Kohler) with the Friar (Sebastian Shaw) in 2.6. The cut of Romeo's jerkin is modern, and his hose are of a workaday, ribbed woollen material. Both lovers wear their hair in styles current in the late 1960s, and their make-up is lighter than that evident in earlier productions. (Compare, for example, Figures 8, 9, 12 and 27.) (1967)

Robert Demeger, Julian Glover and Des McAleer – have achieved a similar effect, and a degree of enthusiastic energy and conviction is usually strengthened by a frank use of argumentative direct address to the audience. Romeo arrives on stage just as Laurence is reflecting on the flower's two aspects, and he speaks just after the Friar has referred to 'the canker death' (2.3.26). Most productions accept this arrangement, although some (1954 for example) have preferred the editorial intervention that brings Romeo on just before his first line. Apart from anything else, the earlier entrance allows the audience to observe Romeo as he makes his way downstage towards Laurence.

The customary prop for the scene is a basket ('this osier cage of ours', 3), but sometimes a more elaborate arrangement has been contrived. Demeger (1986) had been out on his bicycle, and met up with Friar John: they shared coffee from a flask as Laurence amiably explained the properties of flowers and herbs to his colleague. Glover, in 1995, was discovered at a café table. As a clock struck, he checked his watch and exchanged a greeting ('Morning') with the waiter, who brought him his espresso. Rather than produce a specimen from a basket, he picked up a freesia from a glass on the table at 'within the infant rind of this weak flower' (19) and expatiated on its qualities as Romeo appeared upstage and meandered down towards him. In 1997 Richard Cordery was welcomed by an assortment of homely sound effects listed in the promptbook: 'Cock. Birds. Crickets. Dogs'. He washed his hands at a tap after bringing in herbs and basket. More important than the various naturalistic touches brought to the soliloquy is the ease of the relationship between the two men. David Tennant, Romeo in 2000, describes the need to establish

> a familiarity between the pair that was to do with mutual affection and respect. We decided that Romeo, forever in the grip of some existential argument with himself, would be regularly at the Friar's cell, picking his brains and quizzing him on the nature of his own beliefs.   (Tennant)

He came in and knelt by the side of Des McAleer, and he hugged him at the end of the scene. Romeo is more relaxed, less on his mettle, with Laurence than with his other companions, and although he is not allowed an easy ride in accounting for his emotions and behaviour, the humour of the scene leavens the Friar's severity. ('Holy Saint Francis' (61) nearly always gets a laugh.) There has commonly been some stage business at the end to indicate Romeo's anxiety to get on and Laurence's refusal to hurry ('Wisely and slow; they stumble that run fast', 90). In 1954 this became a knockabout between Laurence Harvey and Leo McKern: the promptbook indicates that 'Friar picks up basket. Romeo tries to take basket', and finally 'Romeo pushes Friar off'. In 1989 Mark Rylance eagerly gathered up Patrick Godfrey's gear. But he was dismayed to encounter what he took as a refusal, 'O, she knew well / Thy love did read by rote that could not spell' (83–4), and walked off stage to be brought back by the relenting 'But come young waverer' (85). He picked up Laurence's things again, but was made to wait while the Friar put on his sandals. Michael Maloney (1991) came in, sat down centre stage by the Friar, and opening his arms spoke slowly and earnestly. This solemnity was soon broken, and at the end he dragged Laurence off, joining in on 'they stumble that run fast' as if he had heard the saying a hundred times. Ray Fearon (1997) took up Richard Cordery's basket and went off, obliging the Friar to follow him.

When the lovers meet in Laurence's cell (2.6) (Figures 15 and 16) there has often been an element of humour to qualify their somewhat elevated protestations and the Friar's ominous 'These violent delights have violent ends' (9). In 1986 a clock struck and Robert Demeger looked at his watch on 'Too swift arrives as tardy as too slow' (15). In 1989 Romeo picked Juliet up as she came in and embraced her, and she folded herself round him so effectively that Laurence had to prize them apart before dragging the couple off to the altar. The scene has sometimes been marked by a more general sense of foreboding and solemnity. In 1991 a chill blue light flooded onto the stage through a narrow opening after the warm autumnal glow of the previous scene between Juliet and the Nurse. The Friar's comment on Juliet as she enters, 'O, so light a foot / Will ne'er wear out the everlasting flint' (16–7), lost the moralizing (or wry) three lines that follow on lovers and vanity. Romeo and Juliet embraced and kissed, and the Friar stayed well upstage of them. There was no comic business here, and the dominant effect was of Romeo's mind and tongue racing as he spoke 'Ah, Juliet, if the measure of thy joy . . . ' (24ff.). In 1997 the scene ended with the couple kneeling at the little altar upstage as the lights faded to blackout: the same image was repeated after the interval, at the beginning of 3.1.

Romeo's behaviour in Laurence's cell after his sentence of banishment has occasioned some rough handling from the Friar.

David Tennant even suggests that Romeo is reacting 'like a cornered animal' in lashing out at his friend, and he tried to use the repetitions of 'banished' as though he were trying to wound him (Tennant). The text has often been cut severely, but usually enough remains to give Romeo ample scope. Ian McKellen, a notably extravagant Romeo in 1976, 'wrenched at the Friar's habit in desperation' on 'Thou canst not speak of that thou dost not feel', flung himself to the ground and finally (in Richard David's vivid description) 'pulled out the suicidal dagger with wildly wriggling hands and was hurled against the far wall by the rescuing Friar' (David, 117). In 1986 Robert Demeger, despairing of making his charge see sense, threw up his hands and walked away from Sean Bean on '"Banished"? / O Friar, the damned use that word in hell' (46–7). He relented and came to sit by him, but Romeo pushed him away on 'Hang up philosophy' (57). 'Thou canst not speak of that thou dost not feel' (64) – at the very least an insensitive observation to a selflessly helpful celibate – caused Romeo to collapse sobbing on the stage again. When he drew a knife and threatened immediate suicide (104ff.), Laurence threw himself down by Romeo, knocked it from his hand and hit him angrily on the back. Laurence also struck him to emphasize the argument with each repetition of 'There art thou happy' (136–7, 139). It was hardly surprising (and typical of the natural detail in Bogdanov's production) that after Romeo and the Nurse had gone, Demeger should take a packet of cigarettes from his cassock and light one to steady his nerves. In 1989 the end of the scene was marked by a moment of reconciliation between the Friar and Mark Rylance's self-absorbed Romeo, whose accusation 'Thou canst not speak of that thou dost not feel' had been met with dignified silence (the Friar stayed well away from him at this point). Romeo remained prostrate even while the plan for meeting Juliet was being outlined to him (145ff.), so that the Friar's 'Romeo is coming' (157), spoken while the lover showed every sign of staying sobbing on the floor, drew laughter. On being given Juliet's ring Romeo revived, exclaimed 'How well my comfort is reviv'd by this' (164) and was going straight off without any farewell until the Friar's 'Give me thy hand' (171) brought him back for a leave-taking.

Michael Maloney (1991) showed Romeo's self-absorption by directing much of his anguished meditation on 'banished' to himself, before going across, grabbing Laurence, dragging him downstage and falling down at the front with 'Thou canst not speak of that thou dost not feel'. By now Romeo was crawling around on the forestage. When the Nurse came in and spoke soothingly he embraced her as if he were a child, but he soon became hysterical with the impulse to attack the 'vile part of this anatomy' (105) where his name lodged, and she had to wrestle him to the floor. The Friar nearly hit Romeo but restrained himself, standing over him to argue vehemently. By now Romeo was sitting facing upstage. At the end of the scene the Friar stayed in the centre of the forestage, holding a torch and lost in thought as Romeo hastened off. Julian Glover (1995), by his own account angered by Romeo's killing of Tybalt ('a fight is one thing, murder another'), treated the last sequence as the issuing of orders rather than consolation: Romeo must get out of town, but not before he has consummated the marriage (Glover, 171).

There was a finer inflection of the relationship between the two men in Michael Attenborough's 1997 production. A moment of reconciliation came with Romeo's taking in what was being said at 'Take heed, take heed, for such die miserable' (144). He had pulled away, but after a pause he hugged the Friar, and the encouragement of the instructions to visit Juliet and take refuge in Mantua could now be a temporary sign of hope shared between the two of them. In 2000 David Tennant was revealed hiding in a secret cubbyhole in the set's right-hand wall. When the Friar told him to hide (as the Nurse's knocking was heard outside) he defiantly threw himself on the ground. Although Des McAleer had to use some force to disarm Romeo, by the end of the scene the two were reconciled, and Romeo hugged the Friar with 'But that a joy past joy calls out on me, / It were a grief so brief to part with thee' (172–3).

When Juliet comes to Laurence's cell in 4.1, she has suffered her father's wrath, her mother's chilly indifference and her Nurse's betrayal (Figure 17). Awkwardly, her arrival coincides with the departure of Paris, with whom she has yet another temporizing and equivocal exchange (corresponding to that with her mother after Romeo's secret departure from the Capulet house in 3.3). She endures a kiss, which Niamh Cusack (1986) wiped from her mouth behind Paris's back, and in 2000 Alexandra Gilbreath was even lifted up by Paris in the sexually suggestive manner of their dance in 1.5 (see pp. 143–4) and collapsed on the stage after his departure. The Friar has to watch as Juliet deals with this trial. His ironic response to 'What must be, shall be' – 'That's a certain text' (4.1.21) – has sometimes been an aside, although in 1991 he held up his hand in benediction and Juliet knelt and crossed herself, leaving Paris in the centre of the stage and perhaps indicating that she was about to begin confession. The Friar's powers of persuasion and invention are taxed once again in the dialogue that follows. Juliet is usually quite easily disarmed when she produces the dagger, although in 1991 Laurence held up his hands but did not go to her. In this production the scene was centred in moments of intimacy. On 'And if thou dar'st, I'll give thee remedy' (76) Juliet ran to embrace the Friar, kneeling as she declared herself ready to be chained with roaring bears and undergo other trials of her resolution (most directors have cut some of these lines). The Friar held his ground, remaining a strong centre of authority, and produced a vial from his habit. At 'In this borrow'd likeness of shrunk death' (104) he went to kneel beside Juliet, and she knelt and kissed his hand for a blessing before she departed. Sometimes Juliet's reaction to the idea of the potion has been too impulsive for Laurence's liking. In 1986 Robert Demeger produced a vial from amongst others in a strong box hidden under a paving stone. As Niamh Cusack rushed towards him, he held it back with the warning 'If no inconstant toy nor womanish fear / Abate thy valour in the acting it' (119–20), only offering it when he saw she was resolved. In 1989 Patrick Godfrey had the vial in his pocket,

FIGURE 17 Juliet (Dorothy Tutin) encounters Paris (Barry Warren) when she goes in search of Friar Laurence (Max Adrian), in 1961. (4.1)

but he held it away from Georgia Slowe until he was sure she was in the right frame of mind to use it. Most Friars have had the vial ready, either in a safe hiding place or even (as if anticipating the need) in the folds of their habit or a convenient pocket. Julian Glover (1995), dissatisfied with the logic of ready-mixed potions, had a whole chemical workshop bench at his disposal and made up the prescription as he spoke to Juliet. Richard Cordery (1997) kept his herbal remedies behind the altar, although nothing was made of the possible sacramental connection.

When Juliet is discovered in 4.5 the Friar is seen for the first time in the context of the whole Capulet family. His words of comfort have sometimes lost some of their homiletic force (71–8 have occasionally been omitted) but the image of him as a source of comfort is important at this point, if only as a reminder that even such benign forces are not immune from what is about to happen. As has already been mentioned (p. 59), he often occupies a strong upstage position, as if supplanting Capulet as a figure of authority in the family. In the versions that cut this sequence altogether (Leveaux's in 1991 and Attenborough's in 1997) the action was pushed forward at the expense of this important image. Laurence's spiritual authority is what the family perceives, while his secret, worldly practicality is emphasized for the audience. Julian Glover notes a degree of self-satisfaction in all this, until a 'bubble bursts' and the news of the letter's failure to reach Mantua shatters him. The Friar's part in the final movement of the play, and his emotional state in the last scene, will be discussed in chapter 5.

MERCUTIO

In the last half-century, and particularly since the 1960s, it has become not merely acceptable but almost mandatory for the Friar to be a down-to-earth, argumentative and emotionally involved person, rather than an other-worldly, contemplative soul. Simultaneously Mercutio, once habitually played as a brilliant, witty man-about-town, has become an altogether darker and more numinous figure. Quite apart from any questions about the character's imagined psychology, his behaviour has an important thematic and poetic function. As Joseph Porter has suggested, Mercutio is an equivocal figure. He is named after Mercury, who is the messenger of the gods, the *psychopompos* who leads souls into the next world, and is also a symbol of liminal states of being and equivocal sexuality (Porter, 1988).

Although he 'consorts' with Romeo and other Montagues, and expresses contempt for Tybalt, Mercutio is not a member of either feuding family, but is 'the Prince's near ally' (3.1.111). He is even on the invitation list for the Capulets' feast. Mercutio seems to treat Romeo as a novice in the art of hanging about town and mocks his lovelorn state more cruelly and directly than Benvolio. It seems that he never knows about Romeo's involvement with

Juliet (still less, their marriage). He appears in four scenes: 1.4 (going to the feast); 1.6 (returning); 2.4 (the morning after); and 3.1 (the fight with Tybalt). In the first three he expresses a quizzical, if not cynical, attitude to love and the behaviour of lovers and a talent for bawdy humour and word-play. Himself an accomplished swordsman, in 2.4 and 3.1 he shows his contempt for Tybalt as a fashionable duellist. The 'Queen Mab' speech in 1.4 is a tour de force of fanciful elaboration, which actors have often made grimmer in the last four lines:

> This is the hag, when maids lie on their backs,
> That presses them and learns them first to bear,
> Making them women of good carriage.
> This is she –
>
> (1.4.92–5)

At which point Romeo interrupts with 'Peace, peace, Mercutio, peace. / Thou talk'st of nothing' (95–6). Taken together with his 'conjuring' of Romeo by the parts of Rosaline's body (2.1.17ff.), and the aggressive sexual language he directs at the Nurse (2.4.111ff.), this has been interpreted as reflecting a degree of sexual insecurity in the character. Since the 1960s many reviewers – and some actors and directors – have found this attractive, offering as it does a 'secret' explanation of the character's behaviour.

Roger Allam, who played the part in John Caird's 1984 studio production, has described Mercutio as a friend who cannot bear to part with Romeo: 'His repetitive use of sexual punning seemed neurotic to me, and I saw it as springing from his sense of loss . . . that his closest, most passionate, and intense relationship was ending' (Allam, 112). Romeo's characterization of Mercutio to the Nurse as 'a gentleman . . . that loves to hear himself talk, and will speak more in a minute than he will stand to in a month' (2.4.144–6) itself includes a bawdy pun that unconsciously indicates the extent and influence of his friend's fertile unconscious. But then the play's Verona is as dirty-minded as it is fair, and since the 1960s directors have relished this more openly. Hilary Spurling's *Spectator* review of the 1967 production, in which Norman Rodway played Mercutio, drew attention to the significance of sexual word-play, which by the late 1960s was being given in an increasingly emphatic and outspoken manner at Stratford. The company's laudable 'unobtrusive habit of taking the fig-leaves off Shakespeare' did the play a service: 'The lewdness which runs through this play serves, in the expert hands of Norman Rodway, as a harsh, sardonic counterpoint to the lovers' scenes by moonlight and at sunrise.' Harold Hobson, reviewing the 1976 production, thought that Trevor Nunn must have been most impressed by the actor quoted in the programme as saying that Renaissance Italy reminded him of buggery. Hobson was convinced that the men in the cast kept their distance from the women, reserving hugs and kisses for each other, and that 'an epicene Mercutio thrusts out his bottom in an inviting gesture which will be eagerly discussed by knowing members of school parties later in the year'. To Hobson's perhaps too readily fevered imagination, Nunn seemed to have made 'a fascinating attempt to show the tensions of a homosexual society condemned to act out lives of heterosexual love' (*S. Times*).

Even without appeal to a sense of doubtful sexual identity or repressed desire, a degree of melancholy had often been traced in Mercutio. Interest in Freudian psychology, with its attention to the specifically sexual dimension of the unconscious, was widespread in the arts in the late 1940s – the outstanding Shakespearean example is Olivier's 1948 film of *Hamlet*. There is no explicit reference to such matters in the reviews of Peter Brook's 1947 *Romeo and Juliet*. As Mercutio, Paul Scofield (Figure 18) seemed to be striving for 'an effect of sullen whimsicality' (*Times*) and was 'curiously delicate and un-jovial' (*Time & T.*). Endowed with a surprising degree of 'gravity', his delivery of the 'Queen Mab' speech 'almost, by the way, as a soliloquy' (*Stage*) suggested to Hobson that this was 'a Mercutio who really has seen the fairies and wishes, perhaps, that he had not' (*S. Times*). He

FIGURE 18 Mercutio's death, 1947: Paul Scofield, with Benvolio (John Harrison) supporting him. (3.1)

also observed that the speech 'might have been delivered by the melancholy Jaques'. This did not prevent Alan Dent from finding Scofield 'a keen, witty, bawdy blade with blood in him' (*News Chron.*) or the *Sunday Express* from crediting him with 'an attractive bounce'.

In 1954 and 1958 Glen Byam Shaw treated Mercutio as a conventionally high-spirited man-about-town. In the words of the *News Chronicle*, Tony Britton in 1954 was 'prosy rather than lyrical', and 'an eager cockerel'. Another reviewer thought that the actor brought out Mercutio's 'good, sound, common sense' (*Bristol E. Post*). In 1958 Edward Woodward (Figure 19) effected a more successful version of the same figure, 'gaily sardonic' (*Times*) and 'completely convincing in its power and attack' (*Stage*). A local

FIGURE 19 Mercutio (Edward Woodward) asks Romeo (Richard Johnson) why he has misgivings about going to the feast, while Mercutio's Page (John Davidson, left) and other maskers look on (1.4). The chiaroscuro of Angus McBean's photograph corresponds to the effect indicated in the surviving lighting plots for the 1958 staging.

reviewer, making the fine distinction between offensive and inoffensive bawdy, was impressed by this Mercutio's social standing and his effect on the play's hero:

> After a rather tentative beginning, he creates a character far truer to Shakespeare's text than to recent stage tradition, a young man overflowing with high spirits, who has the cheerful, aristocratic insolence of the Prince's kinsman and whose bawdy jokes, never nudging, but wittily gay, are funny without offence. In his company, Romeo becomes younger and sweeter, and his touching astonishment at his own death, in the full career of his youth, sombrely marks the ending of laughter in the tragedy.   (*SA Herald*)

Since 1958, the sardonic, if not necessarily troubled, dimension has prevailed, although it has been inflected in a variety of ways. In Zeffirelli's 1960 Old Vic production Alec McCowen played Mercutio as a 'disdainful exhibitionist', improvising the Queen Mab speech in response to the group of young men he is with and performing for the gallery even up to the point of his death. This interpretation is reflected in John McEnery's performance in the 1968 film (Levenson, 1987, 98). A year later at Stratford Ian Bannen – unavoidably compared with McCowen – was 'mockingly world-weary' (*E. Standard*), 'dark, sardonic, unloving and ungenerous' (*S. Times*), and 'flashing, quicksilver' (*D. Express*). The *Times* thought that the actor had been 'encouraged by the initial responses of the audience wildly to overplay his hand', and to indulge in excessive and obtrusive naturalism. Bannen's performance was full of inventive (to some minds, inappropriate) clowning: he elaborated the Queen Mab speech with illustrative mime. The *Stratford-upon-Avon Herald* reported an impressive range of 'devil-may-care tongue clicks, cat-calls, hoots, and even a gargle during the duel'. During the bout with Tybalt (Figure 24) he produced a Spanish wineskin, squirted the wine high into the air, caught it in his mouth and gargled with it. More interesting is the degree of sexual equivocation others noticed in the characterization. This was 'a dirty-minded dandy given to sinister giggles and offensive whoops' (*S. Telegraph*) who achieved 'the look of a pirate dangerous to both sexes, as he [strolled] his way through Verona, a straw-hatted troublemaker' (*SA Herald*). Declaring Bannen 'our greatest exponent of psychopaths on the stage today' (he had recently played the manic title character in John Arden's *Serjeant Musgrave's Dance*), Alan Brien in the *Sunday Telegraph* observed that for once his obscenities 'sound as if they were really meant to degrade and infect their hearers'. His early departure from the play was especially unfortunate in a production with an underpowered Romeo.

Productions since Hall's have offered a series of variations on the less debonair and less easily amiable Mercutio. Norman Rodway (1967) played for 'grotesque comedy', and outspoken bawdiness, getting a laugh with the petulance of his sudden high-pitched cry of '*I* am hurt' (3.1.91; my italics) after he received a death blow that seemed – appropriately – to be directed at his groin (*Times*). Michael Pennington (1976) was 'a volatile fantasist, whose jokes [were] always apt to turn dangerous' and who appeared to be stabbed just as he leapt into Tybalt's arms to kiss him (*Times*). He had kept the others waiting by arriving late for the party, was rather delicate and slow in his delivery of the Queen Mab speech, and seemed intent on holding the stage in his private theatre. Roger Allam (1984) delivered 'an angry, dangerous young man' (*Birm. Post*), and Michael Kitchen (1986) 'a laid-back tease with a wicked tongue' (*D. Telegraph*). Mark Lockyer (1995) was 'a compelling mixture of cruel humour, self-lacerating contempt and ambiguous sexuality' (*D. Telegraph*). Class consciousness has featured in the reception of some Mercutios, even when productions have not gone out of their way to suggest contemporary parallels for Verona's culture of rivalry and violence. David O'Hara (1989) was described as 'a lumbering Glaswegian bruiser' (*Times*) and 'a boorish, raw youth, rowdy, unattractive and unfunny' (*S. Times*). J.C. Trewin's comment that Kitchen was 'by no means a Renaissance gallant' (*Birm. Post*) – in a production that was determinedly *not* of the Renaissance – can stand for the conservative critics' reaction to many subsequent Mercutios.

The first encounter with Mercutio, in 1.4, introduces him as an ingredient not announced in the Prologue: Romeo may already be set up as one of a pair of star-crossed lovers, heading with some foreboding but no clear knowledge towards a misadventured, piteous overthrow. However, as far as he and his friends are concerned they are going to perform a socially acceptable form of gate-crashing by turning up as maskers at the Capulet feast. It's a potentially amusing way of spending the evening with a bit of singing and dancing and a spice of danger for the Montagues, and Benvolio has promised it as an antidote for Romeo's infatuation with Rosaline. (She will be there, but so will plenty of other good-looking women.) The basic contrast is between Romeo's lack of interest and the other men's relish for the entertainment, and it's high time they were going – so why, in terms of motivation, does Mercutio take the time and trouble to speak at such length about the fairies' midwife? Some actors have treated this as the occasion to take Romeo aside and spell out a few lessons about imagination and illusion. Allam (1984) began 'seated on a bench: the others on the floor around [him]: Mercutio doing one of his turns'. Then, pausing after 'Through lovers' brains' (1.4.71) he turned directly to Romeo. The actor argued that

> by placing his faith in 'dreams', feeling, love for women, Romeo is being 'inconstant' to Mercutio. He is betraying a relationship based on a higher, truer love, the bond between men. I did most of the second half of the speech directed very strongly at Romeo. When he, finally responding, got up and moved away, I leapt to my feet following him, shouting 'True I talk of dreams', very hurt and angry.
>
> (Allam, 115)

Michael Kitchen (1986) was setting off for the party but turned back to the seat where Sean Bean's drooping Romeo had remained. He sat down at his side and spelled out the lines as if telling a story to a small child: at one point he pulled Romeo's legs across his knees so that they looked like a father (or uncle) and child, and Romeo entered into the joke by sticking his thumb in his mouth. Mark Lockyer (1995), who happened to be wearing a skirt in readiness for his drag act at the party, sat on Romeo's knee, and spoke to him with affectionate earnestness, 'finding' each idea in the speech rather than reeling off a bravura piece he knew by heart. The focus was entirely on Romeo, until the thought of maids lying on their backs began to disturb the speaker. By this point he was down at the front of the stage, his attention distracted away from Romeo and focused on his own imaginings. After he had been interrupted, he said 'True, I talk of dreams' – then paused for a long beat before 'Which are the children of an idle brain' (96–7). The psychological significance of what he had been saying as well as its emotional impact were dawning on him (Figure 20). Then the 'unstable celebration of being one of the boys' (*SA Herald*) took over again: he and the others quickly downed a glass of spirits in what seemed like a college drinking ritual and rushed off. The vulnerability seemed somewhat overplayed.

The age of Mercutio has a direct bearing on this scene, helping to determine whether he is the leader of the pack or its jester – or, indeed, both at once. Kitchen, Allam, and Adrian Schiller (2000) all seemed considerably older than Romeo: Kitchen, apparently giving Sean Bean ten years, was 'an amiable, sardonic bachelor in raffish early middle age' (*S. Times*), and Schiller was described by one reviewer as a 'traditionally jaded, older bohemian roué' (*E. Standard*). Lockyer, by contrast, although companioned with a notably immature Romeo (Zubin Varla), seemed younger than Benvolio and achieved 'amazing transitions from fearless sardonic effrontery to waif-like defenceless[ness]' (*Indep. Sun.*). Observing that he was both sardonic and affectionate, John Peter sensed 'that behind all that flamboyance there is a solitary, inward-looking youngster' (*S. Times*). Apart from the suggestion of physical age, though, the degree of self-confidence and experience carries greater weight. Schiller, an acid, waspish Touchstone in the 2000 season's *As You Like It*, was 'excellent, off-handedly bored and

FIGURE 20 Mercutio (Mark Lockyer) on his way to the Capulets' feast in 1995. He already wears the skirt – but not the brassière and balloons – he needs for his drag act. Balthasar (Godfrey Walters) and Romeo (Zubin Varla) listen. (1.4)

sophisticated' (*Independent*) and 'openly bored stiff by Romeo's indulgent lovesickness' (*FT*): some reviewers thought the Romeo of David Tennant (himself an outstanding Touchstone in 1996) insufficiently lovesick, and more than one suggested that he would have made a better Mercutio. Schiller's seems to have been the most unequivocally sexual rendering: he sat astride the prostrate Romeo and moved his pelvis over his friend's on 'making them women of good carriage' (Figure 21). In 1989

FIGURE 21 In Michael Boyd's 2000 production, Mercutio (Adrian Schiller) sits astride Romeo (David Tennant), to illustrate Mab's effect on maids when they lie on their backs. (1.4)

David O'Hara's 'dour Scot' delivered the description of Queen Mab as though 'gradually . . . seduced by his own rhetoric' (*Guardian*). National prejudice seems to have played its part: a characterization summed up by the *Evesham Journal* as 'a strutting, cocky Glasgow Rangers supporter' (that is, bellicose and uncouth), was praised by Michael Ratcliffe in the *Observer* as 'outstanding': 'behind his pale, angry romantic bearing is a wry, cool, classical style, articulating the verse with considered, deliberate wit and joy'. Irving Wardle characterized the speech as performed 'on a menacing crescendo' (*Times*), and John Peter described a 'long rambling snarl' (*S. Times*), but Michael Billington, as well as finding Mercutio 'seduced by his own rhetoric', thought the speech was delivered well (*Guardian*). In fact O'Hara's performance varied considerably in its degrees of assurance and aggression, often from night to night. On the archive video the speech is given in a measured tone, benefiting from the emphatic consonants of O'Hara's Scottish accent but by no means confrontational. At the beginning of the scene Mark

Rylance's gloomy Romeo seems exceptionally dejected but Mercutio refuses to take him seriously, gyrating his pelvis suggestively on 'You are a lover*rrr* – borrow Cupid's wings' (17). After Romeo's 'I dreamt a dream tonight' (49) there is a long pause, and Mercutio's eventual 'O' is followed by a beat, before 'then I see Queen Mab hath been with you' (53). The progression through each of Mab's victims is deliberate, as though each has to be given the appropriate weight. The speech begins to build on 'Sometime she driveth o'er a soldier's neck' (82) and Mercutio takes the downstage centre position, flourishing his sword. He flexes his knees on 'when maids lie on their backs' (92) and emphasizes Mab's beneficial effect – 'making them women of *good* carriage' (94) – but does not seem to be in a troubled state of mind when he is interrupted. Unlike the Mercutios (such as Lockyer) who have needed comforting by Romeo and, sometimes, by all the other men, O'Hara just reverted at the end to a simpler, more matter-of-fact manner.

In this production the speech seemed to be directed at Romeo, but the Swan's platform stage allowed O'Hara to take in the audience and the bystanders without evident effort or intention. Other Mercutios have been more exhibitionist, performing a showpiece for their onstage audience and perhaps conscious of needing to address the whole of the Royal Shakespeare Theatre's larger and more remote auditorium. The 'huge impishness' of Bannen in 1961 seems to have been focused in this way, as the speech became a 'private game of charades' (*S. Wales E. Arg.*) that reminded one reviewer of Danny Kaye (*Birm. Mall*). Michael Pennington (1976) (Figure 22) was thought by Robert Cushman to be a victim of the general 'busyness' in Trevor Nunn's production: 'instead of building a relationship with Romeo and Benvolio, he has to go through exhausting routines for the entertainment of a crowd of extras'. He ended up 'far more fantasticated' than the Tybalt he affected to despise (*Observer*). Jonathan Hyde, a languid-voiced and 'baleful' Mercutio in 1980, 'did wonders' with the description of Queen Mab, delivered 'in a

FIGURE 22 Mercutio (Michael Pennington, left) and Romeo (Ian McKellen) on their way to the feast in 1976. (1.4)

crouching position to individual members of the gang' (*Times*). Hyde played the different characters of the speech with the help of the Page, who asked the question given to Benvolio in the First Quarto – 'Queen Mab – who's she?' The Page then contributed appropriate bits of business to support the comic routine: for example, he pretended to pass Mercutio money as a 'backhander' to illustrate the lawyer's fees. With 'This is that very Mab' (88) there was no sense of Mercutio becoming engrossed in a private obsession, as he beckoned his friends to come in close to him for the intimate details. In contrast to the sexually explicit or troubled renderings of the sequence, earlier productions seem innocent; in 1947, 1954 and 1958 the other listeners were clearly fascinated, but Romeo's breaking away from the group on 'Peace, peace Mercutio' (95) seems to have indicated impatience rather than disgust.

Once the maskers have arrived at the Capulet house, a more obvious and legitimate opportunity for exhibitionism presents itself. In the next chapter the 'old accustom'd feast' (1.2.20) will be discussed in relation to the meeting of Romeo and Juliet, but it is worth considering the entertainment offered by the maskers in the context of Mercutio's relationship with the larger questions of the play. The young men arrive, masked and therefore conventionally in disguise, and by custom they are to be admitted if they offer some kind of entertainment to the company. ('We'll measure them a measure and be gone', Benvolio suggested at 1.4.10.) Michael Kitchen enlivened the proceedings in 1986, and emulated Tybalt's prowess on the saxophone, by playing a guitar solo from a balcony, jumping down onto the stage, jitterbugging with a female guest and then leaping with her into the small pool down on the right of the forestage. As the dripping couple was helped off, Capulet observed aptly 'this unlook'd-for sport comes well' (1.5.29). Productions in 'period' costume have often featured a brief dance involving sword-play (in 1989 and 1992 for example), and since the 1960s the tendency has been for it to include some element of carnival – broad, bawdy humour. In 1976 the gate-crashers arrived armed with a doll representing Cupid and endowed with an oversize penis, and a similar doll appeared in 1980. In 1984 Balthasar was ready to impersonate the blind bow-boy with wings and a blindfold, and the men sang a Latin song, which Mercutio accompanied on a mandolin. Stratford's most aggressive Mercutio, the 'Veronese Hell's Angel' (*Guardian*) of Bernard Lloyd in Terry Hands's 1973 production, carried with him a life-size foam rubber figure resembling the kind of 'love doll' available in sex shops. This was brandished during the dance – for which he and his friends wore masks with 'long phallic noses and devil's horns' (*New States.*) – but it would not come into its own until the next scene.

In 1995 the Capulet feast was a family party, with a band playing airs from Verdi in the background: Mercutio made a grand entrance upstage centre, dressed in a skirt and wig and flourishing balloons as breasts. Then he led the maskers in a frenetic, carnivalesque dance, contrasting with the gentle waltzing that seemed to be the order of the day. However, the presence of children at this family feast seemed to require a less aggressive mode of behaviour: Mercutio even sat down to play cards with the youngest members of the household. In 2000 the entertainment resembled a fertility rite, as the men wore masks with phallic noses and beat the ground and walls with wands before leading off a chain of dancers. Each of these variations suggested an acknowledgement of animalism and aggressive – even transgressive – sexuality that connected with other aspects of Mercutio's scenes and the bawdy, violent world of the Veronese streets.

Mercutio's 'conjuring' of Romeo on the way home in 2.1, and his commentary on the hero's love-life, have often continued the tone – and used the props – of these contributions to the feast. The most sexually explicit and aggressive performance was in 1973, when Bernard Lloyd dismembered the foam rubber doll as he itemized Rosaline's charms. 'Nothing in the text', fulminated one critic, 'suggests that Mercutio is really a perverted thug' (*Guardian*). In the *Sunday Times* Harold Hobson, already strangely excited by Estelle Kohler's Juliet (see p. 131), found this 'a frightening and terrible thing', but continued:

> Yet his Mercutio, in Stevenson's words, makes the belly move. One reflects, with a thrill of illuminated amazement, that this shameless psychopath is Romeo's chosen friend. It is the keynote of a production which may be disliked or condemned, but cannot be ignored.

As for 'O Romeo, that she were, O that she were / An open-arse and thou a poperin pear!' (2.1.37–8), Benedict Nightingale thought that Lloyd's 'way of clawing such lines up from an acid stomach' suggested that they anticipated 'that extraordinary sexual distaste that pockmarks parts of *Hamlet, Measure for Measure* and *Troilus and Cressida*' (*New States.*). Other Mercutios have relished the scabrous detail of the mockery, but this was the most extreme. In

1980 the 'nervy, foul-mouthed' Jonathan Hyde used the doll of Cupid that he and his friends had taken to the party – a 'huge pink baby with a bobbing phallus' – as a ventriloquist's dummy (*Times*). Benvolio and Mercutio sat down on a bench together, with Benvolio manipulating the doll. Each time a part of the body was named, Benvolio twirled the football rattle he carried. When Mercutio kissed the doll's lips, Cupid hit him; he held up its leg and made its thigh quiver and – rapidly shifting its gender – gave the dummy an erection on 'I conjure only but to raise up him' (29). In 1986 Benvolio and Mercutio were more amiably dissipated. They tottered on and climbed the central staircase, with Benvolio singing in a high tenor voice, trilling the 'R' on Romeo's name. Mercutio made a comic retching sound on '"love" and "dove"' (10), and conjured in Rosaline's name with the help of a champagne bottle, which he shook as he spoke, popping the cork on 'quivering thigh' (19). After 'Romeo, good night' (39) he executed a neat back fall (drawing laughter and applause) which was followed by a long silence. Meanwhile Benvolio had been urinating over the back of the balcony. David O'Hara (1989) leapt onto Benvolio's back to conjure and grabbed his crotch as he reached the 'demesnes' adjacent to Rosaline's quivering thigh (20), and spelled out 'pop-her-in pear'. Mark Lockyer (1995), more fanciful than aggressive, produced a glove puppet of a puppy (filched from one of the Capulet children) and engaged it in conversation. As he exited, the puppy turned and said 'Night, night, Romeo' in a squeaky voice. Chook Sibtain (1997) used Benvolio's foot and leg to demonstrate the parts of Rosaline's body. More suggestive than any of these was Tim McInnerny (1991), who flung himself at the structure that would soon prove to be Juliet's balcony, and clung to it as he invoked Rosaline and the 'open-arse'. It was a vivid but ironically unconscious acting out of the rivalry between Mercutio and the object of Romeo's infatuation, a parody in anticipation of the scene to come with the added element of the imagery of anal penetration, which some actors have made into Mercutio's personal obsession.

After his encounter with Juliet at her balcony window and a quick visit to Friar Laurence to enlist his support, Romeo encounters Mercutio and Benvolio in a scene (2.4) that can be described as 'the morning after'. Like the play's first scene and that of Mercutio's fight with Tybalt (3.1), the location is clearly a public place, and it has often been a café – or, as in Glen Byam Shaw's 1958 production, some Renaissance equivalent of one. In 1947 Brook had Mercutio engaged with a 'case of rapiers' while Benvolio sat reading. The swords were useful when Mercutio wished to illustrate his diatribe against Tybalt, and similar business (though without the reading Benvolio) was used by Byam Shaw in 1954 and 1958. Unsurprisingly, Mercutio and Benvolio have sometimes appeared hung over. In 1986 early morning church bells were heard and Michael Kitchen's Mercutio was discovered slumped at a table, with his straw hat tilted protectively over his eyes. Benvolio entered, ordered a glass of water and dropped an Alka-Seltzer into it. Mercutio pushed over his glass of red wine, indicating that he also needed a tablet. Benvolio obliged, and Mercutio asked silently for a second one. Mercutio drawled the speeches about Tybalt in a working-class London voice, as though the new tuners of accent were upstarts, like the flashy and arrogant new generation of stock market traders of the 1980s. Romeo's arrival was a welcome diversion, and the revelation that he had been shaken out of his lovesick melancholy was a positive tonic. Then the Nurse entered (on a tricycle) and Mercutio was definitively back on form. Against this sociable Mercutio one might set Mark Lockyer's, in the mid-nineteenth century street café of Adrian Noble's 1995 production. After an elaborate performance of being the worse for last night's drinking (an ice pack clutched to his head, the acute annoyance caused by a waiter dropping a tray) Lockyer delivered the verbal attack on Tybalt downstage as a self-absorbed solo turn, while Benvolio remained at the café table engrossed in his newspaper, which seemed to have news of Tybalt's challenge.

Romeo's appearance brings with it a flurry of word-play, which directors have usually dealt with by a double strategy of filleting the text and encouraging bawdy physical business. This can be made to seem a ritual particular to the group, with the young men going through familiar routines as part of their sense of group identity. Terry Hands's 1973 production made a particular point of this. At other times, the sexual innuendo has seemed to go much further, as if sublimating an unacknowledged desire for sex itself. Sometimes this is a barely visible subtext: David O'Hara (1989) kissed Romeo on the lips, 'heartily if not lingeringly', as he welcomed him back to the fold (Wells, 1996, 13). In 1991 – to take an extreme case – Michael Maloney's Romeo ended up on the floor underneath Mercutio and Benvolio, with Tim McInnerny 'punch[ing] his bum' to illustrate Mercutio's memorable description of 'this drivelling love' as 'a great natural that runs lolling up and down to hide his bauble in a hole' and his explanation when asked to 'stop there' that he has 'come to the whole depth of [his] tale' (2.4.91–8). Adrian Schiller (2000) played the speeches sardonically, with intimations of sexual interest that were sparing but surprisingly precise: 'flesh, flesh, how art thou fishified' (38–9) was delivered as though sniffing at Romeo's crotch – in the Queen Mab speech he had knelt down as he mentioned the maids' tainted breaths, as if to suggest that the bad odour was the result of fellatio. Roger Allam (1984) has described the sequence in terms of Mercutio's desire to find out, through as much sexual innuendo as may be necessary, exactly what Romeo has been up to – a desire Allam connects, through the 'open-arse' and 'bauble in a hole' jokes, with a sexuality the character does not admit to himself. The jokes were also used 'to undercut and conceal [his] own sincerity' (Allam, 116–17).

The arrival of the Nurse provides a new incentive. As Mercutio explained that 'the bawdy hand of the dial is now upon the prick of noon' (111–12), in 1947 the three young men all gestured towards the Nurse with their swords, and this was taken up later during the song 'An old hare hoar' (132–7), when, as the promptbook indicates, they 'march[ed] round her beating the ground with their swords'. Jonathan Hyde (1980) threw his 'swizzle stick' (thus named in the promptbook) out at the Nurse mimicking an erection. Brenda Bruce seemed to find this amusing, and simply hit Mercutio on the elbow with her fan. (In 2000 Eileen McCallum, clearly enjoying a rude joke, reacted in the same way.) Michael Kitchen (1986), who had been kissing the hand of Dilys Laye's faux-genteel Nurse, placed it on his crotch, and she withdrew it angrily. He used his cane to flick washing out of the basket on the back of her tricycle, then poked at her with it as she tried to gather the scattered garments, pushing her down onto all fours and sitting astride her. As he left he kissed her on 'Farewell' then added 'ancient lady' (41). She stood fuming, and when Benvolio offered her the carnation that had been on the café table (it was used for the 'pink of courtesy' joke at 59–61) he received a slap on the cheek for his pains. Tony Britton, in 1954, lifted the Nurse's skirt with his foot and Peter laughed tactlessly. Jonathan Hyde (1980) rooted under her skirt, exclaiming 'So ho!' and answering 'No hare, sir' to Romeo's question 'What hast thou found?' (129–30) – the verses 'An old hare hoar' were transposed, and were sung as Mercutio and Benvolio left the stage. Other Mercutios have been rebuked for the 'bawdy prick' with a hit in the crotch with the Nurse's fan. David O'Hara (1989) retaliated by grabbing her buttocks as he uttered the hunting cry 'Soho!' In 1997 Mercutio grabbed the Nurse's bottom, swung her down to a sitting position and made to kiss her. Sometimes this has led to even more savage physical assault: in 1991 Benvolio lifted the nurse up off the floor and Mercutio hoisted her skirts and thrust himself between her splayed legs, taking her from Benvolio's arms and handing her on to the bemused Peter (Figure 23). Adding insult to insult, he knelt with ironic courtesy to kiss her hand on 'ancient lady'.

By 3.1 Romeo and Juliet have been married, but have not yet achieved their wedding night. Directors and actors (and lighting designers) are commonly more anxious than most other readers to know the timing of the play's episodes. In this case it appears that the Nurse set off on her errand to Romeo at nine, and even if the

FIGURE 23 Assaulting the Nurse (Sheila Reid) in 1991: Mercutio (Tim McInnerny) is aided and abetted by Benvolio (Kevin Doyle). (2.4)

bawdy hand of the dial had not in fact reached noon when she found him, she returned to Juliet just after twelve. The marriage will have taken place, according to the plan, in the afternoon. Now the day is still hot, and Mercutio is lingering – against Benvolio's better advice – in a public haunt of men, with Capulets on the prowl. Mercutio's response to his plea to 'retire' and avoid a brawl (3.1.1–4) is puzzling: he characterizes the otherwise pacific Benvolio as an obsessive quarreller, and this has rarely been anything more than a case of Mercutio enjoying the sound of his own voice. Roger Allam, for example (1984), used the lines 'as a ploy to keep him and our companions from leaving' (Allam, 117). Exceptionally, in 1991 Benvolio, played by Kevin Doyle, had been set up from the first scene as moody and violent, and in this sequence he and Mercutio fought a bout that was perilously near to being serious – as he retreated upstage and met Tybalt, Benvolio was rubbing a bruised arm. This was one of the darkest versions of the sequence. To threatening, pulsating background music Mercutio and Tybalt fought in brutal earnest, with moments of tense stillness as they prepared for each attack and ominously increasing volume as they closed with one another. Romeo tried repeatedly to stop them and was pushed back violently. The background sound ceased altogether when Tybalt's sword was thrust home. Mercutio's page (a small boy) had been standing upstage, and ran down to his master to be told to fetch a surgeon. Mercutio walked backwards upstage and fell in the centre, where the men gathered round, supporting him in a group resembling the traditional 'Deposition from the Cross'. Romeo's 'I thought all for the best' (3.1.106) drew a bitter laugh from his dying friend, who was helped from the stage, shouting his final lines: 'I have it, and soundly too. Your houses!' (110).

Peter Brook, in 1947, deployed the two dozen actors available to him as 'extras' to stage the scene as a public spectacle of considerable length and ferocity, relieved by one moment of humour. He emphasized the momentum of the combat by using the steep ramps to either side of his central acting area and choreographing the reactions of 'a sinuous line of onlookers' moving in response to its progress. In the middle of this, members of the Prince's guard arrived and the combatants and the crowd pretended 'innocence' until they departed. Then the fight resumed with its previous ferocity (Levenson, 1987, 75–6). One reviewer found this 'so long drawn out that Romeo's fatal intervention [was] not only ill-timed but incredible' (*Times*), but many reviewers seem not to have been unduly worried by such cool-tempered objections. In Ron Daniels's production (1980) the combat began in earnest, with Jonathan Hyde's Mercutio 'plainly more determined than Chris Hunter's Tybalt on a showdown' (*Times*), and the turning point came with the revelation that Tybalt's stick concealed a blade he was prepared to use. Usually Mercutio's challenge to Tybalt, after Romeo's refusal to fight, is clearly irrevocable and in deadly earnest, even if the first part of it includes comic taunting – in 1997 Chook Sibtain accompanied 'Here's my fiddlestick' (3.1.47) with flourishes with a broomstick, before daggers came out. Adrian Schiller, in 2000, watched Tybalt hit his friend's cheek with impunity and then, as Romeo disappeared offstage, walked across and coolly slapped his challenger. Benvolio made no attempt to part the fighters, and Romeo remained on the sidelines, transfixed, as the fight proceeded to the accompaniment of the production's recurrent and elegiac cello music. A more common tactic has been to start in comic mode, often continuing to the point of Mercutio's death, and sometimes allowing the audience to share his friends' unawareness that he has been mortally wounded.

There has often been a feeling that his death reveals some previously unsuspected (or unconfirmed) 'truth' about Mercutio. Edward Woodward (1958) could have done with more panache throughout the play, thought Felix Barker, but 'he died magnificently. Nothing in his life became him like the leaving of it' (*E. News*). In 1961 Ian Bannen's 'clownish bravado' throughout the duel, as he and Peter McEnery's Tybalt fought up and down the steep staircases of Sean Kenny's set (Figure 24), reminded one displeased reviewer of 'an old Douglas Fairbanks film' (*Birm. Mail*). Another was surprised that Mercutio should be so expert a swordsman that Romeo's intervention seemed pointless, and that neither Romeo nor Benvolio should go to the dying man's assistance, thus robbing the moment of the right emphasis (*Guardian*). 'His final resentment that another's quarrel had robbed him of his life' showed Bannen's true worth as an actor (*Sol. & War. News*), and Alan Brien wrote that his 'elaborate Gasconnades' of wit and insult were complemented by 'cold gusts of rage' (*S. Telegraph*). Harold Hobson had identified this Mercutio

as 'a man trying to exorcise some secret alarm by stimulating his imagination' in the earlier scenes. He suggested that 'at the end, this alarm breaks down all the protections raised around it' (*S. Times*). With a grating cry 'I'm hurt' Bannen staggered off, finally leaving the stage and the play with an indignant yell of 'Your houses!' (*S. Wales E. Arg.*). Jeremy Kingston described the effect when Norman Rodway (1967) received the wound in his groin:

> Even to someone familiar with the story the sight of Mr. Rodway staggering back from Tybalt's thrust comes as a shock. To someone seeing the play for the first time, imagining the incident to be another of Mercutio's jokes, the effect when the joke turns sour must be shattering. The audience became utterly silent. *(Punch)*

Rodway died 'in a welter of blood and curses, writhing and spitting hatred at his friends' (*S. Telegraph*). In the context of Karolos Koun's sombre and restrained production, this was all the more shocking. In 1976 Michael Pennington fixed Romeo with a 'ghastly smile' as he was helped off (Holding, 61). Chook Sibtain (1997) accepted Benvolio's help, but pushed Romeo away with 'A plague o' both your houses' (108). Similarly, in 2000, when Mercutio died he pushed away Romeo's offer of help, and was dragged off unceremoniously into the wings cursing 'Your houses!'

Michael Bogdanov, in 1986, in keeping with the dominant comic tone he had maintained in the first part of the play, began the scene like any other on the piazza, although Capulets were congregating on the opposite side of the stage. Mercutio and Benvolio were sitting at the café table, in its usual position downstage on the right. In the silence, the bored Benvolio clinked a spoon against his glass, much to Mercutio's irritation. The lines

---

FIGURE 24 (*opposite*) Tybalt (Peter McEnery) is taunted by Mercutio (Ian Bannen), who holds the wine skin from which he drank during their fight (3.1). Benvolio (James Kerry, on steps, in white shirt) and Romeo (Brian Murray, right) watch. Sean Kenny's multi-level wooden set for Peter Hall's 1961 production is painted to suggest masonry.

about Benvolio's quarrelsomeness were clearly an attempt to wind him up. At 'claps me his blade [*sic*]' (3.1.6) Mercutio laid his cane across the table – as much to establish it as a weapon as to illustrate the point he was making. Accompanied by two friends, Hugh Quarshie's leather-suited Tybalt arrived behind them in a red Alfa Romeo, crossed to the middle of the stage and stopped. 'A word with one of you' (38) was met with silence. He got out of the car by swinging his legs nonchalantly over the rear wing, paused to polish where he might have scratched it and, for all his desire to affect insolent nonchalance, was clearly angered by Mercutio's taunts ('Make it a word and a blow' – 'You shall find me apt enough to that, sir, and you will give me occasion', 40–2). After Romeo's inexplicably 'calm, dishonorable, vile submission' (72) Kitchen spelt out his insults to Tybalt with unmistakably contemptuous emphasis on the initial consonants ('Good *K*ing of *C*ats . . . ', 76) and responded to Tybalt's 'I am for you [sir]' (81) by kicking him in the crotch. Tybalt flourished the metal chain that was his weapon of choice, and when Romeo first tried to intervene it was Tybalt who pushed him away. The brutality of the fight was real but still comic – at one point Tybalt held his chain round Mercutio's throat while a mêlée of would-be helpers tried to stop him actually strangling his adversary (Figure 25). Mercutio got free, and leapt onto the bonnet of Tybalt's car – there was a moment's pause as Tybalt registered that flailing at Mercutio with the chain would only do irreparable harm to the cherished paintwork. As Mercutio slid off the front of the car he broke the radio antenna, paused for a moment, then threw down some coins on the bonnet as if to pay for it and finally brandished it as a sword, making elaborate passes with it. Tybalt chased Mercutio round the stage, up the stairs (where Mercutio gave him the slip by putting his straw hat on a bystander) and back down again. Pausing by the café table, Mercutio handed Tybalt a glass. They toasted each other, but Tybalt threw the glass's contents in his adversary's face. This was the point at which comedy ceased: long-bladed flick knives came out – Mercutio drawing his first – and

FIGURE 25 The rumble on the piazza in Michael Bogdanov's 1986 production. Tybalt (Hugh Quarshie), in leather, attacks Mercutio (Michael Kitchen) with his chain. (3.1)

Tybalt's gladiatorial demeanor became truly menacing. Romeo's next attempt to intervene was followed quickly by the fatal stabbing. Tybalt ran off, his friends driving the car after him. Mercutio staggered over to the table and held onto the back of a chair. His astonished 'I am – hurt' seemed comic (and drew a laugh from the audience) and the next lines were spoken urgently, but without any particular bitterness until he called out 'Your houses!' as he was helped off stage.

Romeo's response to his friend's death will be discussed in the next chapter, but it is worth pausing over the consequences for the play of Mercutio's early departure. In any production the death of Mercutio, leading as it does to Romeo's killing of Tybalt and its catastrophic consequences, marks a decisive shift to a more sombre mood. On a more practical level, when the actor of Romeo has seemed underpowered the loss of Mercutio's energy has been especially unfortunate. Hardly a production goes by without someone lamenting the loss in this way. One production has dealt more radically with the situation. 'Mercutio's soul / Is but a little way above our heads, /Staying for thine to keep him company', Romeo tells Tybalt as he confronts him (3.1.128–30). In 2000 Michael Boyd took the unusual step of retaining Mercutio as a figure on stage during the final movement of the play. His 'ghost', together with that of Tybalt, watched from above with silent, sardonic detachment as the lovers' fate overtook them. In the Mantua scene, when the Apothecary appeared alongside him atop the curving wall, Mercutio passed the poison across to Romeo's hand (which reached up in a gesture recalling that of the first 'balcony' scene). In some performances both the Apothecary and his understudy were ill, and the ghostly Mercutio spoke the latter's lines, transforming the mercurial wit even more decisively into a literal agent of fate.

4

STAR-CROSS'D
LOVERS

This chapter discusses interpretations of Romeo and Juliet, first in terms of general issues, then with reference to performances of the scenes in which they appear together before the crisis that precipitates their tragedy. The script tells us very little about them, beyond what they say and how they behave. Romeo appears in the context of his friends – in particular Benvolio and Mercutio – and with the Friar. Juliet is seen with her family and, like Romeo, has the Friar as her confessor. The lovers' physical appearance is described only in the most general terms. Both are young, she is 'fair', and he has good manners. He 'bears him like a portly gentleman' and according to Capulet has a reputation in Verona as a 'virtuous and well-govern'd youth' (1.5.65–7). Juliet is of course attractive but that attraction is described figuratively ('she doth teach the torches to burn bright' (1.5.43), etc.) rather than literally: when Romeo mentions her eyes and her cheek (2.2.15ff.) it is to raise her metaphorically to the heavens, rather than to particularize her physical features. We learn more of Rosaline than of Juliet, but that also is only so that she might be grist to a poetic mill – in this case Mercutio's as he enumerates her sexual attractions, from 'bright eyes' to 'quivering thigh, / And the demesnes that there adjacent lie' (2.1.17–20).

In this respect, then, the lovers are blank canvases on which a production can paint whatever it wishes, so long as their looks correspond to whatever notions are current about attractiveness –

or, in more radical interpretations, might be made to stand in opposition to them. There is, however, a more demanding criterion to be met: their demeanour has to seem appropriate to the lines they speak and the actions they take. It is worth summarizing these briefly. Romeo's behaviour before he meets Juliet is described by Benvolio and Montague (1.1.116ff.), and what we learn is qualified by his irony at his own expense when Benvolio accosts him. He is able to exchange wit with Mercutio and Benvolio, and to alternate (or combine) wit and lyrical eloquence in his encounters with Juliet. He is beside himself with anger with Tybalt after the death of Mercutio, and with grief – perhaps to the point of hysteria – in the Friar's cell. In Mantua he is by turns lyrical in anticipating reunion with Juliet, grimly resolute when he learns of her death, and sardonic (somewhat in Mercutio's vein) with the Apothecary. In the graveyard and the tomb he – like Juliet – is passionate in anger and in love. Juliet has to be demure (but not without spirit) with her mother and the Nurse, and both witty and lyrical with Romeo. Her later scenes encompass passion ('Gallop apace . . . ' (3.2.1), the taking of the potion, awakening in the tomb), resourceful equivocation in the face of strong emotions she must disguise (with her mother and the Nurse discussing Tybalt's murder and with Paris at the Friar's cell), and resolution (defying her father over marriage to Paris, threatening suicide and then accepting the potion, and facing the terrors of the tomb).

The lovers' lyrical powers of expression are not the only factor contributing to the sense of their being special and apart from the world around them. The play's poetic texture is characterized by images of darkness and light and also by an insistence on elevation – that is, the supernal, gravity-defying or spiritual – in language and in staging. As well as the 'stars' and 'heavens' invoked as sources of threatening fate or hoped-for grace, the play includes many allusions to what is figuratively or literally 'above'. Juliet's eyes are imagined as having migrated to the heavens (2.2.15–22). Images of rapid flight (thoughts/sun-beams/Venus' doves/a ball) govern Juliet's speech as she anticipates the Nurse's return with news of the rendezvous in 2.5, and similar images with a greater charge of erotic anticipation occur in 'Gallop apace ye fiery-footed steeds' (3.2.1ff.).

Romeo claims that he has been able to 'o'e'rperch' the high orchard walls on 'love's light wings' (2.2.66), and Juliet appears above him at her window. (No stage direction, actual or implicit, requires him to climb up to it, but, as we shall see, many productions have been unable to resist the temptation.) Later he is to use 'cords made like a tackled stair' to help him climb to 'the high topgallant of my joy' in Juliet's bed chamber (2.4.185–6). As Juliet arrives in his cell in 2.6 the Friar observes, with a mixture of admiration and foreboding,

> O, so light a foot
> Will ne'er wear out the everlasting flint.
> A lover may bestride the gossamers
> That idles in the wanton summer air
> And yet not fall, so light is vanity.
>
> (16–20)

Romeo's ascent into Juliet's room, anticipated in the Friar's optimistic instructions in 3.3, is counterbalanced by his descent from it at dawn in 3.5. Juliet's sudden premonition – 'Methinks I see thee, now thou art so low, / As one dead in the bottom of a tomb' (3.5.55–6) – prepares for the lovers' ultimate meeting in what seem to be the lower regions represented by the Capulet tomb.

These examples suggest how the language and action combine to endow the lovers with a sense of specialness, and specifically of elevation. Quite apart from expectations fostered by theatrical and cultural habits and circumstances – the play's reputation and status, even among those who have not seen or read it – Romeo and Juliet themselves are endowed by the script itself with a responsibility to be seen rising above their surroundings. They merit those statues of pure gold not just as a memorial for services rendered posthumously to civil peace or an atonement for injuries done to them, but as a sign of their legendary and unique status – '*never* was a story of more woe' (5.3.308; my italics). In the play's scheme of birth, marriage and death they occupy a central place. Their marriage and death are of course an essential part of the play's story, and birth is connected with them from the outset by the Chorus ('From forth the fatal loins of these two foes', Prologue 5) and used as a metaphor for their nascent love ('Prodigious birth of love it is to me . . . ', 1.5.139).

Even though they may be said to inhere in the play's text – to constitute some of the demands it makes of the players – all of these aspects of the lovers' verbal and physical behaviour are historically contingent. That is, different periods have laid differing degrees of emphasis on each of them, and the qualities themselves have been defined differently. For example, the element of humour in Romeo's speeches, the play's bawdy dialogue in general and the erotic dimension of Juliet's 'Gallop apace' were less perceived or performed in the nineteenth and early twentieth centuries than in recent decades. Just as definitions of 'portly' – that is, gracious and decorous – demeanour have differed over the years, so have the verbal techniques thought appropriate to lyrical speech. In periods when the status of the lovers as 'ideal' has been thought especially important, performers have been measured against current notions of ideal social behaviour, together with whatever other values have been associated with the play's setting in Renaissance Italy. If only in matters of costume and deportment, Romeos and Juliets used to be expected to resemble prototypes in paintings and drawings of the Renaissance itself or in more recent interpretations (such as those of artists associated with the Pre-Raphaelite Brotherhood). Since the middle of the twentieth century, directors have felt less constrained, and productions have been more likely to work against the grain of such idealism. Moreover the pictorial and performance traditions that aligned Juliet and Romeo with the idealized figures and movement of the classical ballerina and the *danseur noble* have by and large been superseded. In the popular imagination, however, remnants of these ideals persist. It is amusing to find Sean Bean, Romeo in Michael Bogdanov's 1986 production (Figure 15), telling a reporter that he is glad to be playing in modern dress: 'I can't stand running around in tights' (*Observer Col. Supp.*).

'Modern dress' is a relative term: many productions since the middle of the twentieth century, although dressed in 'period' costume, have sought to align performances with the youth culture of their own day. In this they have responded to rapid changes in definitions of what it is to be (a) young and (b) in love. The significance of the arrival of 'teenagers' on the British scene has already been considered in the Introduction (pp. 18–20). This influenced interpretations of the play in such matters as relationships between the generations and the nature of the family rivalry – particularly in the wake of *West Side Story* – but the lovers themselves were also directly affected. By the late 1950s, spectacularly enhanced by the advent of rock 'n' roll, the trials of being a teenager in love had become a dominant theme of popular music. In earlier decades, mature actors had been helped by the habit of regarding the characters' development as a graduation from the vague, low-status category of 'young persons' to that of fully fledged lovers. Far from treating adolescence as a necessary but regrettable passing phase, the teenage phenomenon was now celebrated for its ardour, rebelliousness and energy and also for its allegedly 'classless' attitudes. Colin McInnes, writing in 1958, observed that in addition to having more disposable income, a dislike of being 'told', an indifference to the Establishment and a less anxious sex life, modern teenagers were far less interested in class 'than any of the older age groups are or were' (McInnes, 1966, 57).

Some reviews of the play in the early 1950s suggest a desire to see Juliet (if not Romeo) making a miraculous transition from girlhood to maturity without any of the troublesome business of adolescence. According to Cecil Wilson in the *Daily Mail* Claire

Bloom, in the Old Vic production of 1952, 'came skipping on like a child of six rather than 14, but the moment she set eyes on Mr. Alan Badel's Romeo she became in one lingering look a woman embracing all the ecstasy and agony of a first love' (16 Aug). Kenneth Tynan, writing about the same performance, defended Bloom against accusations that she had not served the verse well and praised her refusal to play like the 'average Juliet' who 'sings the part sweetly, chants it demurely, dismissing passion with a stamp of her foot'. This time an actress had acknowledged that 'nine-tenths of Juliet . . . is not in the least demure: she is impatient and mettlesome, proud and vehement, not a blindfold child of milk' (Tynan, 32–3).

CLASS, AGE, FEELINGS AND SEXUAL CHEMISTRY

Because these are high-status roles in an iconic play performed at a prestigious theatre, the press, no doubt fed with information by the publicity department, has often found class a useful angle. In 1947 Juliet, allegedly discovered like David O. Selznick's Scarlett O'Hara after a nationwide search, was the eighteen-year-old Daphne Slater (Figure 36), 'dewy from RADA' and from a sound middle-class background, 'daughter of an official in the Food Ministry' (*S. Mercury*). In 1954 much was made of Zena Walker's being both very young and the daughter of a Birmingham grocer. Judy Buxton, Juliet in 1980 (Figure 13), had 'taken the giant step from television soap opera to the hallowed ground of the Royal Shakespeare Theatre', having appeared as 'Student Nurse Katy Shaw in A.T.V.s "General Hospital"'. It was this, rather than her more 'legit' qualifications – she had recently appeared as Iphigenia in the RSC's production of *The Greeks* – that the *Coventry Evening Telegraph* preferred to headline: 'Dolly-bird who became a Juliet!'

The reception of Michael Bogdanov's 1986 production provides particularly telling examples of these attitudes at work. The

Romeo, Sean Bean, was notable for spells of work in the steel industry and as a council gardener, and for having been chosen at the age of sixteen for the reserve team of Sheffield United. Acting and football, he told the *Observer Colour Supplement*, were very similar: 'There's a brilliant feeling, going out in front of a big crowd. You feel this massive thrill, the hairs on your spine rise.' Another interviewer reported the actor's satisfaction that Romeo was not, as he had always thought, 'wet and soppy', but had 'quite a lot of bottle' (*Times*). There is a note of wonder, as if at the transformation of a male Eliza Doolittle, in *the Bristol Evening Post*'s review: 'Sean Bean, who must be the first former council gardener to step straight into a title role at Stratford, makes his ear-ringed Romeo a noble as well as a suffering figure.' In the *Daily Telegraph* John Barber reached beyond the actor's actual CV to find a simile for the performance: 'rugged as a butcher's assistant'.

Some accounts of Michael Bogdanov's modern-dress production relate the vocal and emotional characterization of the lovers directly to the reviewer's own sometimes shaky sense of modernity. Barber's is the most notable example. Grounded in the belief that 'modern dress must violate a play as poetic as *Romeo and Juliet*', his review insists that this is 'a fiercely hyped-up production whose "Carnaby Street" dandies are constantly at odds with Shakespeare's artificial language, his religious phraseology and elaborate rhyme schemes'. This identification of youth culture, out of date by a decade, also misses the director's attempt to establish the play's world as that of modern Italy. Barber admits that the director 'does make his young sweethearts real', but when the critic identifies a quality to admire in Bean's performance he employs a 'youth' vocabulary redolent more of the 1960s than the mid-1980s: 'Sean Bean's Romeo lacks any tincture of poetry in his make-up but he speaks with a persuasive ardour and throughout suggests a tearaway totally mesmerized by his latest and last dolly bird.'

Niamh Cusack's performance, by contrast, is related to the theatrical heritage: 'Lacking a lower register her voice can become tinny, but she speaks the verse with a shining intelligence and enunciates with the precision of an Ashcroft' (*D. Telegraph*). Stanley Wells, in the *Times Literary Supplement*, offered a sympathetic and appreciative account of the actors' work on the verse, giving a clearer sense of the style: 'The speaking pace in general is steady, opening up the lines rather than assailing us with them.' Observing that the method was a 'serious attempt to root the dialogue in social reality', he felt that it helped 'to release the play's latent comedy'. Bean's Romeo, although 'inept in gesture', played the big emotional moments 'with honest directness if not with technical expertise'. Michael Ratcliffe in the *Observer*, one of the few reviewers to mention the actor's accent, thought the lovers 'young and fair' and found Romeo 'very green . . . with a Yorkshireman's natural gift of elision between syllables: the voice is tender and expressive when intimate, the revenge for Mercutio's death crazy with unpredictable violence, strength and rage'. For Nicholas Shrimpton, who considered Cusack's performance an 'honest, professional job', Bean's Romeo was 'unnoticeably average', so that the 'erotic tension [was] as slight as the sense of tragedy' (*TES*). The *Guardian* reported that Cusack's voice, like Bean's, 'lacked texture and colour' and that she was 'likable but raw'.

Reviewers have often concentrated on the two protagonists in this way, and similar comments could be instanced from reviews of many of the fifteen productions at Stratford since 1947. However, Bogdanov's production is a particularly interesting test case because of the assault it claimed to be making on 'traditional' values both in Shakespearean production and in the wider world. Class was definitely an issue, but the lovers were treated as uniquely virtuous beings in a crass, money-grubbing society. As Stanley Wells pointed out, 'simply costumed, [they] stand outside the production's time scheme'. One notable instance of this was the moment when Juliet, waiting to be left alone in her bedroom with the sleeping draught and the dagger, took up a flute and played a few bars of Debussy: in a production which accompanied a good deal of the action and much of the speech with a 'soft rock' backing, this was a moment of surprising calm and serenity. Even if (in Benedict Nightingale's words) Cusack was not 'distraught or stricken enough at crises' she managed 'to be sweet without cuteness, warm without mawkishness' (*New States.*).

It has long been a common complaint that actors in one or both of the roles have been convincingly youthful, but have lacked the technique or mature insight to give voice to the lyrical and emotionally charged passages. Franco Zeffirelli's Old Vic production of 1960, with John Stride and Judi Dench, is usually singled out (as it was at the time) as the most influential revaluation of the lovers in such terms, but a study of reviews from productions from the late 1940s onwards yields a number of indications of the change already taking place. The eighteen-year-old Daphne Slater, in 1947, was too immature for Ivor Brown's taste: 'her untutored prattling and sobbing of Verona's passion will not do' (*Observer*). In 1954 John Barber, having summed up and dismissed Zena Walker (Figure 26) as 'a plump cutie-pie of 20' and 'a Birmingham fruiterer's daughter', insisted sadly that 'Tragic despair cannot sit on a face with baby dimples' (*D. Express*). Alan Dent in the *News Chronicle* called her 'a dear and roguish little dumpling', prematurely chosen to represent 'an Italian girl ablaze with her first passion and not just a little candle alight on a child's birthday cake'. The anonymous correspondent of the *Times* was sterner: 'the effect of playing which is essentially realistic within a romantic convention is to suburbanize the tragedy'. In the *New Statesman and Nation* T.C. Worsley, who thought the company had achieved the level of 'good provincial repertory', admitted that Walker improved as the play went on but insisted that 'a hot fourteen in Renaissance Italy is not the same thing as the puppy fat and simper of English girlhood'. The complex of social and theatrical attitudes is apparent in these reviews, and Dent's reflects the then current male knowingness about female coming of age in Verona. More sympathetic critics thought Walker successful in the early 'childish' scenes but wanting in the more passionate speeches. Cecil Wilson, in the *Daily Mail*, found the actress

FIGURE 26 Zena Walker and Laurence Harvey as the lovers in Glen Byam Shaw's 1954 production (1.5). Harvey's hair and make-up (and even the modified Renaissance cut of his jacket) maintain his modern 'film star' persona.

'forthright and fiery' but complained that she kept 'Shakespeare's sweetest love story firmly on ground level'. For the *Daily Worker* this was a bonus: 'She is no pale and wilting lover, pining for her Romeo and wallowing in self-pity, but a strong, confident girl, consumed by love, willing to fight to keep it, and, when the feud grips them beyond escape, willing to die for it' (30 Apr).

Several other reviews share this appreciation of Walker's directness. She was 'not afraid to mar her face with tears, to allow emotion rather than Hollywood notions of elegance to dictate her movements' (*SA Herald*). The 'Hollywood' element of the production was provided by the presence of the rising young film star Laurence Harvey (born 1928), who seems to have played 'the Romeo of tradition' (*Leam. Spa Cour.*). Harvey's voice had the 'virile splendour and gravity' required by the role, according to the *Evening News*, but he was thought by some to be too self-conscious, by others to be taking 'a brave if rather stereotyped Shakespearean stand against the general conversational treatment' (*FT*). Eve Chapman, one of the few women reviewing theatre for the national press, contrasted the 'heart-warming charm and spirited acting' of Walker with 'the self-assured Laurence Harvey', who 'far from exhibiting the tremulous tenderness of a love-struck youth performed with the streamlined rakishness of a businessman courting his secretary' (*D. Mirror*).

In both 1958 and 1961 Juliet was played by Dorothy Tutin, first with Richard Johnson in Byam Shaw's graceful, Motley-designed production and then with Brian Murray in Peter Hall's version with its vertiginous wooden set by Sean Kenny. Born in 1930, Tutin was now the 'average' age for performers of the role, and reviews focused in 1958 on her skilful – perhaps too artful – representation of youth. 'A Juliet of utter sincerity and yet of childish passion', according to Philip Hope-Wallace, she managed 'a lovely and impetuous simplicity' in her first scene (*Man. Guardian*). Under the headline 'Tutin's Juliet Echoes Great Ashcroft' Alan Dent wrote ecstatically of 'lovely Juliet, swift as a wagtail, nimble as a trout' (*News Chron.*). The *Times*, like several other reviews, complained of hurried speech: 'her breathless eagerness hardly gives her time to speak what in the part must be conveyed by speaking rather than by acting'. In 1961 Milton Shulman found Tutin 'just a shade too knowing and mature to be wholeheartedly ready to die for love' (*E. Standard*), and reviews in the *Manchester Guardian* and the *Birmingham Post* reflected on the evident sophistication of technique. In the former, Philip Hope-Wallace complained that 'the larger parabolas of poetry' were 'jerkily phrased' in a manner intended to convey 'the breathlessness of thought newly formed and instantly blurted out' but resulting only in a sense of 'plausible simplicity' where she might have gathered 'a growing emotional response from the listener'. In a similarly thoughtful analysis J.C. Trewin admitted that, despite a persistent trick 'of spurting the lines in quick little fountain-rushes' she was able to 'reach and sustain the rapture of the more demanding scenes'. However, three seasons on he still did not find Tutin 'a touching Juliet'.

Richard Johnson, who played Romeo in 1958, was twenty-eight, and in 1961 Brian Murray, catapulted from Benvolio into the leading role at six days' notice, was twenty-four. Johnson lacked 'nobility' according to the *Stage*, and Harold Hobson in the *Sunday Times* found him 'heavy'. The *Times* noted that Johnson seemed more at home among the men, creating 'a more vivid impression by his wild attempts to stop the fight between Mercutio and Tybalt and by his spiritual collapse in Friar Laurence's cell than by any of the scenes with Juliet'. A great deal was said about the length of his hair – the pre-production photos used by some papers indeed show a black mane reaching down to his shoulders, but even the collar-length cut evident in other photographs was thought dangerously epicene in the late 1950s (Figures 27, 19 and 2). In 1961 reviewers concentrated – not always kindly – on Murray's alleged inadequacy, and his 'gauche, straightforward reading' (*E. Standard*), but Zeffirelli's Old Vic production, still in the company's repertoire when Hall's opened, had already set a standard for youthfulness in casting. As for the new Romeo's hair, it struck a more modern but – in some quarters – no welcomer note than Richard Johnson's. The *Stratford-upon-Avon Herald* described 'the looks of a pop singer and the infuriating curls of a modern coffee-bar hero'.

Since 1967 (Ian Holm and Estelle Kohler, Figure 7) actors playing Romeo and Juliet have tended to be cast for their ability to represent modern teenagers, rather than as representatives of ideal grace, beauty and rhetorical accomplishment. As a study of the

FIGURE 27 Peter (Ian Holm) and the Nurse (Angela Baddeley) encounter Mercutio (Edward Woodward), Romeo (Richard Johnson) and Benvolio (Paul Hardwick) in the 'town square' variant of Motley's 1958 set (2.4). A miniature cityscape is set between backdrop and the balustrades to left and right. A pavilion to the same scale, resembling city buildings seen in the background of Italian Renaissance paintings (the work of Pietro Perugino was cited as an influence), is placed behind the platform and steps at the centre. The men wear tights and codpieces, jerkins over white shirts, and ankle boots, and their hair is long by 1950s' standards. Johnson's seems to be collar-length, though earlier publicity photographs show it at shoulder length. Some reviewers still thought it overgrown.

lovers' scenes together will show, these qualities have not always been lacking, but the gradual backward march of the age of puberty and the spread of teenage popular culture over an ever-longer span of years have forced an acknowledgement that performing adolescence is a priority. At the same time, the general acceptance of a wider range of sexual activity among teenagers has altered audience expectations of how the lovers behave. Performances of their parting in 3.5 reflect this most directly, but it is also evident in many versions of the 'balcony' scene. However, even if 'modern dress' is used, the society represented in productions still has to make a degree of repression credible. Among those agreed by several reviewers to be less than convincing as adolescents have been Ian McKellen and Francesca Annis (1976), Michael Maloney and Claire Holman (1991) and David Tennant and Alexandra Gilbreath (2000). Reviewing the performances of Maloney and Holman, Peter Holland insisted: 'It is surely no longer pedantic to complain that these actors were just too old. Neither looks nor can act convincingly adolescent and their childish passion becomes a rather mature affair' (Holland, 1993, 117–18). Alexandra Gilbreath was 'breathy, knowing, . . . more plausibly 40 than 14' and 'never anything but the mistress of her emotions', wrote Georgina Brown (*Mail Sun.*). Benedict Nightingale's notice in the *Times* summed up the contradictions of a Juliet who could be perceived as too impetuous and at the same time too mature (if not necessarily too old): 'She may bang her head or her fists on a wall in frustration, but the very way she walks suggests she's likelier to organize an elopement with Romeo to Mantua than stay at home with those high-dose sleeping pills.' The more determined and self-possessed Juliet is, the more likely she is to raise such commonsense considerations. Matched with a self-confident, exuberant Romeo (Anton Lesser), Judy Buxton in 1980 made Michael Billington wonder why she didn't disguise herself as a page and follow her lover to Mantua. For his part, this Romeo might simply have 'carried her off exultantly into the night' (*Guardian*). Robert Cushman found Lesser 'a clever, self-conscious, rather shallow youth with a violent sense of fun' (*Observer*), and James Fenton suggested that he had stepped straight out of the discotheque, 'his feet still tapping. He is a quicksilver Romeo with a generally passionate disposition, who happens to bump into the lovely Judy Buxton, and of necessity falls in love' (*S. Times*).

Buxton was 'initially sweet and subsequently passionate' (*Coventry E. Tel.*), and in 1997 Zoë Waites, anticipating her night with her husband, lay back on her bed as she contemplated the experience (3.2.26–8). Such unequivocal expressions of sexual longing on the part of Juliet seem not to have been noticed – and probably were not performed – before the later 1960s. In 1947 Daphne Slater even wore a high-necked and forbiddingly enveloping nightdress. The play's young men and servants might revel in bawdy talk, but for a well-born girl to admit desire too graphically was still a surprise. In 1967 Estelle Kohler's performance was hailed as 'urgent yet modest, piteous but never sentimental' (*Punch*) and 'a girl intensely aware of her desire' (*E. Standard*). Reviews of her performance in 1973, opposite an unimpressive Timothy Dalton, suggest that Pandora's box had been opened. Some of the male gazers were fascinated and appalled by a Juliet who seemed to have been reading Kate Millet and Germaine Greer. She was 'flauntingly interested in sex before meeting Romeo' (*New States.*) and gave the fourteen-year-old 'all the open-limbed gawkiness of her girlhood but [made] her always capable of all the functions of a full-grown woman' (*S. Mercury*). Kohler was discovered beating a carpet as she waited for the Nurse's return in 2.5, and she delivered 'Gallop apace' in front of a line with two sheets (the wedding sheets, it seems), which she clutched to her bosom in ecstasy at the prospect of possession. Harold Hobson, who had found her 'brimming with sex appeal' in 1967, was now moved almost to incoherence: 'Miss Kohler's Juliet is deliberately lubricious; her mouth is an invitation to unnamable things, and at the Capulet's ball her relations with Tybalt really do not bear examination' (*S. Times*). More than one reviewer commented on the self-assertiveness of this Juliet. Michael Billington applauded 'the girl's tart-tongued asperity, self-sufficiency and native shrewd-ness' (*Guardian*). Milton Shulman shuddered at the combination of 'man-hunting voraciousness' and, in the later scenes, 'visions of a tiresome shrew that she might have become in middle age had death not saved her' (*E. Standard*).

How much can a Romeo cry without forfeiting his manliness? In 1986 the *Guardian* praised Sean Bean for achieving 'a nice balance between sensitiveness and virility'. The last phrase points to one of the great tasks facing a Romeo in the modern theatre, and one not unrelated to Bean's reported anxiety about playing a 'soppy' character who runs around in tights. In the development of the play's action, Romeo moves to his greatest act of conventional, old-fashioned 'virility' (acting his gender) when he kills Tybalt, but on his next appearance he is in the Friar's cell giving way to 'womanish' transports of grief. This scene (3.3) can perhaps best be understood apart from post-Freudian (and indeed, post-Romantic) notions of psychological realism. As interpreted by the Friar it shows Romeo at his lowest point, 'an ill-beseeming beast' (3.3.112) in seeming both woman in tears and man in shape, and it corresponds to the play's larger scheme of dichotomies (such as 'grace and rude will', 2.3.24). In this it resembles Juliet's protracted scene with the Nurse (3.2, from 32 to the end) just before it, in which she has had to negotiate the difficult emotional territory of grief both for Tybalt's death and for Romeo's banishment. Unfortunately for our impression of Romeo, Juliet reaches a point of resolution and mature self-possession just before he appears as a hysterically 'fearful man' (3.3.1). Moreover, whatever their significance in the 1590s, any symbolic interpretation of Romeo's 'womanish' tears will have very little weight with a modern audience: virility might seem to have gone by the board. The Friar's reference to them (109) has usually been cut. 'Virility' is itself a cultural construct, reflected in and constituted by successive productions of this play as well as by other fictional or factual representations: the sight and sound of a man shedding tears, even in the licensed realm of an old poetic drama, would 'read' differently in 1954 and 2000. Many productions have dealt successfully with the more stylized lamentations around Juliet's supposed deathbed, but Romeo's behaviour in the Friar's cell has remained problematic.

Some actors have integrated these passages even more successfully with Romeo's other moods, usually by a darker emphasis on the character's state of mind in 1.1. Ian Holm, in Karolos Koun's doom-laden 1967 production, exhibited a 'frustrated madness of speech and gesture', which developed into a 'poignant determination to accept his destiny' (*Guardian*). Ian McKellen (1976) began in a Hamlet-like inky cloak, and graduated from melodramatic distraction on Rosaline's account to extravagantly high-spirited antics on Juliet's. Mark Rylance, in Terry Hands's 1989 production at the Swan, began the play 'so deeply sunk in adolescent melancholy and romantic ardour that he, in turn, enforce[d] his viewpoint on the spectator', wrote Irving Wardle. Consequently, his 'key speech' became his line to the Friar, 'Thou canst not speak of that thou dost not feel' (3.3.64), which was delivered 'not with the usual hysterics but as a sober statement of fact'. Everything else in the performance, 'from his gentle submission to Tybalt . . . to the access of murderous wrath as he [broke] into the tomb', went to confirm this (*Times*). Jack Tinker, in the *Daily Mail*, hailed Rylance as 'one of the age's great new romantics, neither sissy nor simpering, but an actor who adds delicate grace notes to his tormented passion'. To Charles Osborne, he seemed 'adept at portraying romantic hysteria' but also 'able to convey gentleness without seeming weak' (*D. Telegraph*). Michael Billington wrote: 'Even his passion for Juliet has a doomed quality: at one poignant moment they simply stare at each other in wordless rapture and Friar Laurence virtually has to prise them apart with a crowbar to get them to the altar.' Rylance delivered the references to fate 'with the quiet certainty of someone aware that happiness is a frail and perilous affair' (*Guardian*). The actor had been announced to play Hamlet later in the season, and a number of reviews referred to his Romeo as a foretaste.

The magic did not work for everyone, though. Michael Ratcliffe found him 'introspective, bookish, self-pitying and somewhat inclined to end up on one whimpering, over-used note in the voice' (*Observer*), and John Peter saw and heard only 'a surly, scruffy boy' who spoke 'clearly but without distinction and [with] only the crudest feeling' (*S. Times*). The *Independent*, missing any indication of Romeo's development, found only a consistent melancholy throughout, even after his meeting with Juliet. In his first scene there was no sense of his 'ridiculousness': 'Rylance twists his scarf and rests his tired head against the pillars, but his eyes suggest genuine introspection and sensitivity.' Jim Hiley, in the *Listener*, noticed how this melancholy ('mesmerized by catastrophe') worked its way through the play. Rylance contrived 'a breathtaking tension' on 'If I profane with my unworthiest hand' (1.5.92), and Juliet's arrival for the marriage was 'greeted by a tiny flicker of what could be horror, before desire overwhelm[ed] them both'.

For Rylance, in Hands's relatively unadorned, 'period' staging, this tactic of emphasizing the character's introspection seems to have paid dividends, but at the risk of allowing Romeo (and Georgia Slowe's Juliet) to be conscious of participating in a tragedy. Two seasons later, in David Leveaux's production, Michael Maloney attempted a similarly dark performance with a similar tactic of self-conscious foreboding. Michael Billington wrote that he 'even approach[ed] Juliet's balcony with lugubrious, fate-filled tread'. He was effective in moments of rage, 'But of the reckless joy of love there [was] scarcely a hint' (*Guardian*). For Charles Spencer this was at first a 'lively, intelligent' Romeo, but his suicidal despair seemed 'embarrassingly overwrought, a self-conscious display of an actor tearing a passion to tatters' (*D. Telegraph*). Peter Holland, commenting that Leveaux's production 'was the least passionate imaginable', observed that Maloney was 'hideously theatrical' and Claire Holman as Juliet 'dully mundane' (Holland, 1993, 117). The reports of the first-night reviewers appeared alongside accounts of two much more successful Stratford productions, *The Alchemist* at the Swan and *The Blue Angel*, directed by Trevor Nunn at The Other Place. The latter, a highly charged and intimate exploration of mature sexual attraction and infatuation, was an unfortunate stablemate for the 'series of glittering tableaux' (*Independent*) (the *Guardian* review was headlined 'watching the scenery') with the pair of passionless lovers that Leveaux had made from Shakespeare's love tragedy.

The Juliets in Terry Hands's 1989 and David Leveaux's 1991 productions, respectively Georgia Slowe and Claire Holman, received 'mixed' notices. The unfavourable reviews reiterate terms used consistently over the half-century to reproach English Juliets: to *Time Out* Slowe was a 'pony club Juliet', while Paul Taylor thought that Holman 'delivere[d] Juliet's poetry as though she were a solid all-rounder having a go at the school verse-speaking competition . . . a prosaic girl who's just putting it all on' (*Independent*). Michael Billington, who had appreciated Rylance's 'doomed intensity', found a corresponding seriousness in Slowe, 'a slight, youthful raven-haired girl given to violent emotional extremes', who 'as the play progresse[d] . . . seem[ed] half in love with easeful death' (*Guardian*). In a considered and sympathetic assessment of Holman's 1991 performance, he observed that she seemed 'more turned on by death than sin', and was 'actually very good' in the 'potion' speech (4.3.14ff.). 'What she lacks is lyrical ecstasy, so that in the balcony scene she seems to be giving a rather tasteful poetry recital instead of expressing unchecked feeling.' These were radically different productions; Hands's being simply staged and swiftly played in the Swan and Leveaux's elaborately tenebrous and tediously slow in the main house. A clue to the relative success of the 1989 lovers may be found in an aspect of Hands's 'sober' production also noted by Billington, implicitly comparing it with Bogdanov's 'victims of society' reading in 1986: 'The current fashion is to play the young lovers as the victims of a money-mad, materialist society: here they seem to be governed by a voluptuous obsession with death.' Quite apart from the question as to their appropriateness as casting, Maloney and Holman were unlikely to overcome their oppressive environment. The lovers in 1991 were beset not only by the materialism of Veronese society, or the machinations of fate, but by the production design and lighting.

Among the demands the play now makes on its eponymous lovers, we should include the collaborative ability to create the impression of 'sexual chemistry'. In 1973 Estelle Kohler had to provide the steam heat for both herself and Timothy Dalton, but Anton Lesser and Judy Buxton (1980) and Sean Bean and Niamh Cusack (1986) appear to have achieved a sense of emotional and sexual rapport, and Cusack's own account indicates the importance she attached to it in their work on the play: it was a major element in the casting process (Cusack, 121–2). Although some reviewers considered them insufficiently altered by the experience of meeting each other, Rylance and Slowe (1989) seem to have convinced most reviewers that they were kindred spirits. In 1991, Maloney and Holman failed. In Peter Holland's words, 'In 3.5, after making love, the two . . . seemed only to have had a cup of tea together' (Holland, 1993, 117). Charles Spencer, in the *Daily Telegraph*, thought they might have been playing Monopoly all night, and other critics vied with each other to find sufficiently tame pursuits to describe the same impression. The age – or apparent age – factor seems to have been decisive: in Holland's words, 'their childish passion became a rather mature affair' (Holland, 1993, 118). Ray Fearon and Zoë Waites (1997) impressed by the energy and ardour of their loving, 'a handsome and genuinely convincing couple, succumbing to the heat of their passion' (*Independent*), with Fearon 'punchily charismatic' and Waites 'urgently youthful' (*Indep. Sun.*). They carried conviction as 'young people with huge passions which they can barely understand, let alone control' (*S. Times*).

Although modern audiences quite reasonably require 'sexual chemistry' between the actors of the title roles, this is not an absolute requirement inherent in the text. The lovers' passion is eloquently present in their own words and in what others say about them, but we have no evidence that audiences in the 1590s expected to see the 'sexual spark' that Charles Spencer missed in Leveaux's production. They may of course have expected to hear it in the lines, and see it expressed in codes of physical behaviour more restrained than those of four centuries later. However the performances by two men achieved conviction in Shakespeare's own theatre, the script they once used now has to be accommodated with an audience's expectations for quite different representations of differently understood passions. At the same time it has to be acknowledged that between the 1950s and the 1990s public and private behaviour (and performances representing it) may have altered, but a sense of sexual attraction and desire, however manifested, was as much a requirement before as after the watershed of the 1960s. Sexual intercourse did not begin (in the words of Philip Larkin's poem '*Annus Mirabilis*') 'between the end of the *Chatterley* ban / And the Beatles' first LP', even if franker intimations of it did become more common then (Larkin, 34).

Romeo's unrequited love for Rosaline, and the attempts of his friends to jolt (or jest) him out of it, is established at various points in the play's first scenes. Mercutio, who does not appear and is not even mentioned until the maskers are on their way to the feast, is the most important and significant of these companions, but Benvolio's importance must not be underestimated. It is a role that rarely gets noticed in reviews, but which (as a kind of Horatio to Romeo's Hamlet) is of great benefit to the principal actor. It is through his conversation with Benvolio in the first scene that we first get a sense of Romeo's intelligence and wit, even when he is suffering from absurd and unrequited love for Rosaline. The scene also establishes, as Jill L. Levenson points out, the 'distinctive language of the young male peer group that will include Mercutio' (Levenson, 2000, 18). Although they are members of the same family, Romeo and Benvolio only appear together in public places, and there are no scenes in the Montague house. Juliet, by contrast, first appears in the bosom of her family with her mother and her nurse, engaged in a conversation about her childhood which is turned to preparation for the prospect of marriage to Paris, a good match socially ('the county Paris', 3.5.114) and personally ('stuff'd', Capulet later observes, 'with honourable parts', 181). Quite apart from its bearing on the Capulet household's standing and aspirations, this is the scene in which Juliets are shown at their youngest. Dorothy Tutin, in 1958, was 'enchantingly childlike' in her 'glee . . . on hearing that the ball is about to begin' (*S. Times*). The location has sometimes been characterized as a teenage girl's room. In 1980 Judy Buxton was sitting at the mirror of a large dressing table when the Nurse ushered in her mother, and in 1995 Lucy Whybrow's dressing table was provided with toys. It is her demeanour, her relationship with the Nurse, and the physical rapport between the two of them, rather than any set dressing, that establish the youthfulness of Juliet in this scene. Apart from its comedy, the Nurse's relentless reminiscence sets up an image of the childhood from which Juliet will presently be liberated, if she has not left it already. In 1967 *Plays and Players* noted a distinct shift in conventions: 'Instead of a portrait equally compounded of sweetness and light, we have here quite a tough and at times almost abrasive teenager.' Estelle Kohler was 'a very different girl from the dark, dewy-eyed young thing the youthful Claire Bloom twice offered'. Peter Holding comments that in 1973 Kohler's 'I'll look to like, if looking liking move' (1.3.97) seemed 'more like a cautious equivocation than the conventional response of a dutiful Elizabethan daughter' (Holding, 53).

MEETING: CAPULET'S FEAST

Capulet's 'old accustom'd feast' in 1.5 has ranged in scale and status from densely populated Renaissance magnificence (1947, 1954, 1958 and 1961) to a bourgeois family birthday party, with children, a band and a cake (1995), and even a town-square festival with wine in unlabelled bottles and candles in glass jars (1997). As the guests move into the hall for dancing, the focus shifts from the servants' work (clearing dinner, making sure of their own entertainment) to the arrival of the maskers and the dancing that will bring Romeo and Juliet together. The scene has to be staged so that the audience sees clearly the moment when Romeo sees Juliet (and, frequently, that when she sees him), and three encounters have to be convincingly set aside from the continuing festivities: Capulet's nostalgic reminiscences with his cousin, Tybalt's anger over a Montague's presence, and the lovers' first conversation.

The formal patterns of Renaissance social dancing allow for Romeo to watch Juliet as she leads off the first 'measure' of the evening either with her father or with Paris – 'yonder knight' whose hand she enriches when Romeo asks a servant who she is (1.5.40–1.) Dorothy Tutin, in 1961, was 'glimps[ed] . . . as Romeo sees her for the first time, dancing in the lamplight under an arch' (*Times*). Then she held a torch high in the air and led a double column of masked cavaliers down towards the promontory on Sean Kenny's vertiginous set where Romeo had found a vantage point. Some directors have preferred to 'freeze' and silence the party-goers and dancers for the duration of the lovers' meeting: Karolos Koun, in 1967, was able to do so as part of a general strategy of stylization that expressed his emphasis on the formal tragic nature of the play. Others have preferred to invent some realistic pretext for leaving the pair alone, and have often shunted the party upstage. Michael Bogdanov (1986) sent his guests up to a barbecue and a bar, at which on one occasion (the daily production reports show) he himself served as a waiter, and Adrian Noble (1995) offered a firework display to be watched through the gates at the back. Peter Hall (1961) immobilized the guests in groups in the depths of the upstage area under and around Sean Kenny's central structure while the lovers spoke. David Leveaux (1991) had a screen across the middle of the stage with a colonnade-like row of doors through which the dinner table was seen being cleared as the scene opened, and behind which the dancers later retreated to leave Romeo and Juliet on the forestage. Terry Hands in 1989 used the full, bare depth of the Swan stage to combine stylization and naturalism. Capulet and his cousin talked on a bench in the centre of the stage while the dancers slowly circled round them; then the dancers moved upstage for subdued conversation. They fell silent and turned to look as Capulet slapped Tybalt's face, but resumed in response to the host's 'cheerly, my hearts!' (1.5.87). For the lovers' exchange, however, the upstage action 'froze'. The other dancers were bathed in a warm amber light, while a white spotlight isolated the couple downstage. In a subtle touch, Hands allowed Juliet to observe Tybalt's anger (expressed in direct address to the audience) and go to follow him off. But Romeo grasped her hand to detain her, and the situation juxtaposed the birth of their love and the figure that would provide its nemesis. This also provided, as few other directors have managed to, a moment to help explain Juliet's subsequent grief over Tybalt's death: Hands's earlier production and Michael Boyd's in 2000 both had Juliet dance at one point with Tybalt.

Another strategy is to empty the stage by leading the guests off in a dance. Peter Brook in 1947 had the maskers enter and kneel to do obeisance to the ladies, then each took a partner to dance with. They continued dancing 'wildly' through Capulet's conversation with his cousin (30–40) and then Brook simply cleared the stage of all activity for the lovers' meeting. In 1997 the party began with a waltz, after which Juliet danced a steamy tango with Paris. This sensual party piece was followed by a change in the music to samba rhythm for a conga line led off by the Nurse. It formed up downstage on the audience's right and then went up and round the Swan's platform stage counter-clockwise before leaving the stage altogether. Juliet detached herself and continued on round the stage alone and thoughtfully until she came face to face with Romeo (Figure 28). In 2000, as on some other occasions, the whole character of the earlier dancing suggested a combination of party-time and fertility rite: in Boyd's version it was initiated by the maskers (see p. 104) and continued with a slow, lavolta-like measure in which the women were lifted up by the pelvis and slid down their partner's body with a leg crooked around him. On this occasion, Juliet's partner was Paris. (A similar direct expression of sexual dominance and acceptance was incorporated in Sue Lefton's choreography for the 1991 production.) In 1980 the feast had been 'a real rout complete with garlanded dancers, throbbing South American music and a sacrificial lamb with a rose stuck in its mouth' (*Guardian*). (It resembled a Mexican *piñada*, and the revellers were garlanded in what seemed like a medley of folkloric

FIGURE 28 The lovers (Ray Fearon and Zoë Waites) meet in Michael Attenborough's 1997 Swan production. The sole festive element in Romeo's party attire is his embroidered waistcoat. (1.5)

references.) As the dancers continued upstage behind them, Anton Lesser and Judy Buxton were left side by side, downstage centre, their garlands suddenly making them look like a bride and groom.

The lovers now meet, speak a sonnet together, and kiss twice. The speeches begin formally and together the lovers develop a metaphor. Romeo contrives to move deftly past the first hurdle – her insistence that 'palm to palm' is how pilgrims kiss – to touch her lips with his (106), and the final five-stress line is shared between them across a kiss:

> Give me my sin again.
>   You kiss by th'book.
>   (109)

How frank and sensual is Juliet's response? As one might expect, productions of the 1940s and 1950s favoured chaste salutes above passionate responsiveness. Daphne Slater and Laurence Payne (1947) achieved 'a moment of wide-eyed rapt ecstasy in their first meeting' (*Birm. Post*, 7 Oct). Some found Dorothy Tutin's 1961 performance in this sequence too artful, and therefore mature, for the performance of youthfulness she had managed in the scene with her Nurse and her mother. Kenneth Tynan thought her 'an intense little elf, far too joyless in the early scenes and vocally too limited for the later arias' (*Observer*), and Bamber Gascoigne, in the *Spectator*, admitted that she had great charm but lacked 'the sweet enchantment of love at first sight'. This impression might be turned in the opposite direction, though: the *Daily Telegraph* reviewer was apparently pleased that 'even as early as the ball scene she [gave] hints of a maturity of spirit as yet unrealised'. Tutin's Romeo, Brian Murray, seems to have responded to his first sight of Juliet with 'nervous laughs', which suggests a welcome acknowledgement that the youth might be thrown off balance by the experience as well as being more conventionally enraptured (*E. News*). Roger Warren found Anton Lesser's Romeo (1980) too mannered and comedic in this as in other passages, noting that 'Sin from my lips? O trespass sweetly urg'd' (108) won a laugh (Warren, 1981, 151). Sometimes the rapture has seemed best when expressed simply: Amanda Root and Simon Templeman (1984) came to the end of the 'grave decorous dance' and removed their masks to gaze at each other 'in delighted awe' (*Guardian*). In Boyd's production (2000) Romeo had kept his distance from the revelry until he noticed Juliet. The couple stood gazing at one another as the chain dance left the stage, and she followed it while he spoke 'O, she doth teach the torches to burn bright' (43) and asked her name. When the dancers returned it was Juliet who grabbed Romeo's hand and forced him to join in.

In Ron Daniels's 1980 version, after the 'near orgiastic event' of a dance 'half-way between disco and mardi gras' (*E. News*), Anton Lesser reacted to his first kiss from Judy Buxton 'as if [he'd] had a whiff of pot' (*SA Herald*). Niamh Cusack (1986) has described the encounter in terms of Juliet's greater thoughtfulness:

> Though they talk the same language they are not saying quite the same things: she's obviously taking her part in the flirtation, but she manages ostensibly to talk about lips being used for prayer. She tries to be careful, while all he can do is think, 'Give us a kiss.'
>
> (Cusack, 126)

Roger Warren thought that the shared sonnet 'became the shy, tentative statement of two people coming together in defiance of their environment' (Warren, 1987, 85). In 1991 Michael Maloney and Claire Holman rubbed each other's hands as they spoke the first lines, then moved closer to clasp hands on 'lest faith turn to despair' and he came slowly towards her, moving into an embrace on 'though grant for prayer's sake' (103–4). She put her arms round him, and a lingering embrace was followed by 'You kiss by th'book' – here spoken with a degree of recognition as well as surprise. One of the most convincingly mutual versions of the sequence was that of Zoë Waites and Ray Fearon (1997): he took her left hand with his right just as Tybalt spoke his ominous exit line, the couple's fingers touched on Romeo's offer to 'smooth that rough touch with a tender kiss' (95). They took hands on 'Good pilgrim' (96), Romeo kissed Juliet on 'Give me my sin again' and – most important – she kissed him back on 'You kiss by th'book.' Without the Nurse's interruption, it seemed as though they might have gone a lot further (Figure 28). Alexandra Gilbreath (2000) was even more active, reaching up to Romeo's other hand after the initial contact of one palm to palm then moving closer and, putting her arm round him when he kissed her for a second time and holding the moment for several seconds. Charles Spencer noted that 'she seem[ed] to glow from within when she first encounter[ed] Romeo' (*D. Telegraph*). This production was one of the few to follow the scene with the second Chorus, gratingly chanted and played by a sardonic choir of servants and musicians from above the wall on the audience's right. 'Passion lends them power' (13) was accompanied with a mime of intercourse on the part of Gregory and Sampson, subsiding into mock post-coital gasps as Romeo appeared.

AT JULIET'S WINDOW

Any reading of the lovers' meeting has to take on board their acknowledgement of the moment's seriousness: as Niamh Cusack observes, 'Left alone afterwards [Juliet] passionately vows that she would die rather than have anyone else' (Cusack, 126). Romeo, for his part, is already moving away from both the idealized posturing represented by his suit to Rosaline and the bawdy enjoyed by the friends who try to find him after they have left the feast (2.1). Neither Romeo nor Juliet knows that their encounter at the feast is going to move so precipitately towards marriage in the course of the 194 lines of the scene (2.2). Despite the scene's customary name – and a well-established theatrical and pictorial tradition – the lines nowhere refer to a 'balcony', and the action does not necessarily require one: but simply appearing at a window allows Juliet little scope for movement, and many Romeos have preferred the opportunity of giving physical (if not always very athletic) expression to their ardour by climbing up the architecture.

Designs for the main house at Stratford have usually allowed for the need to bring the scene as close as possible to the audience, while making it visible to the furthest reaches of the auditorium. For Peter Brook's 1947 staging Rolf Gérard provided an architectural unit evocative of Italian Renaissance painting, combining bedroom and balcony exterior and interior (Figure 29), and in 1954 the first of the very different stagings designed by Motley for Glen

FIGURE 29 Rolf Gérard's set for the Capulet household in 1947. Juliet's bedroom is on the left of the upper level, with the balcony at the extreme right. The shallow forestage, false proscenium and lateral 'assembly areas' of the 1932 theatre are evident in this photograph.

Byam Shaw's two productions offered a sweep of balustraded upper level on an austere permanent set with opposing 'houses' at each end and a downstairs niche for Juliet's bed resembling the accommodation in a railway sleeping car. In 1958, having returned to the more painterly Italianate style of their 1935 London production, they created an elegant structure of loggias and arcades from which the central segment was removed to afford a view of the silver-tipped orchard trees (see Mullin, 141–2, 151–2). In 1961 Sean Kenny's set, full of jutting platforms and stairs, had the balcony down on the audience's right, more or less six feet above stage level. The neo-Elizabethan set used by Trevor Nunn in 1976 placed the balcony on a jutting platform just in front of the proscenium arch on the audience's right (Figure 30), and in 1989 the Swan's highest gallery offered Romeo a challenge he wisely

FIGURE 30 Francesca Annis and Ian McKellen as the lovers in 1976. The 'Elizabethan' stage is bare and evenly lit, and audience members are visible on galleries at the rear. The balcony itself is set against the proscenium arch on the left-hand side of the theatre. Behind its promontory is a gap in the wooden set to allow free passage for the safety curtain. (2.2)

ignored – until in the 'farewell' scene (3.5) he had to descend from it with a ladder of cords and (after a bad case of skinned hands) a pair of thoughtfully provided protective gloves (Figure 31). In the main house both Michael Bogdanov (1986) and David Leveaux (1991) placed the scene downstage on the audience's right, and both made a point of including the structure (a platform in front of the proscenium arch in 1986, a metal frame pushed forward in 1991) in the action of earlier scenes. In 1986 Juliet looked down

FIGURE 31 Mark Rylance makes his death-defying descent from Juliet's balcony at dawn (3.5) in Terry Hands's 1989 Swan production.

from it at Romeo as she left the party, and in 1991 Mercutio clambered up the 'balcony' in 2.1 as he conjured up Romeo. Robert Smallwood compared this balcony to 'a child's playpen on stilts' and objected to the ease with which Romeo was able to reach Juliet: 'It immediately becomes obvious what satisfaction he could have tonight, and there is no reason whatever for all the bother with rope-ladders later' (Smallwood, 347–8).

In 1980 and 2000 Juliet had no window or balcony as such, but simply appeared above a wall, which was a movable set unit in 1980 (Figure 32), and a more solid fixture in 2000. The 1980 sets

FIGURE 32 Anton Lesser and Judy Buxton contrive to touch hands across the expanse of the peeling plaster wall in Ron Daniels's 1980 production. (2.2)

proved difficult to manipulate and unworkable for the sight-lines on tour and in London. The Aldwych promptbooks show that the set was redesigned, with permanent scenic units, and a window with grille and curtains. In what must be one of the most inadvertently radical rethinkings of the scene, Juliet now came down from her room to meet her lover centre stage. Perhaps the least practical Stratford staging was that of Hands's 1973 production (Figure 33), for which Farrah designed a metal walkway like a gantry, evoking yet again the fire escapes of *West Side Story*. This could move up and down the stage, but even at its furthest position forward it allowed audiences in the uppermost level (and some of the dress circle patrons) only a glimpse of the lower half of Estelle Kohler's body and muffled the actor's voice. To add to the oddity of the situation, Timothy Dalton's Romeo could have climbed straight up to the balcony by one of the lateral stairways, but made a show of being unable to: at one point he

FIGURE 33 Farrah's 1973 set, with its high steel gallery and lateral hanging bars, suggests both urban landscape (*West Side Story*, again) and shades of the prison house already closing in on the lovers (Estelle Kohler and Timothy Dalton) at their second encounter. (2.2)

reached up to touch Juliet's hand but fell off the platform he was on – a few steps more, in fact, and he might have held her in his arms.

On her wide steel balcony, Kohler in 1973 proved one of the most energetic Juliets. In Jeremy Kingston's words, she was 'permanently on heat' (*Punch*). Benedict Nightingale in the *New Statesman* thought he detected the director's instructions to the lovers to 'swirl' and 'bounce':

> He grins and flings his arms loosely about a good deal, boyishly dashing hither and thither, before settling into a sort of gangling, flailing angst, all arms and legs like a demented tree in a hurricane. She gasps, throbs and bubbles breathlessly, squeaking and squealing with girlish glee as she jumps from side to side of her absurd balcony.

After what he found a 'perfunctory' ball scene, Frank Marcus complained that this Juliet spent the balcony scene 'squealing from her bridge', and he was reminded of a council house tenant 'shouting her shopping list from the balcony to the delivery boy below' (*S. Telegraph*). One might wonder how many occupants of 1970s public housing were still served by delivery boys. Harold Hobson, having already found her 'deliberately lubricious', read Juliet's energy as 'seeking in frenzied desperation for means of physical release which have some, but not an essential, connection with love' (*S. Times*). The eroticism passed by the critic of the Birmingham *Sunday Mercury*, who observed simply that the frenetic movement 'captured all that high-flying feeling of first love'. B.A Young felt that Dalton's running and jumping served only to mask the emptiness of his performance, whilst Kohler, previously restrained in Karolos Koun's formal and sombre production, now seemed younger than in 1967, and able to indulge 'teenage passions free of the inhibitions of grand theatre' (*FT*). The promptbook shows that Dalton jumped up and hung briefly from the balcony, and that Kohler knelt and touched his hand before – as noted already – he fell off.

The 1973 production has been dwelt on at such length because, despite Dalton's ineffective Romeo, it indicates the degree to which the scene might now express physical desire, fully sensed but not yet to be fulfilled. Unsurprisingly, earlier readings seem to have suggested a less sensual rapture. By the time Brook's production was seen in London, in October 1947, it was observed that Daphne Slater had gained in assurance: 'She now carries us enthusiastically to the end of the balcony scene, always blithe and alert in new-found wonder' (*Birm. Post*). Zena Walker in 1954, credited by many reviewers with freshness, forthrightness and good sense, was 'not dumbfounded by love' (*E. News*). It was due to her, wrote Patrick Gibbs, 'that the balcony scene held the attention not as an operatic duet but as a charming and credible conversation' (*D. Telegraph*) – one of many comments indicating a pleasing but unexciting performance. Laurence Harvey, 'manly at all costs' (*D. Mail*), was 'hunched with yearning as he gaz[ed] up at the balcony' (*FT*). Dorothy Tutin and Richard Johnson had to play the scene 'in semi-darkness' in 1958, which W.A. Darlington suggested might explain why it seemed to make so little impression on the audience: '"I have forgot why I did call thee back [170]," which is usually received with a sympathetic stir in the auditorium, tonight went for nothing at all' (*D. Telegraph*). The *Daily Herald*'s reviewer, by contrast, thought her 'lighter than air and likely any moment to take off into space' – a comment that should be taken alongside others in the same vein, indicating the tip-toe quality of her physical performance. *Education* hazarded the opinion that 'the great ballerinas apart, no one [had] ever moved more lightly across the stage . . . Her feet seem[ed] scarcely to touch the boards.' In 1961 Tutin was credited with 'sweet and touching urgency' on Juliet's 'Do not swear at all. / Or if thou wilt, swear by thy gracious self . . . ' (112ff.) and 'clear thinking alongside her impulsiveness' (*Evesham J.*), and was the only actress Felix Barker could recall 'to put such separate and subtle inflection on both the words "sweet" and "sorrow" in the famous line' (184) (*E. News*). There is also an earthier dimension to be found in what follows. Several Juliets have elicited a laugh from the audience with 'What satisfaction canst thou have tonight?' (126) – a response which occurs when both performers make clear the erotic urgency of Romeo's state and also Juliet's understanding of it.

Humour seems to have become increasingly important in this sequence. Even in 1961 Bernard Levin, reflecting on the general levity he found in Peter Hall's production, claimed that 'there seems even to be an attempt to make the balcony scene seem a bit of a giggle' (*D. Express*), and, for all her lyrical ability, Tutin was accused by the *Bristol Evening Post* of 'agitated flirting and fluttering'. The promptbook shows that both she and Romeo laughed on 'What satisfaction canst thou have tonight?' Mark Rylance (1989) played Romeo's seriousness, rather than sadness or melancholia, at the beginning of the scene, and was genuinely taken aback when Juliet appeared: 'It *is* my lady, O [momentary pause as he takes the impact of the thought] it is my love!' (10; my italics). Rylance favoured the musicality of the verse, unafraid to be lyrical as occasion demanded. Despite this, he and Georgia Slowe were able to inflect the 'satisfaction' with a degree of comedy. Here the audience's laugh came on his response to her simple 'I gave thee mine before thou didst request it' (128). This was followed by another tiny pause, then he uttered another 'O'. By now he had earned himself more exclamations: 'O, O, O [*sic*] blessed, blessed night' was rapturous, but cut short by 'I am afeard, / Being in night, all this is but a dream' (139–40). Towards the end of the scene, when Juliet reappeared and called him back, his response 'My nyas' (167) was amusingly high-pitched, but 'And I'll still stay to have thee still forget, / Forgetting any other home but this' was followed by a pause of some thirty seconds before Juliet's ''Tis almost morning, I would have thee gone' (174–6). David Tennant and Alexandra Gilbreath (2000) embraced the comedy in the scene without sacrificing the seriousness: as Tennant has pointed out, 'there is a conflict of interests . . . with Juliet full of the practicalities of the danger Romeo is in and the need for him to get to safety and Romeo's desire to flout the risks to tell how enchanted he is' (Tennant). The freedom granted by the scene's wit, and Gilbreath's natural and youthful body language (leaning with her head on her hands, lolling full length along the top of the 'balcony' wall with her feet crossed behind her), made her seem more genuinely a teenager than at other points in the performance. 'O Romeo, Romeo' was not at all lyrical but expressed her frustration at acquiring a lover from the wrong household: she even head-butted her arms on 'wherefore art thou Romeo?' (33).

The reception given to Mark Rylance's fundamentally serious young man, surprised by passion, suggests that such Romeos fare better than those who key the performance of this scene to exuberance and physicality. Ian McKellen (1976), generally considered over-energetic throughout the play, 'seemed to be compensating for his own maturity by overstressing the lad's moonstruck teenage rapture' (*Guardian*). In this scene, thought Robert Cushman, Romeo was 'bewildered by his luck' in contrast to the 'confident and generous' Juliet of Francesca Annis (*Observer*). Anton Lesser (1980) lay back on the ground and hugged himself in ecstasy at the sound of Juliet's voice, and leapt in the air 'with a Baryshnikov-like frenzy' when she made her vow of fidelity (*Guardian*). 'He is scrawny', wrote Felix Barker, 'with a leaping, nervous agility and legs like indiarubber.' Lesser 'parod[ied] his romantic extravagances' (*E. News*). Gareth Lloyd Evans wrote in the *Stratford-upon-Avon Herald* of 'sexual grunts and gestures' accompanying the speeches here. Another reviewer observed that this 'callow, unromantic youth' was 'so uncertain of his emotions that he writhes, chokes and stammers not merely with them but with the embarrassment of having them', and could not recall any previous occasion when the audience had found the scene funny (*S. Telegraph*). In 1986 there were laughs on Sean Bean's observation 'she speaks' (25), when he suddenly presented himself centre stage with 'I take thee at thy word' (49), and on his diffident but resourceful explanation 'With love's light wings did I o'erperch these walls' (66). No doubt because

Bogdanov's production accepted the play's potential for comedy, the performers were able to control and modulate the mood of this scene, having defused any false solemnity attached to it by tradition. The comedy was offset by moments of stillness and emotional simplicity: Juliet's thoughtful pause after the first mention of his name, and her loving emphasis on the second in 'O Romeo, Romeo . . . '; the strong emphasis on the last four words in 'But that thou overheard'st, ere I was ware, / *My true-love passion*' (103–4; my italics); and the long pause after "Tis twenty year till then' and before 'I have forgot why I did call thee back' (169–70).

Should Romeo and Juliet touch hands at any point? In Zeffirelli's 1960 Old Vic production, John Stride and Judi Dench had tried in vain to reach each other's fingertips. Ian Holm and Estelle Kohler (1967) stretched out their hands just enough to touch, then 'separate[ed] into the night with their fingers pressed to their mouths' (*Times*). In 1973 Timothy Dalton attempted to reach Estelle Kohler, and touched hands but (as has been noted) fell off the stairs. In John Caird's 1984 production at The Other Place, Amanda Root and Simon Templeman did not touch each other, 'but the air between them quivered with feeling' (*S. Times*). Adrian Noble (1995) placed Juliet's window high on a centre-stage wall, and there was no attempt at contact. The dizzy elevation of the balcony in Terry Hands's Swan production (1989) kept Georgia Slowe well out of Mark Rylance's reach. In productions where the lovers have touched hands, the most favoured moments have been the last section of the scene. Peter Brook seems to have had Romeo reaching up in vain on his attempted declaration 'Lady, by yonder blessed moon I vow . . . ' (107) and again at Juliet's "Tis almost morning, I would have thee gone' (176). Byam Shaw's 1954 promptbook indicates that Juliet should drop down with her head through the balcony railings, so that they can hold hands before Romeo's 'I would I were thy bird' (182). In the same director's 1958 staging Juliet knelt down and stretched her hand down on 'And with a silken thread' (180).

In 1961 Brian Murray and Dorothy Tutin stood looking at each other, Romeo leaning against a pillar and gazing up, at "Tis almost morning'. He took her hand on 'Like a poor prisoner' and she slowly withdrew it during the speech (179–83). In 1980 Anton Lesser reached up across the expanse of peeling wall to take Judy Buxton's hand on 'Sweet, so would I' (182) (Figure 32). David Leveaux (1991) brought Romeo up onto the balcony, or at least as far as its outer rail. Michael Maloney flung himself up the side of it with 'O wilt thou leave me so unsatisfied?' (125) and Claire Holman's startled 'What satisfaction canst thou have tonight?' (126) provoked a laugh. After a pause she leaned against the rail on the audience's right, while he craned forward over the rail opposite, reaching out to stroke her cheek on 'Th'exchange of thy love's faithful vow for mine' (127). She took his hand on 'I gave thee mine before thou didst request it' (128) and moved towards him to embrace him. After her first exit and return, Juliet leaned down over the rail and took Romeo's hand on 'thy purpose marriage' (144). Romeo now hung onto the front of the balcony. Once again, a pause was held while the lovers looked at each other, this time before "Tis almost morning' (176).

In 1997, the 'balcony' was 'a distinctly modest thing, with potted geraniums, green shutters and lace curtains' (*Guardian*), a window set a few feet above stage level in a wall at the back of Robert Jones's compact set of an Italian square. Ray Fearon and Zoë Waites made the most of their proximity. She was already leaning down to him as she professed she would 'prove more true / Than those that have more coying [*sic*] to be strange', and straightened up with 'I should have been more strange, I must confess' (100–2). Romeo knelt as he attempted to vow by the moon 'That tips with silver all these fruit-tree tops' (108), and remained kneeling until Juliet's 'Too like the lightning, which doth cease to be / Ere one can say "It lightens"' (119–20). Juliet took his hand two lines later on 'when next we meet' (122). Romeo reached his left hand up to her on 'Wouldst thou withdraw it?' and she knelt to take his hand in her right as she reassured him with 'But to be frank and give it thee again' (130–1). At the end of the scene, when Juliet leaned over the balcony and Romeo grasped her hand on 'Good night, good night' (184), the couple were confirming what had already become established as a gesture of their love, rather than suddenly arriving at it.

MARRIAGE AND SEPARATION

After the scene at Juliet's window and before their meeting in Friar Laurence's cell (2.6) Romeo and Juliet have a busy day. Romeo secures the Friar's agreement to marry them, and the Nurse meets Romeo and carries back his message about the rendezvous. The cumulative effect of these scenes is to place the lovers in a series of contexts: the Friar's preoccupation with the apparently perplexing duality of nature, the bawdy sociability of Romeo's friends, and the garrulous domestic common sense of the Nurse. Between the marriage and their first night together, the catastrophic murders of Mercutio and Tybalt intervene. Juliet, having waited for the Nurse at the beginning of 2.5 with rapturous but comic anticipation, waits for Romeo in 3.2 with a more exalted and erotically charged speech – ironically ignorant of the events of the preceding scene. After this, the actress has to negotiate a scene of 111 lines in which she receives news of a death, discovers that it is Tybalt that is dead rather than Romeo, learns that Romeo has murdered her cousin and is banished – and must reconcile grief for a kinsman with dismay at her lover's exile. Unlike the later sequence in which she equivocates with her mother over punishments for Romeo (3.5.64–125), in this scene Juliet's feelings are divided rather than dissembled. In the last six lines of 3.2, Juliet, despondently holding the 'cords' that were to be her lover's highway to her bed, responds immediately and fervently to the Nurse's assurance that 'Romeo will be here at night' (140). She sends him a ring – although it is his 'last farewell' that she anticipates (143).

Romeo's killing of Tybalt has often been a savage, frenzied but still technically premeditated murder after the accidental death of

Mercutio – at the end of what has sometimes been a comic fight. It is before the news of Mercutio's death that Romeo exclaims against his tame acceptance of Tybalt's insult, which he expresses in terms of Juliet's love having made him 'effeminate' (3.1.116). When he knows Mercutio is dead and sees Tybalt 'in triumph' he rejects 'respective lenity' (124–5) and takes vengeance.

In 1947 and 1954 Romeo killed Tybalt suddenly, but without excessive brutality, on 'This shall determine that' (133). Subsequent Romeos have been more brutal. David Leveaux, in 1991, had Romeo grapple hand to hand with Tybalt, forcing him to the ground and slamming his head against it before he pulled out a knife and stabbed repeatedly his by now helpless victim. After a hysterical rendition of his brief soliloquy ('This gentleman, the prince's near ally . . . ', 111ff.) Zubin Varla (1995) turned on Tybalt furiously, paused for a moment after 'Mercutio's soul / Is but a little way above our heads, / Staying for thine to keep him company' (128–30) and flung himself at Tybalt. He stabbed him twice, brutally, leaving the corpse sprawling face down across the café table (Figure 34). Refusing to fight fairly is an important indication of Romeo's unbounded anger. Sean Bean (1986), after a brief struggle, forced Tybalt down onto his car and stabbed so frenziedly at his exposed chest that he had to be dragged off. In 1989 Mark Rylance, shouting 'Mercutio' hysterically, kicked the floored Tybalt's sword away and closed in with a dagger. In 1997, in keeping with the rustic ambience, sickles and machetes appeared as weapons, and Tybalt, less a duellist than a well-equipped small-town bully, used his fists and a short, vicious-looking knife. Ray Fearon as Romeo jettisoned all decorum and went for him with a flail.

After the death, Romeo stands 'amaz'd' (136), unable to move, despite Benvolio's urging him to be gone: when he does run off, it is with a cry of 'O, I am fortune's fool' (138), confirming his earlier realization that 'This day's black fate' hangs ('doth depend') over more days to come (121). Most productions have placed an interval after the explanations, lamentations and sentencing to

FIGURE 34 Tybalt (Dermot Kerrigan) lies dead across a café table in Adrian Noble's 1995 evocation of mid-nineteenth-century Italy. The Capulets (Christopher Benjamin and Darlene Johnson) look on in dismay. Benvolio (Michael Gould, extreme right) explains to the Prince (Christopher Robbie). (3.1)

banishment that conclude this scene. In 1991 Leveaux had Juliet appear upstage and run down to a position just behind one of the doorways in the screen, which descended just behind the proscenium arch. As the lights faded to a blackout she had raised her arms to touch the top of the door-frame, as if about to begin 'Gallop apace'. After the interval she was discovered lying on the apron of the darkened stage, isolated in a pool of light. Claire Holman delivered the first section of the speech in somewhat explanatory mode, but moved down to left of centre for the more passionate 'Come, night, come Romeo . . . ' (3.2.17) 'Give – me – my – Romeo' (21) was stretched out ecstatically, and she rolled on her back for 'O, I have bought the mansion of a love / But not possess'd it' (26–7). The stage grew lighter as she reached the more domestic image of 'an impatient child that hath new robes / And may not wear them' (30–1). Adrian Noble (1995), having taken an interval before the fight scene, closed tableau curtains to conceal a clearance of the stage after the Prince's departure, and reopened them to reveal Lucy Whybrow on a garden swing. Although the speech was paced and phrased sensitively, it had an oddly detached and explanatory feel: 'Give me my Romeo' was followed by 'and when I shall die' as if a new, bright thought had struck her, and the yearning of 'O, I have bought the mansion of a love' was more wistful than erotic. In keeping with the overall juvenility of her performance, Whybrow twirled round hysterically and collapsed in a heap on the news of Romeo's banishment – a confirmation of the Nurse's later description of her 'weeping and blubbering' (3.3.87) that few Juliets have favoured. Zoë Waites, kneeling with a pillow at the centre of the bed that was now placed centre stage – replicating the position of the bier in the funeral with which the production had begun – lay back on 'O, I have bought . . . ' but then sat up on 'But not possessed it' as though recognizing what she was missing.

Again, the earlier productions favoured a simpler staging that lends itself less obviously to the speech's erotic dimensions. Zena Walker (1954) simply leaned back against the railing on the set's upper level and looked longingly into the distance (Figure 35). Reviews yield no details of this scene, but the consensus on her overall performance (represented by the *Financial Times*) suggests that 'spirited defiance' and down-to-earth determination would not have elicited any great erotic or emotional charge. 'She has . . . none of the youthful arrogance of love nor finally does she suggest its ecstasy.' On Dorothy Tutin's two renditions of this scene, in 1958 and 1961, and Estelle Kohler's first, in 1967, the archive also offers little of substance, beyond such comments as J.C. Trewin's that in 1961 Tutin could 'reach and sustain the rapture' (*Birm. Post*) and the promptbook's evidence that on both occasions the speech was played on the bed. Kohler's 1967 performance undoubtedly contributed to the impression of an 'urgent, spontaneous and deeply felt' Juliet (*Times*), and was consistent with Peter Lewis's view that she conveyed 'the youth, the

impetuousness, the breathless discovery of the depth of her feeling with a bruised and lovely smile that sees every moment of joy smashed flat by fate' (*D. Mail*). In Terry Hands's 'violent delights' production of 1973, having beaten a carpet as she waited for the Nurse's news in 2.5, Estelle Kohler now stood in front of a pair of sheets hanging from the same line, embracing them rapturously as she imagined the delights of her wedding night (*Punch*). In 1976 Francesca Annis was 'bloodlessly ethereal and apt to turn breathy or shrill in moments of crisis'. She brought 'considerable music' to the elegiac passages and 'extract[ed] stabs of feeling in unfamiliar places' (*Times*). However, Irving Wardle insisted, 'her passion [was] well insulated within the decorum of classical delivery'.

In Michael Bogdanov's 1986 production Niamh Cusack embraced fully the speech's sexual dimension, in what seems to have become the accepted approach. Cusack described her reading of 'die' in 'when I shall die' (21) in these terms:

> the white of the stars, and his body in white, and the white of him ejaculating inside me, and the cutting up in little white stars, linking . . . with the idea of spiritual death, which immediately afterwards breaks into the scene in reality with the news of Tybalt's death. (Cusack, 129)

Even when performances (such as Alexandra Gilbreath's in 2000) seem over-explicit in spelling out the succession of images, the energy required by the speech and the degree of physical expressiveness are acknowledged. At the opening of the play's second part Gilbreath ran down from the back of the stage to the very edge of the apron, teetering as though her passion were restrained only by some invisible elastic rope.

FIGURE 35 (*opposite*) Motley's permanent set of light, natural wood for Glen Byam Shaw's 1954 production. Juliet (Zena Walker) stands on the upper level. Steps lead down to the shallow forestage, and curtains can be used to vary the appearance of the structure. Juliet's bedroom is at ground level on the right, and the balcony above on the left.

Romeo's scene with the Friar and the Nurse, 3.3, has been discussed above (pp. 73–4). By the end of it Romeo is heartened by the prospect of a wedding night, described with a characteristic superlative as 'a joy past joy' (172), but a short scene between Capulet, his wife and Paris prepares another unanticipated blow to the lovers' hopes: Capulet is perfectly confident his daughter will be 'ruled' by him in accepting the offer of the Count's hand in marriage, and the ceremony will take place in a few days' time. Even if the audience does not recall that Lady Capulet was supposed to see Juliet before going to bed (either she was tired or reluctant, or the playwright forgot), the impending dilemma colours its understanding of the lovers' farewell, which occupies the first fifty-nine lines of the next scene. The whole of 3.5 requires careful staging. The first section has to take place 'above', and after her mother's summons, presumably from stage level, Juliet *'goeth down from the window and enters below'* – in the First Quarto's explicit stage direction. In the Swan Theatre (1989), Terry Hands used the topmost gallery for the lovers' scene, after which Romeo made a vertiginous descent to stage level (Figure 31), and similar use was made in Trevor Nunn's 1976 pseudo-Elizabethan staging of the balcony established at the left side of the proscenium arch. Hands had employed the steel gantry in his 1973 staging. None of these located the opening conversation between the lovers in Juliet's bedroom, still less in her bed.

Peter Brook, in 1947, opened the tableau curtains to reveal Juliet on her bed on the upper level, with Romeo already up and dressed and leaning over her head (Figure 36). Juliet started up to a sitting position with her first words, 'Wilt thou be gone?' (3.5.1) as though wakened by him, and the lovers' embraces were performed with him kneeling by the bed. Romeo's departure could then take him over the side of the upper level, and Juliet could come down the staircase to meet her mother downstage. Motley's set for Glen Byam Shaw's 1954 production placed the bed on the lower level, to the audience's right. The grey drape used to

FIGURE 36 The awakening scene (3.5) in 1947. Daphne Slater and the fully clothed Laurence Payne on a neatly turned down bed.

mask the structure for the Friar's cell was raised, and Juliet was again discovered lying on the bed. This time Romeo had reached the top of the stairs and was leaning against the top rail as she spoke her line. She then got out of bed and climbed up to him. His descent then followed by way of the corded ladder to the front of the set, so that he could be centre stage for her premonition, 'Methinks I see thee, now thou art so low, / As one dead in the bottom of a tomb' (55–6), and his final adieux. In 1961 Dorothy Tutin was discovered on the bed on an upper level, and as the scene began Romeo was getting up to draw aside the curtains that surrounded it. Juliet knelt and they embraced, and she put her arm round his neck to restrain him with the assurance that the light was 'some meteor' rather than daybreak (13). She drew him back onto the bed and they kissed as he spoke 'I have more care to stay than will to go' (23). They embraced again and there was a pause before the Nurse's warning (37). In 1967 Ian Holm clasped Estelle Kohler's face with 'Come death, and welcome' (24) and they embraced on 'This doth not so, for she divideth us' (30). (In this production, as in most others, the lark/loathed toad lines at 31–4 were cut.) Leveaux, in 1991, placed the scene on a platform thrust out precariously from one of the screens, more or less in the centre of the stage. As Romeo came out and stood on the edge, Juliet appeared behind in the doorway. They kneeled facing each other at the front of the platform, and embraced on his resolve to stay and be put to death, but she pulled away with 'It is not day' (25). The Nurse came in at the door behind them, interrupting a kiss, on 'More dark and dark our woes' (36), and after Romeo dropped down to the stage Juliet knelt to hold hands with him from above. As her mother came in, she exited and the balcony was pulled off. David Tennant and Alexandra Gilbreath (2000) played the scene on top of the set's left-hand curving wall (see cover photograph), previously used in the 'balcony' scene and subsequently the point from which the Apothecary, aided by Mercutio, handed down the poison to Romeo (see pp. 176–7).

Placing the lovers centre stage in a bed adds to the potential for 'sexual chemistry' but creates its own problems. Not every couple has been able to satisfy the reviewers' enhanced expectations for post-coital behaviour, and at least two Romeos – Lesser in 1980 and Varla in 1995 – have been reproved for going to bed with their trousers on. More important is the opportunity for anticipating the furnishings of the family vault, so that the lovers will be seen lying together in the same position here and in the play's final sequence. In 1980, 1984 and 1997 the inclusion of Juliet's funeral reinforced the effect foreshadowed in Juliet's line just after meeting Romeo: 'If he be married, / My grave is like to prove my wedding bed' (1.5.133–4). Juliet, of course, took the sleeping draught and fell back onto the same bed, and Zoë Waites had even spoken 'Gallop apace' on it.

In 1986 the scene opened with slow music and early-morning birdsong. Sean Bean and Niamh Cusack were lying on the bed. He swung his legs sideways to pull on his trousers, prompting 'Wilt thou be gone?' With 'Let me stay' (17, replacing 'Let me be ta'en') he took his shirt off again, but she rose and crossed upstage to the venetian blinds, insisting 'It *is* the lark' (27; my italics). The Nurse entered behind the blinds and Romeo and Juliet walked across to the right-hand side of the stage, disappearing briefly before appearing on the balcony, from which he could climb down. In Adrian Noble's less efficient version of the same kind of staging (1995) the bed came up, with the lovers in it, on a trap in the centre of the forestage. Curtains were flown in behind the bed, concealing the scenic unit with the 'balcony'. Once again, Romeo sidled deftly out of bed to put his trousers on, looping his embroidered braces over his shoulders, and, appropriately enough, birdsong was heard. Having agreed to part, the couple hastened upstage behind the curtains, which opened to reveal them just as they arrived on the balcony. A lighting change now 'lost' the bed. Romeo clambered down from the window. As Juliet came down from the window the curtains closed and her mother entered on the forestage. Michael Attenborough (1997), having placed the bed in the middle of the Swan's stage, cut references to Romeo's descent from Juliet's room, thus losing the moment of eerie premonition ('Methinks I see thee, now thou art so low . . . ', 55) but gaining an effective central position for a very intimate version of the parting. The lovers were indeed naked. As he accepted the danger of being caught rather than give up possession of her, Ray Fearon rolled Juliet over onto her back with 'How is't, my soul?' (25). Juliet put on her shirt and he pulled on shorts and trousers, carefully buttoning up his flies, as they prepared for his departure: there was no sudden and embarrassing huddling into his clothes for this Romeo. One reviewer found Fearon's delivery of 'what envious streaks / Do lace the severing clouds in yonder east' (7–8) too matter of fact, 'giving us a fair idea of the view, but not much more', whereas Zoë Waites filled similarly descriptive language 'with a moving sense of love clouded by impending loss' (*Independent*).

TOWARDS CATASTROPHE

IN JULIET'S BEDROOM

Juliet, having received the sleeping draught from Friar Laurence, has returned home, shown herself submissive to her father's wishes, and prepares for bed. The Capulets' reactions to their daughter's behaviour, and those of the Nurse and the Friar, have been discussed already. Apart from any other considerations, they contribute to the sense of isolation in which Juliet takes the draught: 'My dismal scene I needs must act alone' (4.3.19). Her soliloquy, with its picture of Tybalt's ghost and the terrified Juliet dashing out her brains 'with some great kinsman's bone' (53), is especially demanding, and is rhetorically and emotionally more formidable than her relatively brief death scene.

Peter Brook's promptbook (1947) reflects the difficulty he seems to have felt in pacing the production at this point. The scene began on stage level, and then Juliet climbed slowly up the stairs to her 'bedroom' during the potion speech, in which she appeared 'genuinely frightened' (*S. Times*). Among other revisions made late during rehearsal, Brook cut the household bustle of 4.4, so that Juliet's collapse onto the bed was followed by the Nurse's arrival to wake her. After the discovery of her inert body, a further drastic revision moved the dialogue directly to the Friar's instructions beginning 'Dry up your tears' (4.5.79–83). Originally this had been transposed to follow such of the musicians' dialogue as had been included. Zena Walker, in 1954, blew out the candle in her bedroom as the Nurse departed, and there was a pause before 'God knows when we shall meet again' (4.3.14). 'Come, vial' (20) was followed by a longer pause (a musical fermata in the promptbook). The speech built to a climax emphasized by another pause before 'O look, methinks I see my cousin's ghost' (55), and Walker 'follow[ed] ghost round' as the imaginary Tybalt stalked Romeo. She then drank from the vial, climbed onto the bed, drew the curtain and swooned with her head on the stage. In 1961 Dorothy Tutin gave what Bernard Levin called a 'marrow piercing' delivery of the speech (*D. Express*). A pause preceded her vision of her kinsman's ghost (55–7), and she threw herself face down on the bed after 'Stay, Tybalt, stay!' then, after another long pause, sat up and drank. After a moment during which she looked round, Juliet lay down and pulled the covers over her. In Terry Hands's 1973 production Estelle Kohler's bed was garlanded as if for the wedding: the rendering of the speech was unsparing, with the actress unafraid to show the agonies of anxiety and imagined torment (Figure 37). Like her depiction of sexual passion earlier in the play, Kohler's performance had a physicality and directness that made no concessions to old-fashioned notions of gracious-ness or decorum. This was a terrified but resolute woman.

Michael Bogdanov (1986) managed to include all the scene's elements, beginning with a remarkable moment of peace and ending with the comic confrontation between Peter and the musicians. In a blackout the bedroom was set as it had been for 3.5, with high venetian blinds flown in upstage of the bed. As the lights came up Juliet was discovered kneeling downstage on the left-hand side, playing Debussy's *Syrinx* on a flute. She put the flute away in its case, carefully, as the Nurse showed her a dress before laying it out on the bed. The Nurse went off singing to herself. After drinking from the vial, Juliet fell on the bed with her head downstage, having taken care to hide the dagger under the pillow. The lights faded out on the bed, and came up on the forestage and

FIGURE 37 Juliet (Estelle Kohler), standing on her garlanded bridal bed, imagines the possible consequences of taking the potion and waking up in the family vault. (4.3, 1973)

behind the blinds. To the accompaniment of cheerful 'hurry' music, figures crossed and re-crossed at the front and Capulet gave instructions from the steps centre stage. During this the revolve turned three times, and the sun was seen rising at the back as the Nurse peeped through slats of the central blind. By Capulet's 'her blood is settled' (4.5.26) the offstage music provided by Paris had already become very loud. Bogdanov included the Friar's words of comfort to Juliet's parents (66–78), but, in line with the production's overall tendency, 'The most you sought was her promotion' (71ff.) was accusatory, as if chastising them for their social ambitions. After the Friar's instructions, stagehands came in to remove the bed, and the Friar hurried downstage to take Juliet's knife from under her pillow. A brief version of the musician's dialogue was interrupted by Peter's arrival: he gave them the 'gleek' – a rude gesture accompanied by a raspberry – and they departed.

Georgia Slowe, in Hands's simply staged Swan production (1989), had already impressed Michael Billington as 'half in love with easeful death', even in the balcony scene. She exhibited 'a kind of horrified thrill' at the prospect of 'waking alone in the tomb and madly playing with her forefathers' joints' (*Guardian*). Paul Taylor accused her of 'hysterically bellow[ing]' the speech in an 'operatic display' that cancelled out pathos and concentrated 'exclusively and shrilly on her childish fears', and complained that neither lover showed the maturity and 'rapid moral enlargement' required by the play (*Independent*). As in Hands's 1973 version, the lamentations were spoken simultaneously. The Friar's words of consolation were included, and 'The most you sought was her promotion' was spoken reprovingly (as it had been in 1986). After the family departed, the lights faded down on the bed, and the musicians' scene with Peter was played downstage. Juliet's funeral was accompanied by a tolling bell and soft clarinet music: the body was set downstage in the centre and gates were pulled across under the gallery. This would allow Romeo to be seen at the back of the stage when he reached the graveyard, and then break into the monument by forcing one of the gates.

Such elegant solutions to the notorious traffic problems of the scene were not available in the main house. In 1991 Juliet's bed was laid out on the platform that had been thrust out 'above' for the lovers' parting. This time a flight of steps was placed at the left-hand side of it. A wedding dress hung ready on a dressmaker's dummy, and the Nurse (like Dilys Laye in 1986) sang happily to herself as she left. Juliet began her 'dismal scene' on the steps, pausing as she began to call the Nurse back, then continuing up to the platform, the lights shifting so that only the bed was illuminated. 'God knows when we shall meet again' was faint, but within a few moments, by 'Come vial', Juliet was resolved.

Then doubt set in again. On 'Stay' she thrust away the imaginary ghost with her outstretched arms. Romeo's name in the final line was spoken slowly three times like an incantation, and high, ethereal voices were heard as she drank. Juliet slumped with an involuntary 'O'. Servants then crossed and re-crossed in front of and below the upper platform, and they were still busy with household preparations during the Nurse's discovery of Juliet's apparent death. With 'Lady! Lady! Lady!' (4.5.13) the Nurse turned Juliet over, and crossed herself at what she saw. The lamentations were drastically cut down, becoming a formal duet on the forestage for Capulet and his wife, accompanied by offstage music. The director took the unusual step of removing Friar Laurence altogether from this scene, perhaps assuming that his instructions to Juliet in 4.1 would have carried the plot point. Lucy Whybrow's performance of the speech in 1995 was remarkable for its rapidity and the constant rise in pitch. After drinking, she lay down and remained in the bed in the centre of the forestage, as Capulet talked from the window above to servants who contrived to be oblivious of the bed's presence. Alexandra Gilbreath (2000), still in the black mourning dress she had worn to go to the Friar's cell, was lit by footlights as she sat on the bed: they cast ominous shadows on the walls behind her, and as she imagined her cousin's ghost, Tybalt entered rapidly from upstage and walked past the bed and down through the audience. After drinking from the vial, apparently in some distress and pain, she subsided onto the bed and pulled the sheets over her. In some productions where the bed has remained undisguised at ground level the busy servants of the next sequence have worked round her sleeping form: in 2000 they even tossed logs across her and jumped over the bottom of the bed. Usually Capulet's anxious interference in the wedding preparations has been placed well downstage. (In 1973 Jeffery Dench stopped a servant carrying a cake, tasted the green decoration and pronounced 'Good [tastes the cake decoration] – angelica!' – removing at a stroke the one possible reference to the Nurse's name (4.4.5).)

The stylized grieving of the Capulet family, after the discovery of the apparently dead Juliet in 4.5, is one of the most intractable of the play's impassioned passages for the modern actor and director. Glen Byam Shaw, in 1954 and 1958, arranged a painterly tableau to accommodate it (Figure 3). It has often been trimmed, and sometimes (in 1973, 1989, 1995 and 2000) the speeches have been spoken simultaneously with the effect of an operatic quartet. In 1991 the sequence was whittled down to a brief duet for the parents. Most productions have allowed the scene its proper time and space, although the repetitious lines ('Beguil'd, divorced, wronged, spited, slain' (55) etc.) have often been abbreviated. Byam Shaw cut the same way in both his productions. He omitted three lines from Capulet's development of the image of Death as son-in-law (38–40) and trimmed the lamentations of Capulet, his wife and Paris by seven lines including their 'lists' so that only the Nurse was allowed an incantatory effect. In 1967 Karolos Koun, advised by John Barton, removed similar lines from Capulet and Paris, but Peter Hall's version (1961) included the 'lists' and both Terry Hands (1973) and Trevor Nunn (1976) allowed the scene to be heard in its entirety. In 1973 the voices chimed in on one another, rising to a crescendo before Friar Laurence called a halt. At The Other Place in 1984 John Caird, unusually, cut only the Nurse's repetitions (51–4), leaving everything else intact. Polly James thus became one of the most concise Nurses in the play's Stratford career, confining herself to 'O woe! O woeful, woeful, woeful day' (49). Brook and Byam Shaw, in both his productions, omitted the dialogue between the musicians and Peter (100–41). It began to make a comeback in the versions used by Hall and Koun in 1961 and 1967 (omitting only a half-dozen of the lines), and in 1973 Hands surprised reviewers by including the whole sequence. In 1976 Nunn again cut only a few lines, allowing Richard Griffiths to make a great impression with the depth of feeling suddenly evinced in Peter. As well as amplifying Peter's role, it adds an additional element – clumsily, sincerely affectionate – to the emotional composition of the household, and it is true to the form set down in the play's first scene that this one should be concluded with a dispute between unmoved professionals and a grieving but aggressive servant.

In 1995, when Paris arrived he was accompanied by a group of singing bridesmaids, including children. The lamenting speeches were simplified and spoken as overlapping. Peter slumped, speechless, at the side of the stage, too overcome to join in (*SS*, 242). In 2000 Eileen McCallum bustled cheerfully around Juliet's bed until the very last moment when Juliet's state became unavoidably apparent (Figure 14). The jauntiness faded suddenly from the last 'Lady!' in her attempt to wake Juliet as she realized what had happened. After calling out above the swelling offstage din of the bridegroom's drums and discordant trumpets, the Nurse took a swig from her flask of aqua vitae. When Lady Capulet came on she lifted Juliet's limp body up to a standing position, and Capulet then took his daughter in his arms ('Let me see her . . . ', 25) and placed her tenderly on the bed. The lamentations, which were again overlapped, became increasingly strident and cacophonous (taking over from the wedding music) until the Friar silenced them in a stentorian, rebuking voice. At the end of the scene the Friar followed the family off and the Nurse was the last to leave, taking Peter's lines, 'Honest good fellows, ah put up, put up, / For well you know this is a pitiful case' (97–8). After deciding to 'tarry for the mourners' (140–1) the musicians, who had appeared on top of the left-hand wall, retired.

IN MANTUA

Mantua, where Romeo learns from Balthasar that Juliet is dead, resolves to join her and buys poison, has often been characterized by directors and designers as a place of death, taking a cue from Friar John's lines about its citizens' fear of the plague (5.2.8–11). Attractive as such stage pictures may be, they anticipate the action of a scene that begins with Romeo in high spirits ('My bosom's lord sits lightly in his throne', 5.1.3) after awakening from the all too flattering 'truth' of sleep. Balthasar's news prompts Romeo to new resolution, defying the stars, but the speech in which he describes the Apothecary and his shop (5.1.37ff.) is a strange tour de force. Its presence is perhaps justified by its contributing – like Juliet's 'potion' soliloquy – to the preoccupation with decay and death that dominates the play as it moves towards the Capulets' monument.

Peter Brook (1947) played the scene on an empty stage, with Romeo discovered in his black cape and tights, leaning against a tall tree set right of centre (Figure 38). This dreamy, serene and romantic isolation echoed Romeo's first appearance in the play, in the same costume on a stage littered with discarded weapons. The promptbook indicates that his exchanges with Balthasar were increasingly urgent and his description of the Apothecary more deliberate. The tableau curtains closed in the course of this and the Apothecary emerged through them onto the forestage at the end of it, so that the sliding stage could move the tomb set into place during the last few lines. Despite his need to hasten the play's final movement to its conclusion, Brook retained the whole of Romeo's descriptive speech about the Apothecary and his shop. In 1954 Glen Byam Shaw began part three of the production with this scene, in a street crowded with revellers, one of them singing and playing a musical instrument. In 1989 Terry Hands staged the scene simply and without elaborately 'gothic' effects: the prize for these must go to David Leveaux, whose 1991 production offered 'a stark, skull-scattered deathscape that could make Golgotha look like a popular picnic spot' (*Independent*). A procession of figures in death's-head masks snaked down and across the stage before the scene, and a cage-like platform descended bearing what one assumed was the sleeping Juliet. Upstage, dimly visible, was a pile of coffin-like boxes, with skulls littered around. The detailed description of the Apothecary's shop was cut, and at the end of the speech he came down from the back of the stage, carrying a pedlar's pack, 'grey and tottering' and with 'a voice rustling like a dry wind over white bones' (*SA Herald*). In this case, Romeo and

FIGURE 38 Romantic isolation in Mantua, 1947. Laurence Payne's Romeo leans against the solitary tree. (5.1)

Juliet proved less impressive than their surroundings: Romeo's reaction to the news of Juliet's death was 'absurdly bloodless' (*Times*). For Adrian Noble's 1995 production the designer Kendra Ullyart created an expressionist cityscape with a forced perspective of high walls and tiny lighted windows. In the Swan in 1989 Terry Hands, having placed Juliet on the darkened platform, was able to play the Mantua scene in unusually and ironically bright light on the gallery above. The 1997 staging in the same space also left Juliet's bed – now become her bier – on the stage, and simply played the Mantua scene (minus the Apothecary) upstage.

Michael Bogdanov in 1986 offered one of the most elaborate versions of the scene, here keyed to the ironic contrast between the lovers' feelings and an uncaring society rather than to any sense of destiny or approaching death. A band marched across the stage, and took up its position at the back behind the structure on the revolve. This was carnival time in Mantua, and a roller skater, an acrobat and a stilt walker crossed, followed by three actors wearing 'big heads' caricaturing Ronald Reagan, Helmut Kohl and (handbag over arm) Margaret Thatcher. Romeo lingered down-stage as a crowd gathered at the back to watch the acrobat and applaud. Laughter punctuated his exchange with Balthasar at 'her body sleeps in Capel's monument' and 'ill news' (5.1.18, 22), and by now the music had become discordant and distorted. 'Then I defy you, stars!' (24) coincided with applause upstage.

How much does an audience need to hear about the Apothecary? The 1954 version of the speech was complete, but in 1958 Byam Shaw cut Romeo's description of the shop's stock-in-trade (42–8) and four later lines, one of them (71) perhaps because 'contempt and beggary' did not hang so evidently on this apothecary's back. Peter Hall (1961) and Karolos Koun (1967) cut more deeply elsewhere, but both omitted only three lines (44–6) of the seven-line inventory. In Koun's version, with its chorus-like use of the plague-stricken Mantuan citizenry, a blind pedlar circled silently upstage, while Romeo encountered the Apothecary. In 1973 Romeo bought his poison from a figure more emblematic than picturesque, the ominous hooded figure (variously construed as Fate and Death by reviewers) that had presided on the high gantry at the back at moments of crisis. Michael Boyd, in 2000, having created an even more harsh and unforgiving society for the play, identified the Apothecary with the presiding and mocking forces of destiny rather than with the social world of the play. He brought him on at the top of the left-hand wall of his austere set, where the 'ghosts' of Tybalt and Mercutio had already taken their places to preside over the fate of the lovers. Romeo reached up for a vial of poison, passed to him by Mercutio, in a gesture recalling the 'balcony' and 'farewell' scenes, which had been played in the same position. What the promptbook describes as the 'caustic chorus' of musicians and servants watched from the right-hand wall.

Effective as these numinous figures might have been, the most chilling remains Brian Lawson's 'wonderfully sinister, scar-faced apothecary' (*S. Times*) in Bogdanov's carnival-obsessed Mantua. As Romeo called out 'What ho! Apothecary!' (57) the crowd rushed down and off, engulfing him as they went, but a solitary leather-jacketed figure walked slowly down from underneath the stairways. This was clearly one of the local drug dealers. In paying him Romeo threw banknotes down on the stage, which he picked up and stuffed into the pocket of his blouson. Like Capulet, the Apothecary was a man of business.

IN THE CAPULETS' MONUMENT

From this point onwards directors have tended to hasten what is already a rapid movement towards the Capulet vault. The brief scene in which Friar John reports how he was prevented from delivering the all-important letter to Romeo (5.2) has usually been hurried through. Bogdanov (1986) was one of the few directors to make anything of it, and had John bicycle on in the dark, recalling his more relaxed encounter with Laurence when they shared a flask of coffee in the early morning after the Capulets' party. One event omitted by the playwright, though, has proved attractive.

David Garrick, in 1748, had added Juliet's funeral to his version of the play, with an appropriate 'dirge'. It became an expected feature of productions long after his text had been forsaken, and the notion of showing Juliet being placed in the family vault still has its appeal. Two Stratford productions (1984 and 1997) began the play with the funeral of the lovers, and three (1980, 1989 and 1991) have included Juliet's funeral in proper sequence, immediately before 5.1. In 1980 Ron Daniels had Juliet carried on

FIGURE 39 Juliet's funeral (before 5.1) in Ron Daniels's 1980 production. A torch-lit ceremony is presided over by the Prince (Bruce Purchase) rather than the Friar, and accompanied by Stephen Oliver's setting of 'Brightness falls from the air', lines from a lyric in Thomas Nashe's *Summer's Last Will and Testament* (1592).

from upstage centre to the accompaniment of Stephen Oliver's setting of Thomas Nashe's 'Brightness falls from the air' (a 'swinging funeral ode', according to the *Financial Times*) while the stage filled with hooded figures bearing torches. Most of the actors not required immediately were used for this impressive effect – I counted seventeen hooded figures filing in from the central opening between the two 'wall' flats at the back (Figure 39). The *Times* noted that the script of this sequence was now not only very full but also augmented – an unwelcome addition in what was already a long evening. In fact, as was noticed by another reviewer, Romeo's reference to Tybalt (5.3.97–100) was omitted and his body left out of the tomb: possibly for the sake of the symmetrical arrangement of the stage around Juliet's bier (*SA Herald*). Hands's 1989 arrangement has already been commented

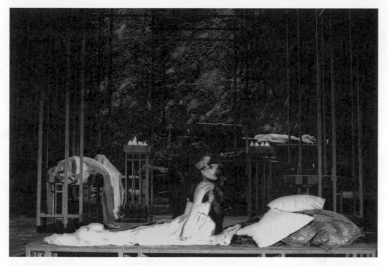

FIGURE 40 Romeo (Michael Maloney) takes his last farewell of Juliet (Claire Holman) in the cage-like tomb of David Leveaux's 1991 staging. (5.3)

on: it offered one of the best 'solutions' to the problems of staging the scene on a quasi-Elizabethan stage. In the main house in 1991 the family tomb had made half its descent from the flies before the Mantua scene. For the final scene it was lowered to stage level, revealing a 'high tech cube' that in a period when the British banks were regrouping themselves and revamping their corporate images was compared by one reviewer to 'a new high street branch of the Natwest' (*Observer*). Robert Smallwood, in *Shakespeare Quarterly*, suggested that it resembled some giant birdcage (349) (Figure 40).

Violence, or the threat of it, accompanies the lovers into the tomb, with an increasing sense of the grotesque and macabre. Having arrived in the graveyard, Romeo threatens to tear Balthasar joint from joint 'and strew this hungry churchyard with [his] limbs' (5.3.36), and as he approaches the Capulets' monument he addresses it as a 'detestable maw . . . womb of death, / Gorg'd with the dearest morsel of the earth' (45–6). Romeo encounters Paris, who has probably assumed, like her parents, that Juliet took her life because she was distraught at Tybalt's death, and accuses 'vile Montague' of having come to pursue vengeance beyond death (54–5) – presumably by defiling Tybalt's corpse. (Paris's graceful rhymed poem of mourning at 12–17 – 'Sweet flower, with flowers thy bridal bed I strew' – has frequently been cut.) Romeo fails to recognize his rival until after he has killed him and only then remembers Balthasar's report of the planned marriage with Juliet. His death speech (88–120) represents Death as a rival wooer, and his life ends with a kiss. Productions have regularly trimmed the scene of most (often all) of Romeo's threats and explanations to Balthasar, and the latter's exchange with the Friar (123–35). The intervention of the watchmen has been simplified, and the Prince's interrogation of Paris's page and Balthasar (270–89) has usually been removed altogether.

Quite apart from its relationship with other aspects of the play's verbal and physical imagery, the final sequence thus contains a complex of information and relationships, some known and others unknown to the characters. Harley Granville-Barker observed: 'as it is a tragedy less of character than of circumstance, upon circumstance its last emphasis naturally falls' (Granville-Barker, 69). Only by hearing at least a good deal of the Friar's long speech will everyone on stage be able to piece the story together, but many directors have considered this an unnecessary trouble for the audience. The thirty-five lines of explanation (230–65) have sometimes been filleted (as by Hall in 1961 and Koun in 1967) or on occasion deleted altogether, notably in the wholesale revisions of Brook and Bogdanov. Brook appears to have rehearsed the sequence following Juliet's death before cutting it at a late stage (Trewin, 35). Byam Shaw's otherwise very full 1958 promptbook indicates a second set of cuts that remove the whole of 232–65, perhaps for the tour. This reduces the Friar's statement to 'I married them', followed by his offer to submit himself to 'the rigour of severest law' (265–8). Hall (1961) cut twelve lines of the Friar's long speech, Koun (1967) twenty, and Nunn (1976) eight. Among more recent directors Michael Attenborough and Michael Boyd (1997 and 2000) made extensive cuts in the sequence, losing fifteen and seventeen lines respectively between 227 and 263, then moving directly to 290 ('Where be these enemies? Capulet, Montague' – Boyd cut the first half of this line).

Fuller accounts have been rare. Hands, in 1973, cut only two lines here and also included, unusually, most of the passage of explanations that follows line 270. Here as elsewhere in the play, John Caird's 1984 production at The Other Place trimmed the text only slightly, removing Romeo's explanation of his conduct ('Why I descend unto this bed of death . . . ', 28–32) and the dialogue between the Friar and Balthasar (121ff.), and simplifying the watchmen's lines. The Prince lost six lines beginning 'Seal up the mouth of outrage . . . ' (215–20). This fixed attention firmly on the Friar and on those who were to learn from his account, from which only four lines were cut, the Friar's offer to place Juliet in a sisterhood (156–7) and the news of Lady Montague's death (209–10). The play's final lines have often been treated as an epilogue, most obviously when the same actor has played 'Chorus' as well as Escalus. The scene's darkness is gradually invaded by light in the form of torches and lanterns carried by a succession of new arrivals culminating in the watch, the Prince and the members of the rival households. Morning brings only a 'glooming peace', and the 'sun for sorrow will not show his head' (304–5), but some kind of chilly dawn light is usually arrived at in the final moments.

From the point of view of staging, if the script is followed to the letter (it rarely is) the last scene will require Romeo to appear outside the monument and break his way into it, with an instantaneous shift of location to its interior. On two occasions (1976 and 2000) Juliet has been placed, Ophelia-like, in a grave below the stage, from which Romeo has had to lift her. Usually she has been on a bier, which (as we have seen) may also have been seen as her bed or will at least resemble it. When this is the case, Romeo is re-enacting the wedding night, and on occasion he has failed to reach her in time to achieve this.

In 1947 the monument was a scenic unit trundled in on the sliding stage, and resembled 'a fragment of bomb damage' (*Time & T.*). Like many other directors, Brook simplified the arrivals of Romeo and Paris in the churchyard and omitted the exchange (122–39) between the Friar and Balthasar. Of Laurence Payne's performance, the reviewers have little to say, but Brook appears to have denied Romeo any final consolation: the promptbook shows that on 'Thus with a kiss I die' (120) he 'makes to kiss her' but is interrupted by a 'paroxysm' and 'turns, lying across her'. In a moment of intimacy the 'Friar takes Romeo in arms from bier as Juliet sits up and rises. Juliet from standing [down right] of bier, turns in, sees Romeo in Friar's arms falls on him on bier.'

Motley's plain set endowed the final scene of Byam Shaw's 1954 production with what the *Stage* considered 'solemn cold formality . . . with stars pricking through the canopy' (Figure 41a). In a literal-minded reading of the staging, another reviewer wondered why an intruder needed to prise open the gates of a tomb when he might simply jump down into it from above (*Sol. & War. News*). Laurence Harvey, thought the anonymous reviewer in the *Times*, was good only in this scene – and by then it was too late. The waking Juliet seems to have sat bolt upright, 'with scarcely a sign of dawning dismay' (*S. Wales Arg.*). Byam Shaw made a substantial cut (over 100 lines) in the final minutes, moving from the watchmen's discovery of the bodies (180) to the Prince's 'Where be these enemies?' (290).

In 1958 black drapes closed off the upstage area, and an ornate cross was suspended over a dais in the centre of the stage, which was surrounded by elegant metal screens that Romeo would have

FIGURE 41a (*opposite*) The final tableau in Byam Shaw's 1954 production. The promptbook diagram (Figure 41b) shows the placing of the lovers, as seen in the photograph.

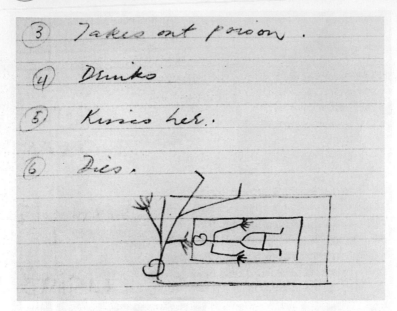

FIGURE 41b Promptbook diagram showing the placing of the lovers in Figure 41a.

to break through after descending a flight of stairs from the left-hand upper level. Sean Kenny's set for Hall's 1961 production was far grimmer: 'a charnel house [was] lowered from the flies, through the grilles of which the corpses of the departed Capulets [were] proffered to our gaze', and from which Juliet was 'drawn like a loaf from a baker's oven' (*Oxf. Mail*) (Figure 42). Timothy O'Brien's designs for Koun's 1967 production had already suggested a Verona hastening towards the churchyard, and Ian Holm 'seem[ed] to have one foot in the tomb from the start' (*Plays & P.*). In his final moments he paused after 'Thus with a kiss', and 'I die' was allowed to 'fall gently to earth' (*Leam. Spa Cour.*).

FIGURE 42 (*opposite*) The stacked sepulchres of Sean Kenny's 1961 set for the final scene. Friar Laurence (Max Adrian) and the Prince (Tony Church) stand above, left. Capulet (Newton Blick) and Lady Capulet (Cherry Morris) stand to the right of the bodies of Paris, Romeo and Juliet.

Hands's direction of the lovers' deaths in 1973 was agreed to have erred in the direction of melodrama: Timothy Dalton was too strident in his final speech, and Estelle Kohler's body was drenched in blood after she had stabbed herself. One of the most striking performances of the scene was that in Nunn's 1976 production. Ian McKellen's Romeo descended to stage level from one of the galleries at the back: the grave itself was a trap, and the references to Tybalt's corpse were cut so as to simplify the stage picture. After taking the poison, transported by grief Romeo held the unconscious Juliet in a standing position for a last embrace. He then lowered her to the edge of the trap and sat with her in his arms, facing upstage so that her arm was stretched across his back. Without his being able to see or feel it, the arm began to stir. As Roger Warren observed, 'what has usually seemed a blemish, the purely accidental nature of the tragedy, was turned into a positive feature: stressing what a close thing it was intensified the pathos of their deaths' (Warren, 1977, 171). Juliet, for her part, slumped on top of Romeo after her suicide, with her hand brushing his face in a final caress as she fell. What followed showed that this was not at all a sentimentalized version of the play. John Woodvine's Capulet carried his anger into the tomb, and was even ready to assault the Friar until he was prevailed on to take Montague's hand. Nothing would be easy in the days that followed (Figure 43).

The *Sunday Times* found Bogdanov's ending of the play in 1986 'brash and unromantic where Shakespeare's own is brash and romantic'. Juliet was placed on her bed centre stage, and eerie 'horror' music was heard as the scene began. Paris appeared on the right-hand balcony with a flashlight and came down. The exchange with Balthasar was omitted, and Romeo was already on stage at 'Thou detestable maw . . . ', 45. After a fight (to appropriate music) downstage, Romeo identified Paris and pulled him somewhat unceremoniously out of the way before climbing onto the bier. In early performances he then took out a syringe and injected himself: daily production reports show that later the actor insisted on drinking the poison from a vial, which presents a

FIGURE 43 The families gather round the grave in Trevor Nunn's 1976 production, Friar Laurence (David Waller) holds Romeo (Ian McKellen) to the left of the grave, Capulet (John Woodvine) and Lady Capulet (Barbara Shelley) hold Juliet (Francesca Annis), while Montague (Ian Beavis) sits disconsolately at the right. The Prince (Griffith Jones) reads the letter which Romeo gave Balthasar (5.3.274–7).

less shocking image but makes more sense for Juliet's desire to 'drink' what remains. Music swelled to a climax as he collapsed. After her final speech, Juliet placed Romeo's dagger in his hand, and impaled herself on it in a movement suggesting sexual penetration. The last caress was a gesture literally representing love-in-death. A cacophony of voices was heard offstage as the Friar pleaded with Juliet to leave and its volume increased as she died. Dramatic music faded in again, and the lights dimmed quickly to blackout. They snapped on again a few moments later, to reveal a pair of golden statues on a plinth. In front of it the Prince was reading the Prologue from cards, as if delivering a statement to a news conference. Photographers and reporters and a camera crew had rushed up the aisle and onto the stage.

A photo-call was set up, lining up those involved in the tragedy in front of the statues – including the Nurse and the Friar posing with the cords, and even the Apothecary. The press exited, and Lady Montague (her death had not been announced) came back to lay a single rose against the plinth. Benvolio, who had been sitting at the café table, crossed, stood looking at the statues for a moment and exited. The play then ended with a sudden blackout. The *Financial Times* dismissed this loftily: 'as kitsch, the ending is hard to beat. Strictly for school children in deprived inner cities.' In fact, the reviewer had touched on exactly the resonance Bogdanov wanted to achieve, and an audience he would have liked to woo.

Paul Taylor thought that Mark Rylance (1989) seemed too angry ('bawling') as he approached the Capulets' monument – he was one of the few Romeos to include the threat to Balathasar (*Independent*). In a continuance of his rage Rylance attacked Paris in an 'access of murderous wrath' (*Times*), much as he had gone for Tybalt. Like McKellen in 1976, in his final moments this Romeo wound the unconscious Juliet's arms around himself. There was a moment of tension in the final sequence, when Capulet moved to retrieve the dagger from his daughter's body and the Montague men reached instinctively for their swords. Finally, though, Capulet and Montague held hands across the bed in a familiar gesture of reconciliation. The final sound in the production was the dawn chorus, faded up under the Prince's last lines. It poignantly recalled the end of the two scenes played at Juliet's balcony. Like most of his predecessors, Michael Maloney (1991) did not speak Romeo's explanation or the threats to Balthasar. The staging – as has often been the case – made an uneasy compromise between achieving a credible sense of darkness and the need for the audience to see what happens: Romeo and Paris fought just upstage of an exceptionally well-lit tomb, and Romeo's failure to recognize his adversary was incomprehensible. After disposing of Paris, Romeo moved onto the structure that housed Juliet on what seemed to be a mattress and Tybalt on a more substantial bier

(Figure 40). He lifted and took her in his arms after 'This vault a feasting presence, full of light' (86) and laid her down on 'A dateless bargain to engrossing Death' (115) before taking his poison. As he embraced Juliet her arm moved, unnoticed by him, 'as if to return his embrace' – a gesture recalling that of Francesca Annis in 1976 (*Times*). Romeo's death was rapid and agonizing. He lay on top of Juliet to take his kiss, then rolled off downstage of her but still on the bier. The usual cut removed the Friar's exchange with Balthasar, and the Friar did not propose to place Juliet in a 'sisterhood' (156–7). The sequence was simplifed to 'Come, come away. Come, go, good Juliet, I dare no longer stay.' The hovering high soprano plainchant was heard again as Juliet insisted 'let me die' (169) and torchbearers came in quickly after she expired. Capulet's wife knelt at the head of the bier, and after an abbreviated version of the Friar's speech and reactions to it, the Prince stood downstage of the bier with Capulet and Montague on either side of him as they shook hands. 'Go hence to have more talk of these sad things' (306) was addressed to them, rather than to the assembled company or the world at large. As with so many elements of David Leveaux's staging, this was perceptive in detail and eloquent in musical and pictorial gesture – but the stately pace, the lateness of the hour, and the general dissatisfaction with the lovers themselves deprived it of its power.

Adrian Noble (1995) took the unusual step of allowing his Romeo to threaten Balthasar, but Zubin Varla softened the tone with the more conciliatory 'So shalt thou show me friendship' after his man's understandable haste in assuring him 'I will be gone sir, and not trouble ye' (40–1). After his fight with the well-lit but once again inexplicably unrecognized Paris, Romeo proceeded to Juliet's bed-like bier. After taking the poison he fell at the side of it, and Juliet woke to find his head on her lap. In the concluding moments Capulet and Montague clasped hands across the dead bodies, music crept in under the first words of the final speech, and all on stage looked out towards the audience as a slow fade to black seemed to confirm the sun's reluctance to shine.

In 2000 Boyd was accused of 'robbing the last act of its torch-lit sense of sanctuary' (*Mail Sun.*). 'Plague seep[ed] through the final scenes' (*D. Mail*) but not in any picturesque way: the cast wore surgical masks when they came to the graveyard, as if fearful of its health hazards. Juliet was not discovered on stage at the beginning, but was uncovered when Romeo prised open the 'grave' trap that had served earlier as Friar Laurence's herb garden. Unceremoniously he hauled her halfway out of it to take his last embrace – Lyn Gardner remarked that 'the lovers lug[ged] each other around like sacks of potatoes' (*Guardian*). The Romeo, David Tennant, felt that his final speech had 'a strong sense of someone who has come home' and certainly invested it with this, in contrast to the more extravert grief of such performances as McKellen's or Maloney's (Tennant). Boyd switched effectively from realistic to symbolic action: the dying Juliet descended into the grave, taking Romeo with her, and the covering was closed. It was opened again when the Prince arrived. The Friar was kept under close guard to one side of the stage, and the Prince's 'We still have known thee for a holy man' (269) was delivered without warmth after the twenty lines of his shortened explanation. Laurence then began a 'long, slow walk' offstage (*Time Out*), down the gangway into the audience. As the Montagues and Capulets began their gestures of reconciliation and the aged, crippled Prince tried to sum up the case, Romeo and Juliet rose from the grave. As Capulet spoke of them as 'Poor sacrifices of our enmity' (303) they walked off the stage and down the gangway while the final lines of the play were being spoken (Figure 44).

In an article occasioned by Franco Zeffirelli's 1960 Old Vic production, John Russell Brown argued persuasively for the integrity and importance of the last scene. Zeffirelli had made radical cuts in the whole of the play's final movement (his screen version followed the same pattern) and had pushed forward to the finale without allowing the Friar's explanations to be heard (Brown, 151). Most of the productions discussed above have preserved a good deal of the Friar's long speech at 228–68, albeit

FIGURE 44 Romeo (David Tennant) and Juliet (Alexandra Gilbreath) have risen from their grave and peer into it before leaving the stage down the ramp through the auditorium in Michael Boyd's 2000 production. (5.3)

with generous cuts in the speeches that follow. Even in a truncated version, this rehearsal of what the audience already knows allows a production to show most of those on stage beginning to grasp what has caused the catastrophe they are involved in. Of the productions that cut the scene most radically, Brook's seems to have been more hasty than impressive, whereas Bogdanov's was working towards a commentary on the play's events other than that explicitly provided in the original text. Boyd's, in 2000, created an especially strong sense of the ineffectiveness of virtue in the face of a cruel world governed by an arbitrary Fate. The 'caustic chorus' and the persistent ghosts of the slain presided over a catastrophe that left the Friar unpunished but without consolation – and from which the lovers simply departed through the audience. In any case, the final lines of the play promise 'more talk of these sad things' (306) and postpone the dispensation of pardon and punishment. In Stratford the script's concluding *Exeunt* has usually been replaced by a slow fade to blackout, as it was even by Hands at the Swan (1989), on whose platform stage a general *Exeunt* without a fadeout might have been managed. Ending with a rhyme on the lovers' names, as all but Bogdanov's production have done, the play returns to them as representative figures, and to a sense that the dawn is bringing at least some kind of peace however 'glooming' it may be. Boyd's production undercut even this. As David Tennant, Stratford's first Romeo of the twenty-first century – or last of the twentieth – observed: 'The real tragedy is left for those who have to rebuild this ruined society. One suspects that their problems are bigger than a couple of gold statues can mend'.

PRODUCTION CREDITS AND CAST LISTS

Programmes supply production credits and cast lists; in every case the listing is that announced for the first performance. They reveal how by the end of the 1970s the lavish cast numbers of earlier years had been halved. Characters are listed in the order given by the Arden edition of the play (p. 80). Variations in spelling (e.g. Abram/ Abraham) have not been noted, but some programmes list characters not included by Arden ('Ladies', 'Women', 'Page to Mercutio', etc.) and some famous 'ghosts' (notably Rosaline and 'the lively Helena'). Watchmen and musicians have been listed collectively in the order given in the programme. The number of theatre band musicians is given, where they were listed as distinct from the named characters (e.g. 'James Soundpost') played by actors. 'Prince' here replaces 'Escalus', the name that appears only in the stage direction for his first entrance but has often been adopted in cast lists. In cases where children appear, either in a list or with alternative names divided by a slash (e.g. the Pages), only half of the number or one of a pair would have appeared at any one performance. The date given is that of the press night in Stratford, rather than the first performance: from the 1960s some late dress rehearsals became 'club performances', and preview performances available to the general public became customary in the 1970s. 'Transfer' notes performances at the Barbican and elsewhere, including tour venues. Unless otherwise stated, all productions were staged at the Royal Shakespeare Theatre (known until 1960 as the Shakespeare Memorial Theatre).

1947

Director	Peter Brook
Designer	Rolf Gérard
Music	Roberto Gherard
Lighting	Mark Pritchard
Duelling	Rex Rickman and Patrick Crean

PRINCE	Robert Harris
MERCUTIO	Paul Scofield
PARIS	Donald Sinden
MONTAGUE	Michael Golden
LADY MONTAGUE	Gwen Williams
ROMEO	Laurence Payne
BENVOLIO	John Harrison
ABRAM	George Cooper
BALTHASAR	William Avenell
CAPULET	Walter Hudd
LADY CAPULET	Muriel Davidson
JULIET	Daphne Slater
TYBALT	Myles Eason
UNCLE TO CAPULET	Douglas Seale
NURSE	Beatrix Lehmann
PETER	Leigh Crutchley
SAMPSON	William March
GREGORY	Anthony Groser
FRIAR LAURENCE	John Ruddock
FRIAR JOHN	John Blatchley
APOTHECARY	Douglas Seale
CHORUS	John Harrison

CITIZENS, MASKERS, GUARDS, WATCHMEN AND GUESTS:
Joss Ackland, Julian Amyes, Helen Burns, Margaret Courtenay, Anne Daniels, Elizabeth Ewbank, Sol Glabman, Margaret Godwin, David Hobman, Maxwell Jackson, Lois Johnson, Pamela Leatherland, Keith Lloyd, Joanna Mackie, Diana Mahony, David Oxley, Lennard Pearce, John Randall, Richard Renny, Herbert Roland, Duncan Ross, Irene Sutcliffe, John Warner, Beryl Wright, Kenneth Wynne

Number in company	45
Press night	5 April 1947
Transfer	London, Haymarket

1954

Director	Glen Byam Shaw
Designer	Motley
Music	Antony Hopkins
Lighting	Peter Streuli
Fights	Bernard Hepton and John Greenwood
Dance	Pauline Grant

PRINCE	Raymond Westwell
MERCUTIO	Tony Britton
PAGE TO MERCUTIO	Raymond Sherry
PARIS	Donald Pickering
PAGE TO PARIS	Ian Holm
MONTAGUE	Philip Morant
LADY MONTAGUE	Joan MacArthur
ROMEO	Laurence Harvey
BENVOLIO	Powys Thomas
ABRAM	John Turner
BALTHASAR	Jerome Willis
CAPULET	William Devlin
LADY CAPULET	Jean Wilson
JULIET	Zena Walker
TYBALT	Keith Michell
TYBALT'S PAGE	David O'Brien
CAPULET'S COUSIN	Ian Mullins
NURSE	Rosalind Atkinson
PETER	Geoffrey Bayldon
SAMPSON	Mervyn Blake
GREGORY	Bernard Kay
ANTHONY	Ian Bannen
POTPAN	David King
OLD MAN (SERVINGMAN)	George Hart
FRIAR LAURENCE	Leo McKern
FRIAR JOHN	Edward Atienza
APOTHECARY	Peter Duguid
WATCH	Edward Atienza
CHORUS	James Grout

CITIZENS OF VERONA AND MANTUA, KINSFOLK OF BOTH
HOUSES, GUARDS, WATCHMEN, MUSICIANS AND SERVANTS:
Geoffrey Adams, Philip Anthony, Annette Apcar, Jan Bashford, Jill
Cary, Richard Coe, Beverley Cross, Ron Haddrick, Jane Holland, Kevin
Miles, Jean Morley, Timothy Parkes, Audrey Seed, James Villiers, Frank
Waters

Number in company   43
Press night   27 April 1954

1958

Director	Glen Byam Shaw
Designer	Motley
Music	Leslie Bridgewater
Fights	Bernard Hepton
Dances	Pauline Grant

PRINCE	Anthony Nicholls
MERCUTIO	Edward Woodward
PAGE TO MERCUTIO	John Davidson
PARIS	Michael Meacham
PAGE TO PARIS	Roy Spencer
MONTAGUE	Donald Layne-Smith
LADY MONTAGUE	Stephanie Bidmead
ROMEO	Richard Johnson
BENVOLIO	Paul Hardwick
ABRAM	Thane Bettany
BALTHASAR	Kenneth Gilbert
CAPULET	Mark Dignam
LADY CAPULET	Rachel Kempson
JULIET	Dorothy Tutin
TYBALT	Ron Haddrick
TYBALT'S PAGE	Gordon Souter
CAPULET'S COUSIN	Donald Eccles
NURSE	Angela Baddeley
PETER	Ian Holm
SAMPSON	Peter Palmer
GREGORY	Julian Glover
ANTHONY	Edward de Souza
POTPAN	John Grayson
FRIAR LAURENCE	Cyril Luckam
FRIAR JOHN	Edward de Souza
APOTHECARY	Donald Eccles
WATCHMEN	Antony Brown, John Salway
PRINCE'S GUARDS	Roger Bizeley, Roy Dotrice, Paxton Whitehead
CHORUS	Anthony Nicholls

CITIZENS OF VERONA AND MANTUA, GUESTS, MUSICIANS,
SERVANTS AND WATCHMEN:
Peter Anderson, Eileen Atkins, Zoë Caldwell, Miranda Connell, Mavis
Edwards, William Elmhirst, Pamela Taylor, Stephen Thorne

Number in company	37
Press night	8 April 1958
Tour	Leningrad/Moscow, December 1958–January 1959

1961

Director	Peter Hall
Settings	Sean Kenny
Costumes	Desmond Heeley
Music	Raymond Leppard
Lighting	John Wyckham
Fights	John Barton
Dances	Pauline Grant

PRINCE	Tony Church
MERCUTIO	Ian Bannen
PAGE TO MERCUTIO	Michael Stephens
PARIS	Barry Warren
PAGE TO PARIS	Bruce McKenzie
MONTAGUE	Michael Murray
LADY MONTAGUE	Edith Macarthur
ROMEO	Brian Murray
BENVOLIO	James Kerry
ABRAM	Peter Holmes
BALTHASAR	Terry Wale
CAPULET	Newton Blick
LADY CAPULET	Cherry Morris
JULIET	Dorothy Tutin
TYBALT	Peter McEnery
PAGE TO TYBALT	Barry Stockwell
CAPULET'S COUSIN	Ronald Scott-David
NURSE	Edith Evans
PETER	Russell Hunter
SAMPSON	Sebastian Breaks
GREGORY	Richard Barr
POTPAN	William Wallis
FRIAR LAURENCE	Max Adrian
FRIAR JOHN	Michael Warchus
APOTHECARY	Gordon Gostelow
WATCHMEN	Julian Battersby, Brian Wright
CHORUS	Tony Church

CITIZENS OF VERONA AND MANTUA, GUESTS, MUSICIANS,
OFFICERS AND SERVANTS:
Paul Bailey, Adrian Blount, Rosalind Knight, Narissa Knights, Bruce
McKenzie, Ronald Scott-Dodd, Michael Warchus, Georgina Ward,
Brian Wright

Number in company   33
Press night   15 August 1961

1967

Director	Karolos Koun
Designer	Timothy O'Brien
Assistant to designer	Tazenna Firth
Music	Guy Woolfenden
Lighting	David Read
Fights	John Barton
Dances	Pauline Grant
PRINCE	Jeffery Dench
MERCUTIO	Norman Rodway
PARIS	John Bell
PAGE TO PARIS	Alton Kumalo
MONTAGUE	Hector Ross
LADY MONTAGUE	Clare Kelly
ROMEO	Ian Holm
BENVOLIO	David Weston
ABRAM	Mike Billington
BALTHASAR	Ray Callaghan
CAPULET	Nicholas Selby
LADY CAPULET	Sheila Allen
JULIET	Estelle Kohler
TYBALT	Ian Hogg
CAPULET'S COUSIN	Terence Greenidge
NURSE	Elizabeth Spriggs
PETER	Richard Moore
SAMPSON	Philip Hinton
GREGORY	Peter Gordon
ANTHONY	David Kincaid
POTPAN	Oscar James
CLOWN	Bruce Myers
FRIAR LAURENCE	Sebastian Shaw
FRIAR JOHN	Peter Rocca
APOTHECARY	William Eedle
MUSICIANS	Dallas Adams, Louis Mahoney, Colin McCormack

WATCHMEN   David Ashford, Robert Davis,
                           Chris Malcolm
CHORUS   Michael Jayston

TOWNSPEOPLE, DANCERS AND ATTENDANTS:
Christopher Bond, Ann Constant, Amaryllis Garnett, Don Henderson,
Patricia Hope, Roger Lloyd Pack, Edward Lyon, Gerald McNally, Helen
Mirren, Lynn Moore, Matthew O'Sullivan, Matthew Robertson,
Katherine Stark, Ted Valentine, James Vallon, Anna Volska, Richard
Williams

Number in company   49
Press night   13 September 1967

1973

Director	Terry Hands
Assistant to the director	Barry Kyle
Designer	Farrah
Music	Ian Kellam
Lighting	John Bradley
Fights	B.H. Barry
Choreography	John Broome

PRINCE	Clement McCallin
MERCUTIO	Bernard Lloyd
PARIS	Anthony Pedley
PAGE TO PARIS	Colin Mayes
MONTAGUE	Richard Mayes
LADY MONTAGUE	Janet Whiteside
ROMEO	Timothy Dalton
BENVOLIO	Peter Machin
PAGE TO BENVOLIO	John Abbott
ABRAM	Lloyd McGuire
BALTHASAR	Nikolas Grace
CAPULET	Jeffery Dench
LADY CAPULET	Brenda Bruce
JULIET	Estelle Kohler
TYBALT	David Suchet
CAPULET'S COUSIN	Denis Holmes
NURSE	Beatrix Lehmann
PETER	Brian Glover
SAMPSON	Gavin Campbell
GREGORY	Colin Mayes
FRIAR LAURENCE	Tony Church
FRIAR JOHN	John Abbott
ROSALINE	Janet Chappell
APOTHECARY	Ray Armstrong
CITIZENS	Ray Armstrong, Michael Ensign
MUSICIANS	John Abbott, Ray Armstrong, Michael Ensign

WOMEN   Annette Badland, Janet Chappell,
Louise Jameson

CHORUS   Clement McCallin

Nine musicians

Number in company   25

Press night   28 March 1973

1976

Director	Trevor Nunn with Barry Kyle
Assistant director	Anna Raphael
Designer	Chris Dyer
Permanent stage for the season designed by	John Napier with Chris Dyer
Music	Stephen Oliver
Lighting	Clive Morris
Fights	Robert Anderson with Peter Woodward
Dances	Laverne Meyer

PRINCE	Griffith Jones
MERCUTIO	Michael Pennington
PARIS	Richard Durden
PAGE TO PARIS	Paul Whitworth
MONTAGUE	Ian Beavis
LADY MONTAGUE	Judith Harte
ROMEO	Ian McKellen
BENVOLIO	Roger Rees
ABRAM	Duncan Preston
BALTHASAR	Greg Hicks
PAGE (CAPULET)	Peter Woodward
CAPULET	John Woodvine
LADY CAPULET	Barbara Shelley
JULIET	Francesca Annis
TYBALT	Paul Shelley
CAPULET'S COUSIN	Norman Tyrrell
NURSE	Marie Kean
PETER	Richard Griffiths
SAMPSON	David Howey
GREGORY	Leonard Preston
FRIAR LAURENCE	David Waller
FRIAR JOHN	Dennis Clinton
APOTHECARY	Clyde Pollitt
MUSICIANS	David Howey, Keith Taylor, Jacob Witkin
WATCHMEN	Brian Coburn, Jacob Witkin

LADIES	Lea Dregorn, Susan Dury, Pippa Guard, Judith Harte
CHORUS	John Bown

CITIZENS AND SERVANTS:
Dennis Clinton, Brian Coburn, Clyde Pollitt, Leonard Preston, Keith Taylor, Jacob Witkin

Nine musicians

Number in company	30
Press night	29 March 1976
Transfer	Newcastle, Theatre Royal, 15 March 1977
	London, Aldwych Theatre, 5 July 1977

1980

Director	Ron Daniels
Designer	Ralph Koltai
Costumes	Nadine Baylis
Music	Stephen Oliver
Lighting	Mark Pritchard
Fights	Peter Woodward
Choreography	David Toguri

PRINCE/CHORUS	Bruce Purchase
MERCUTIO	Jonathan Hyde
PARIS	Peter Settelen
PAGE TO PARIS	Stuart Lyell/Richard Porter
MONTAGUE	Shay Gorman
LADY MONTAGUE	Eve Pearce
ROMEO	Anton Lesser
BENVOLIO	Allan Hendrick
ABRAM	Michael Siberry
BALTHASAR	Killan McKenna
CAPULET	Trevor Baxter
LADY CAPULET	Barbara Kinghorn
JULIET	Judy Buxton
TYBALT	Chris Hunter
CAPULET'S COUSIN	Dennis Clinton
NURSE	Brenda Bruce
PETER	Jimmy Gardner
SAMPSON	Sion Tudor-Owen
GREGORY	Ned Vukovic
FRIAR LAURENCE	Edwin Richfield
FRIAR JOHN	Brett Usher
APOTHECARY	Jimmy Gardner
SIMON CATLING	Ned Vukovic
HUGH REBECK	Brett Usher
JAMES SOUNDPOST	Philip Dennis
WATCHMEN	William Armstrong, Dennis Clinton, Brett Usher
LADIES	Jo Anderson, Sara Moore, Julia Tobin

YOUNG PETRUCHIO   William Armstrong
SON OF OLD TIBERIO   Timothy Walker

Eight musicians

Number in company   28
Press night   16 April 1980
Transfer   Newcastle, Theatre Royal,
                   23 February 1981
                   London, Aldwych Theatre,
                   9 October 1981

1984

Director	John Caird
Designer	Bob Crowley
Costumes	Priscilla Truett
Music and sound tape	Ilona Sekacz
Lighting	Brian Harris
Movement	Geraldine Stephenson
Fights	Malcolm Ranson
PRINCE	Martin Jacobs
MERCUTIO	Roger Allam
PARIS	Steven Pinner
PAGE	Jeremy Sullivan
MONTAGUE	Donald McKillop
LADY MONTAGUE	Liz Moscrop
ROMEO	Simon Templeman
BENVOLIO	James Simmons
BALTHASAR	Jimmy Yuill
CAPULET	George Raistrick
LADY CAPULET	Penny Downie
JULIET	Amanda Root
TYBALT	Andrew Hall
NURSE	Polly James
PETER	Charles Milham
GREGORY	Hepburn Graham
LADY	Alison Rose
FRIAR LAURENCE	Frank Middlemass
FRIAR JOHN	Guy Fithen
APOTHECARY	Roger Allam
[CHORUS	Martin Jacobs]

Other parts played by members of the company

Number in company	19
Stratford venue	The Other Place
Press night	1 May 1984
Tour	National, from 10 October 1983
Transfer	Newcastle, Gulbenkian Theatre, 25 February 1985

1986

Director	Michael Bogdanov
Assistant Director	Jude Kelly
Designer	Chris Dyer
Costumes	Chris Dyer and Ginny Humphreys
Music	Hiroshi Sato
Lighting	Chris Ellis
Fights	Malcolm Ranson
Choreography	Kenn Oldfield
PRINCE	David Glover
PRINCE'S AIDE	Stan Pretty
MERCUTIO	Michael Kitchen
PARIS	Robert Morgan
MONTAGUE	Roger Watkins
LADY MONTAGUE	Eileen Page
ROMEO	Sean Bean
BENVOLIO	Martin Jacobs
ABRAM	Malcolm Hassall
BALTHASAR	Philip Sully
LADIES (MONTAGUE)	Jenni George, Cornelia Hayes
CAPULET	Richard Moore
LADY CAPULET	Anna Nygh
JULIET	Niamh Cusack
TYBALT	Hugh Quarshie
CAPULET'S COUSIN	Dennis Edwards
NURSE	Dilys Laye
PETER	Donald McBride
SAMPSON	John Patrick
GREGORY	Sean O'Callaghan
LADIES (CAPULET)	Lucy Hancock, Caroline Johnson
FRIAR LAURENCE	Robert Demeger
FRIAR JOHN	Stanley Dawson
APOTHECARY	Brian Lawson
POLICEMEN	Stanley Dawson, Patrick Robinson

CHILDREN:
Timothy Luckett, Paul McGrevvey, Simon Townsend, Daniel Wadhams

Other parts played by members of the company
'Rock group' of five and 'Carnival band' of nine musicians

Number in company	27 (plus 4 children)
Press night	8 April 1986
Transfer	Newcastle, Tyne Theatre,
	17 February 1987
	London, Barbican, 14 April 1987
Video recording	29 October 1986

1989

Director	Terry Hands
Designer	Farrah
Music/music director	Claire van Kampen
Lighting	Mark Pritchard
Fights	Malcolm Ranson
Dances	Anthony van Laast

PRINCE	Rob Heyland
MERCUTIO	David O'Hara
PARIS	Michael Howell
PAGE TO PARIS	Richard Doubleday
MONTAGUE	Michael Loughnan
LADY MONTAGUE	Katherine Stark
ROMEO	Mark Rylance
BENVOLIO	Patrick Brennan
ABRAM	Ben Miles
BALTHASAR	William Oxborrow
CAPULET	Bernard Horsfall
LADY CAPULET	Linda Spurrier
JULIET	Georgia Slowe
TYBALT	Vincent Regan
CAPULET'S COUSIN	Griffith Jones
NURSE	Margaret Courtenay
PETER	Evan Russell
SAMPSON	Francis Johnson
GREGORY	Jared Harris
FRIAR LAURENCE	Patrick Godfrey
FRIAR JOHN	Ben Miles
APOTHECARY	Griffith Jones
LADIES	Jennie Heslewood, Hilary Tones
WATCH	Peter Carr
CHORUS	Rob Heyland

SERVANTS, GUESTS, CITIZENS OF VERONA AND MUSICIANS:
Members of the company

Four musicians, including Claire van Kampen

Number in company	23
Stratford venue	Swan Theatre
Press night	5 April 1989
Tour	RSC/British Telecom tour,
	12 September 1989 to 11 January 1990
Transfer	London, Barbican (The Pit),
	4 January 1990
Video recording	14 April 1989

1991

Director	David Leveaux
Designer	Alison Chitty
Design assistant	Rob Howell
Music	Ilona Sekacz
Lighting	Jean Kalman
Sound	Paul Slocombe
Fight director	Malcolm Ranson
Movement director	Sue Lefton

PRINCE	Julian Glover
MERCUTIO	Tim McInnerny
PARIS	Valentine Pelka
PAGE TO PARIS	Simon Blinkhorne/Lee Broom
MONTAGUE	Randal Herley
LADY MONTAGUE	Jan Shand
ROMEO	Michael Maloney
BENVOLIO	Kevin Doyle
ABRAM	Andrew Dumbleton
BALTHASAR	Charles Daish
CAPULET	Jonathan Newth
LADY CAPULET	Celia Gregory
JULIET	Claire Holman
TYBALT	Sean Murray
CAPULET'S COUSIN	Michael Poole
NURSE	Sheila Reid
PETER	Scott Ransome
SAMPSON	Ken Sabberton
GREGORY	Simeon Defoe
SERVINGMAN	Howard Crossley
FRIAR LAURENCE	Robert Langdon Lloyd
FRIAR JOHN	Peter Bygott
APOTHECARY	Anthony Douse
CHORUS	Julian Glover

SERVANTS, CITIZENS AND WATCH:
Peter Bygott, Mairead Carty, Hilary Cromie, Simeon Defoe, Emily Joyce, Ken Sabberton, Lucy Tregear

CHILDREN:

Liam Askins, Gavriely Gavriel, Matthew Reeve/Thomas Horton

Five musicians, plus the six Stephen Hill singers

Number in company	28 (plus 4 children)
Press night	8 April 1991
Transfer	Newcastle, Theatre Royal,
	3 March 1992
	London, Barbican, 24 June 1992
Video recording	18 January 1992

1995

Director	Adrian Noble
Designer	Kendra Ullyart
Costumes	Nadine Baylis
Original music	Shaun Davey
Lighting	Hugh Vanstone
Fights	Terry King
Movement	Sue Lefton
PRINCE	Christopher Robbie
MERCUTIO	Mark Lockyer
PARIS	Paul Bettany
PAGE TO PARIS	Ralph Birtwell
MONTAGUE	Jeffery Dench
LADY MONTAGUE	Anita Wright
ROMEO	Zubin Varla
BENVOLIO	Michael Gould
BALTHASAR	Godfrey Walters
CAPULET	Christopher Benjamin
LADY CAPULET	Darlene Johnson
JULIET	Lucy Whybrow
TYBALT	Dermot Kerrigan
CAPULET'S COUSIN	Christopher Robbie
NURSE	Susan Brown
PETER	Gary Taylor
SAMPSON	Justin Shevlin
GREGORY	Paul Hilton
FRIAR LAURENCE	Julian Glover
FRIAR JOHN	Gary Taylor
APOTHECARY	Jeffery Dench
ROSALINE	Lisé Stephenson
LADIES	Joanna Hole, Rachel Sanders
WATCH	Christopher Tune
WAITER	Ralph Birtwell
CHORUS	Christopher Robbie

CHILDREN:

Lolly Austen, Alexander Bennison, Francesca Bradley, Benjamin Hunt, Ferdinand Kingsley, Emilie-Jane Lecocq, Emily Organ, Sam Whybrow

Ten musicians

Number in company	22 (plus 8 children)
Press night	5 April 1995
Transfer	Newcastle, Theatre Royal, 1 March 1996
	London, Barbican, 23 April 1996
Video recording	27 April 1995

1997

Director	Michael Attenborough
Designer	Robert Jones
Music	Stephen Warbeck
Lighting	Tim Mitchell
Fights	Terry King
Movement	Terry John Bates

PRINCE	Neil Philips
MERCUTIO	Chook Sibtain
PARIS	Oliver Fox
MONTAGUE	Louis Mahoney
MONTAGUE'S WIFE [*sic*]	Sandra Clarke
ROMEO	Ray Fearon
BENVOLIO	Lawrence Wood
ABRAM	Jack Tanner
CAPULET	David Lyon
CAPULET'S WIFE [*sic*]	Jan Chappell
JULIET	Zoë Waites
TYBALT	Nigel Caluzel
NURSE	Sandra Voe
PETER	Russell Layton
SAMPSON	Russell Layton
GREGORY	Oliver Fox
HELENA	Amanda Perry-Smith
LIVIA	Jo Keating
FRIAR LAURENCE	Richard Cordery
FRIAR JOHN	Louis Mahoney
CHORUS	Neil Philips

Other parts played by members of the company
Four musicians, including Neil Philips

Number in company	17
Stratford venue	Swan Theatre
Press night (Stratford)	18 November 1997
Transfer	London, Barbican (The Pit), 5 November 1997
Tour	National and international, February–July 1998

2000

Director	Michael Boyd
Designer	Tom Piper
Music	Stephen Warbeck
Lighting	Chris Davey
Fights	Terry King
Movement director	Liz Ranken
Sound	Mic Pool

PRINCE	Alfred Burke
MERCUTIO	Adrian Schiller
PARIS	Nicholas Khan
PAGE TO PARIS	Claire Adamson
MONTAGUE	Vincent Brimble
LADY MONTAGUE	Helen Weir
ROMEO	David Tennant
BENVOLIO	Anthony Howell
ABRAM	Jalaal Hartley
BALTHASAR	Christian Mahrle
CAPULET	Ian Hogg
LADY CAPULET	Caroline Harris
JULIET	Alexandra Gilbreath
TYBALT	Keith Dunphy
CAPULET'S COUSIN	Sam Cox
NURSE	Eileen McCallum
PETER	Robert Goodale
SAMPSON	Tim Treloar
GREGORY	Andrew Pointon
POTPAN	Paul Ewing
FRIAR LAURENCE	Des McAleer
APOTHECARY	Sam Cox
PRINCE'S GUARD	Sam Cox, Graeme Mearns
CHORUS	Sam Cox, Paul Ewing, Andrew Pointon, Tim Treloar

(CHORUS in Prologue to Act 1 spoken by Romeo)

GUARDS AND TOWNSPEOPLE:
Citizens of Stratford-upon-Avon (indicated in programme, but not included in performance)

Nine musicians

Number in company	22
Press night	5 July 2000
Transfer	Newcastle, Theatre Royal, 14 November 2000 London, Barbican, 17 January 2001
Video recording	7 October 2000

REVIEWS CITED

1947

Birmingham Post, 7 April 1947, T.C. K[emp]
Birmingham Post, 7 October 1947
Coventry Evening Telegraph, 5 April 1947
Daily Herald, 7 April 1947
Daily Mail, 7 April 1947, Lionel Hale
Daily Telegraph, 7 April 1947, W.A. Darlington
Daily Worker, 8 April 1947
Evening Standard, 14 April 1947, Beverley Baxter
Irish Times, 7 April 1947
Manchester Guardian, 7 April 1947, G.P.
News Chronicle, 11 April 1947, Alan Dent
Observer, 13 April 1947, Ivor Brown
Stage, 10 April 1947
Sunday Express, 6 April 1947, Stephen Watts
Sunday Mercury (Birmingham), 6 April 1947, W.H. Bush
Sunday Times, 6 April 1947, H[arold] H[obson]
Time and Tide, 12 April 1947
Times, 7 April 1947

1954

Bristol Evening Post, 29 April 1954
Daily Express, 28 April 1954, John Barber
Daily Herald, 28 April 1954
Daily Mail, 28 April 1954, Cecil Wilson
Daily Mirror, 28 April 1954, Eve Chapman
Daily Sketch, 28 April 1954, Harold Conway
Daily Telegraph, 28 April 1954, Patrick Gibbs
Daily Worker, 28 April 1954, Donald Douglas

Evening News, 28 April 1954, Stephen Williams
Financial Times, 28 April 1954, Derek Granger
Leamington Spa Courier, 30 April 1954, N.T.
Liverpool Daily Post, 29 April 1954
Liverpool Post, 28 April 1954
New Statesman and Nation, 15 May 1954, T.C. Worsley
News Chronicle, 28 April 1954, Alan Dent
Observer, 2 May 1954, Ivor Brown
Solihull and Warwick County News, 1 May 1954, Janet Latimer
South Wales Argus, 28 April 1954, Beatrice Worthing
Stage, 29 April 1954
Stratford-upon-Avon Herald, 30 April 1954, Ruth Elllis
Sunday Times, 2 May 1954, Harold Hobson
Times, 28 April 1954

1958

Daily Herald, 9 April 1958
Daily Mail, 9 April 1958, Cecil Wilson
Daily Telegraph, 9 April 1958, W.A. Darlington
Education, 23 April 1958
Evening News, 9 April 1958, Felix Barker
Manchester Guardian, 9 April 1958, Philip Hope-Wallace
News Chronicle, 9 April 1958, Alan Dent
Observer, 13 April 1958, Kenneth Tynan
Stage, 10 April 1958, R.B. M[arriott]
Stratford-upon-Avon Herald, 11 April 1958, Rosemary Anne Sisson
Sunday Times, 13 April 1958, Harold Hobson
Times, 9 April 1958

1961

Birmingham Mail, 16 August 1961, W.H.W.
Birmingham Post, 16 August 1961, J.C. Trewin
Bristol Evening Post, 19 August 1961
Daily Express, 16 August 1961, Bernard Levin
Daily Mail, 16 August 1961, Robert Muller
Daily Telegraph, 16 August 1961, W.A. Darlington
Evening News, 16 August 1961, Felix Barker

Evening Standard, 16 August 1961, Milton Shulman
Evesham Journal, 18 August 1961, J.H.B.
Financial Times, 16 August 1961, T.C. Worsley
Gloucester Echo, 16 August 1961, D.M.
Leamington Spa Courier, 18 August 1961, N.T.
Manchester Guardian, 18 August 1961, Philip Hope-Wallace
Observer, 20 August 1961, Kenneth Tynan
Oxford Mail, 16 August 1961, Don Chapman
Punch, 23 August 1961, Eric Keown
Solihull and Warwick County News, 19 August 1961
South Wales Evening Argus, 16 August 1961, Ken Griffin
Spectator, 18 August 1961, Bamber Gascoigne
Stage, 19 August 1961, Eric Johns
Stratford-upon-Avon Herald, 18 August 1958, Edmund Gardiner
Sunday Telegraph, 20 August 1961, Alan Brien
Sunday Times, 20 August 1961, Harold Hobson
Times, 16 August 1961
Western Independent (Plymouth), 20 August 1961, 'Prompter'

1967

Birmingham Post, 14 September 1967, Keith Brace
Daily Mail, 14 September 1967, Peter Lewis
Evening Standard, 14 September 1967, Milton Shulman
Financial Times, 14 September 1967, B.A. Young
Guardian, 14 September 1967, Gareth Lloyd Evans
Leamington Spa Courier, 15 September 1967, F.M.A.
New Statesman, 22 September 1967, Philip French
Plays and Players, November 1967, Peter Roberts
Punch, 19 September 1967, Jeremy Kingston
Spectator, 22 September 1967, Hilary Spurling
Sunday Telegraph, 17 September 1967, Alan Brien
Sunday Times, 17 September 1967, Harold Hobson
Times, 14 September 1967, Irving Wardle

1973

Evening Standard, 29 March 1973, Milton Shulman
Financial Times, 29 March 1973, B.A. Young

Guardian, 29 March 1973, Michael Billington
New Statesman, 6 April 1973, Benedict Nightingale
Plays and Players, April 1973, Robert Cushman
Punch, 4 April 1973, Jeremy Kingston
Sunday Mercury, 1 April 1973
Sunday Telegraph, 1 April 1973, Frank Marcus
Sunday Times, 1 April 1973, Harold Hobson
Times, 29 March 1973, Irving Wardle

1976

Birmingham Post, 2 April 1976, J.C. Trewin
Coventry Evening Telegraph, 2 April 1976, David Isaacs
Financial Times, 2 April 1976, B.A. Young
Guardian, 3 April 1976, Michael Billington
Observer, 4 April 1976, Robert Cushman
Stage, 9 April 1976, R.B. Marriott
Stratford-upon-Avon Herald, 9 April 1976, Gareth Lloyd Evans
Sunday Times, 4 April 1976, Harold Hobson
Times, 5 April 1976, Irving Wardle

1980

Birmingham Post, 10 May 1980, J.C. Trewin
Cahiers Elisabéthains, 18 (October 1980), 105–6, Jean Fuzier and
    Jean-Marie Mayuin
Coventry Evening Telegraph, 24 April 1980, Peter McGarry
Evening News, 24 April 1980, Felix Barker
Financial Times, 25 April 1980, B.A. Young
Guardian, 24 April 1980, Michael Billington
Observer, 27 April 1980, Robert Cushman
Stratford-upon-Avon Herald, 16 May 1980, Gareth Lloyd Evans
Sunday Telegraph, 27 April 1980, Francis King
Sunday Times, 27 April 1980, James Fenton
Times, 24 April 1980, Irving Wardle

1984

Birmingham Post, 2 May 1984, Richard Edmonds
Cahiers Elisabéthains, 26 (October 1984), 120–3, Jean Fuzier

Guardian, 3 May 1984, Nicholas de Jongh
Sunday Times, 6 May 1984, John Peter

1986

Birmingham Post, 9 April 1986, J.C. Trewin
Bristol Evening Post, 9 April 1986
Daily Telegraph, 10 April 1986, John Barber
Financial Times, 9 April 1986, Martin Hoyle
Guardian, 10 April 1986, Michael Billington
New Statesman, 18 April 1986, Benedict Nightingale
Observer, 13 April 1986, Michael Ratcliffe
Observer Colour Supplement, 6 April 1986
Punch, 16 April 1986, Sheridan Morley
Sunday Times, 13 April 1986, John Peter
Times, 10 April 1986, Irving Wardle
Times Educational Supplement, 18 April 1986, Nicholas Shrimpton
Times Literary Supplement, 25 April 1986, Stanley Wells

1989

Daily Mail, 6 April 1989, Jack Tinker
Daily Telegraph, 7 April 1989, Charles Osborne
Evesham Journal, 13 April 1989
Financial Times, 7 April 1989, Michael Coveney
Guardian, 7 April 1989, Michael Billington
Independent, 7 April 1989, Paul Taylor
Listener, 27 April 1989, Jim Hiley
Observer, 9 April 1989, Michael Ratcliffe
Sunday Telegraph, 9 April 1989, John Gross
Sunday Times, 9 April 1989, John Peter
Time Out, 12 April 1989, Paul Arnott
Times, 7 April 1989, Irving Wardle

1991

Cahiers Elisabéthains, 41 (April 1992), 56–8, P.J.S.
Daily Telegraph, 30 August 1991, Charles Spencer
Guardian, 30 April 1991, Michael Billington

Independent, 30 August 1991, Paul Taylor
Observer, 1 September 1991, Michael Coveney
Shakespeare Quarterly, 43 (1992), 341–56, Robert Smallwood
Stratford-upon-Avon Herald, 6 September 1991, Paul Lapworth
Times, 19 August 1991, Benedict Nightingale

1995

Daily Telegraph, 7 April 1995, Charles Spencer
Guardian, 7 April 1995
Independent, 7 April 1995, Paul Taylor
Independent on Sunday, 9 April 1995, Irving Wardle
Shakespeare Survey 49 (1996), 234–67, Peter Holland
Stratford-upon-Avon Herald, 15 April 1995, Paul Lapworth
Sunday Times, 9 April 1995, J[ohn] P[eter]
Times, 7 April 1995, Benedict Nightingale
Times Literary Supplement, 21 April 1995, Kate Bassett

1997

Guardian, 6 November 1997, Michael Billington
Independent, 8 November 1997, David Benedict
Independent on Sunday, 9 November 1997, Robert Butler
Stratford-upon-Avon Standard, 14 November 1997
Sunday Times, 9 November 1997, J[ohn] P[eter]
Times, 7 November 1997, Benedict Nightingale

2000

Daily Express, 7 July 2000, Robert Gore-Langton
Daily Mail, 6 July 2000, Michael Coveney
Daily Telegraph, 7 July 2000, Charles Spencer
Evening Standard, 6 July 2000, Patrick Marmion
Financial Times, 7 July 2000, Ian Shuttleworth
Guardian, 13 July 2000, Lyn Gardner
Independent, 10 July 2000, Paul Taylor
Mail on Sunday, 5 July 2000, Georgina Brown
Observer, 9 July 2000, Susannah Clapp
Spectator, 15 July 2000, Patrick Carnegy

Sunday Times, 16 July 2000, Robert Hewison
Time Out, 12 July 2000, Jane Edwardes
Times, 10 July 2000, Benedict Nightingale

ABBREVIATIONS

Birm. Mail	*Birmingham Mail*
Birm. Post	*Birmingham Post*
Bristol E. Post	*Bristol Evening Post*
Cahiers Elis.	*Cahiers Elisabéthains*
Coventry E. Tel.	*Coventry Evening Telegraph*
D. Express	*Daily Express*
D. Mail	*Daily Mail*
D. Mirror	*Daily Mirror*
D. Telegraph	*Daily Telegraph*
E. News	*Evening News*
E. Standard	*Evening Standard*
Evesham J.	*Evesham Journal*
FT	*Financial Times*
Glos. Echo	*Gloucester Echo*
Indep. Sun.	*Independent on Sunday*
Leam. Spa Cour.	*Leamington Spa Courier*
Liv. D. Post	*Liverpool Daily Post*
Mail Sun.	*Mail on Sunday*
Man. Guardian	*Manchester Guardian*
New States.	*New Statesman*
New States. & Nat.	*New Statesman and Nation*
News Chron.	*News Chronicle*
Observer Col. Supp.	*Observer Colour Supplement*
Oxf. Mail	*Oxford Mail*
Plays & P.	*Plays and Players*
S. Mercury	*Sunday Mercury*
S. Telegraph	*Sunday Telegraph*
S. Times	*Sunday Times*
S. Wales Arg.	*South Wales Argus*
S. Wales E. Arg.	*South Wales Evening Argus*

SA Herald	Stratford-upon-Avon Herald
SA Standard	Stratford-upon-Avon Standard
Sol. & War. News	Solihull and Warwick County News
SQ	Shakespeare Quarterly
SS	Shakespeare Survey
TES	Times Educational Supplement
Time & T.	Time and Tide
TLS	Times Literary Supplement
Warwick Adv.	Warwick Advertiser
Western Ind.	Western Independent

BIBLIOGRAPHY

PRODUCTION ARCHIVES

The primary source for productions at Stratford-upon-Avon is the collection of the Shakespeare Centre Library. Its holdings include promptbooks and production documents for each post-war production of *Romeo and Juliet*, together with cutting books ('Theatre Records'), programmes, photographs and colour slides. Fixed-camera video recordings are available for the productions in 1986, 1989, 1995 and 2000. Other reviews, including notices of productions outside Stratford-upon-Avon, have been consulted in the Shakespeare Institute Library and Birmingham Shakespeare Library.

BOOKS AND ARTICLES

Addenbrooke, David, *The Royal Shakespeare Company: The Peter Hall Years* (London, 1974)

Allam, Roger, 'Mercutio', in Russell Jackson and Robert Smallwood (eds), *Players of Shakespeare 2* (Cambridge, 1988), 107–19

Beauman, Sally, *The Royal Shakespeare Company: A History of Ten Decades* (Oxford, 1982)

Bennett, H.S. and George Rylands, 'Stratford productions', *Shakespeare Survey 1* (Cambridge, 1948), 107–11

Bergonzi, Bernard, *Wartime and Aftermath: English Literature and Its Background, 1939–1960* (Oxford, 1963)

Berlioz, Hector, *The Memoirs of Hector Berlioz*, trans. David Cairns (revised edition, London, 1970)

Berry, Cicely, *Text in Action* (London, 2001)

Booker, Christopher, *The Neophiliacs: A Study of the Revolution in English Life in the Fifties and Sixties* (London, 1970)

Brook, Peter, *The Shifting Point: Forty Years of Theatrical Exploration, 1946–1987* (London, 1988)

Brooke, Nicholas, *Shakespeare's Early Tragedies* (London, 1968)

Brown, John Russell, 'S. Franco Zeffirelli's *Romeo and Juliet*', *Shakespeare Survey 15* (1970), 147–55

Bruce, Brenda, 'The Nurse in *Romeo and Juliet*', in Philip Brockbank (ed.), *Players of Shakespeare 1* (Cambridge, 1985)

Chambers, Colin, *Other Spaces: New Theatre and the RSC* (London, 1980)

Comfort, Alex, *Sex in Society* (Harmondsworth, 1966)

Cusack, Niamh, 'Juliet', in Russell Jackson and Robert Smallwood (eds), *Players of Shakespeare 2* (Cambridge, 1988), 121–35

David, Richard, *Shakespeare in the Theatre* (Cambridge, 1978)

Dawson, Anthony B., *Watching Shakespeare: A Playgoer's Guide* (London, 1988)

Dench, Judi, 'Judi Dench talks to Gareth Lloyd Evans', *Shakespeare Survey 27* (Cambridge, 1974), 137–42

Dessen, Alan C., 'What's new? Shakespeare on stage in 1986', *Shakespeare Quarterly*, 38 (1987), 90–6

Donaldson, Peter S., *Shakespearean Films / Shakespearean Directors* (Boston, 1990)

Garebian, Keith, *The Making of 'West Side Story'* (Toronto, 1995)

Gibbons, Brian (ed.), *Romeo and Juliet*, The Arden Shakespeare (London, 1980)

Glover, Julian, 'Friar Lawrence in *Romeo and Juliet*', in Robert Smallwood (ed.), *Players of Shakespeare 4* (Cambridge, 1998), 165–76

Goldman, Michael, *Shakespeare and the Energies of Drama* (Princeton, N.J., 1972)

Granville-Barker, Harley, *Prefaces to Shakespeare: 'Romeo and Juliet'* (London, 1930; illustrated edition with notes by M. St Clare Byrne, London, 1963)

Green, Benny, *Revolt into Style: The Pop Arts in Britain* (Harmondsworth, 1972)

Hennessy, Peter, *Never Again: Britain, 1945–1951* (London, 1993)

Hewison, Brian, *Too Much: Art and Society in the Sixties, 1960–75* (London, 1986)

Hewison, Brian, *Culture and Consensus: England, Art and Politics since 1940* (London, 1995)

Holding, Peter, *Text and Performance: 'Romeo and Juliet'* (London, 1992)

Holland, Peter, 'Shakespeare Performances in England, 1990–1', *Shakespeare Survey 45* (1993), 115–44

Holland, Peter, *English Shakespeares: Shakespeare on the English Stage in the 1990s* (Cambridge, 1997)

Hunt, Albert and Geoffrey Reeves, *Peter Brook* (Cambridge, 1995)

Kahn, Coppélia, 'Coming of age in Verona', in Carolyn Ruth Lenz, Gayle Greene and Carol Thomas Neely (eds), *The Woman's Part: Feminist Criticism of Shakespeare* (Urbana, Ill., and Chicago, 1983), 171–93

Larkin, Philip, *High Windows* (London, 1974)

Levenson, Jill L., *Shakespeare in Performance: 'Romeo and Juliet'* (Manchester, 1987)

Levenson, Jill L. (ed.), *Romeo and Juliet*, The Oxford Shakespeare (Oxford, 2000)

MacInnes, Colin, *Absolute Beginners* (Harmondsworth, 1959)

MacInnes, Colin, *England, Half English: A Polyfoto of the Fifties* (Harmondsworth, 1966)

Mahood, M.M., *Shakespeare's Wordplay* (London, 1957)

Marwick, Arthur, *British Society since 1945* (3rd edition, Harmondsworth, 1996)

Marwick, Arthur, *The Sixties* (Oxford, 1999)

Melly, George, *Revolt into Style: The Pop Arts in Britain* (Harmondsworth, 1970)

Mullin, Michael, *Design by Motley* (Newark, Del., and London, 1996)

Partridge, Eric, *Shakespeare's Bawdy* (Revised edition, London, 1955)

Porter, Joseph, *Shakespeare's Mercutio: His History and Drama* (Chapel Hill, N.C., and London, 1988)

Pringle, Marian J., *The Theatres of Stratford-upon-Avon, 1875–1992: An Architectural History* (Stratford-upon-Avon, 1994)

Rolph, C.H. (ed.), *The Trial of Lady Chatterley: Regina v. Penguin Books Limited* (Harmondsworth, 1961)

Schofield, Michael, *The Sexual Behaviour of Young People* (revised edition, Harmondsworth, 1968)

Scott, Clement, *From 'The Bells' to 'King Arthur'* (London, 1897)

Shellard, Dominic, *British Theatre since the War* (New Haven, Conn., 1999)

Sissons, Michael and Philip French, *The Age of Austerity, 1945–1951* (Harmondsworth, 1964)

Smallwood, Robert, 'Shakespeare at Stratford-upon-Avon', *Shakespeare Quarterly*, 43 (1992), 341–56

Snyder, Susan, *The Comic Matrix of Shakespeare's Tragedies* (Princeton, N.J., 1979)

Spencer, T.J.B. (ed.), *Romeo and Juliet*, The New Penguin Shakespeare (Harmondsworth, 1967)

Spencer, T.J.B. (ed.), *Elizabethan Love Stories* (Harmondsworth, 1968)

Tennant, David, 'Romeo', in Robert Smallwood (ed.), *Players of Shakespeare 5* (Cambridge, forthcoming)

Trewin, J.C., *Peter Brook: A Biography* (London, 1971)

Tynan, Kenneth, *Tynan Right and Left* (London, 1967)

Warren, Roger, 'Theory and practice: Stratford, 1976', *Shakespeare Survey 30* (Cambridge, 1977), 169–79

Warren, Roger, 'Shakespeare in performance, 1980', *Shakespeare Survey 34* (Cambridge, 1981), 149–60

Warren, Roger, 'Shakespeare at Stratford-upon-Avon, 1986', *Shakespeare Quarterly*, 38 (1987), 82–9

Wells, Stanley, *Royal Shakespeare: Four Major Productions at Stratford-upon-Avon* (revised edition, Manchester, 1977)

Wells, Stanley, 'Juliet's Nurse: the uses of inconsequentiality', in John F. Andrews (ed.), *'Romeo and Juliet': Critical Essays* (New York and London, 1993), 197–214

Wells, Stanley, 'The challenges of *Romeo and Juliet*', *Shakespeare Survey 49* (1996), 1–14

THEATRE YEARBOOKS AND SOUVENIRS

The following are listed in chronological order of publication.

Shakespeare Memorial Theatre 1948–50: A Photographic Record with Forewords by Ivor Brown and Anthony Quayle. Photographs by Angus McBean (London, 1951)

Shakespeare Memorial Theatre, 1952 (with reprinted article by Anthony Quayle) (Stratford-upon-Avon, n.d.)

Shakespeare Memorial Theatre 1954–56: A Photographic Record with a Critical Analysis by Ivor Brown. Photographs by Angus McBean (London, 1956)

The Shakespeare Memorial Theatre, 1955. Introduction by Ivor Brown (Stratford-upon-Avon, n.d.)

Shakespeare Memorial Theatre 1958, ed. John Goodwin (Stratford-upon-Avon, 1958)

Royal Shakespeare Company, 1960–63, ed. John Goodwin (London, 1964)

Royal Shakespeare Company Yearbook, 1984/85, ed. Simon Trussler (Stratford-upon-Avon, 1985)

INDEX

This index includes actors, directors, critics and other individuals mentioned in the main text who are connected with a theatre or film production of *Romeo and Juliet*. It also includes references to other Shakespeare plays. Individual productions, listed under Shakespeare, are identified by director and year. Page numbers in bold refer to illustrations.